D0568109

THE ALASKANS

CANDLE CREEK.

THE ALASKANS

By the Editors of

TIME-LIFE BOOKS

with text by

Keith Wheeler

TIME-LIFE BOOKS / ALEXANDRIA, VIRGINIA

Time-Life Books Inc.
is a wholly owned subsidiary of

TIME INCORPORATED

Founder: Henry R. Luce 1898-1967

Editor-in-Chief: Hedley Donovan
Chairman of the Board: Andrew Heiskell
President: James R. Shepley
Vice Chairman: Roy E. Larsen
Corporate Editor: Ralph Graves

TIME-LIFE BOOKS INC.

Managing Editor: Jerry Korn
Executive Editor: David Maness
Assistant Managing Editors: Dale M. Brown, Martin Mann, John Paul Porter
Art Director: Tom Suzuki
Chief of Research: David L. Harrison
Director of Photography: Melvin L. Scott
Planning Director: Philip W. Payne
Senior Text Editor: Diana Hirsh
Assistant Art Director: Arnold C. Holeywell
Assistant Chief of Research: Carolyn L. Sackett

Chairman: Joan D. Manley
President: John D. McSweeney
Executive Vice Presidents: Carl G. Jaeger (U.S. and Canada), David J. Walsh (International)
Vice President and Secretary: Paul R. Stewart
Treasurer and General Manager: John Steven Maxwell
Business Manager: Peter G. Barnes
Sales Director: John L. Canova
Public Relations Director: Nicholas Benton
Personnel Director: Beatrice T. Dobie
Production Director: Herbert Sorkin
Consumer Affairs Director: Carol Flaumenhaft

THE OLD WEST

EDITORIAL STAFF FOR "THE ALASKANS"
Editor: Thomas H. Flaherty Jr.
Picture Editor: Robert G. Mason
Text Editors: Gregory Jaynes, Gerald Simons
Designer: Edward Frank
Staff Writers: Susan Bryan, Stuart Gannes, David Johnson, John Manners, Michael Roberts
Researchers: Karen Bates, Jane Coughran, Jean Getlein, Tonna Gibert, Lois Gilman, Jane Jordan, Roger Warner
Art Assistant: Daniel McSweeney
Editorial Assistant: Diane Bohrer

EDITORIAL PRODUCTION
Production Editor: Douglas B. Graham
Operations Manager: Gennaro C. Esposito
Assistant Production Editor: Feliciano Madrid
Quality Control: Robert L. Young (director), James J. Cox (assistant), Michael G. Wight (associate)
Art Coordinator: Anne B. Landry
Copy Staff: Susan B. Galloway (chief), Patricia Graber, Florence Keith, Celia Beattie
Picture Department: Dolores A. Littles, Alex George
Traffic: Barbara Buzan

THE AUTHOR: Keith Wheeler spent more than a year in Alaska as a World War II correspondent for the Chicago *Times,* and he returned 30 years later for an extended visit before writing *The Alaskans.* He began his career with the Huron, South Dakota, *Evening Huronite,* before moving to the *Times* and in 1951 to LIFE, where he was a staff writer until 1970. Now a freelancer, he has written five novels and five nonfiction works, including *The Railroaders, The Townsmen* and *The Chroniclers* in the Old West series.

THE COVER: Weary gold seekers haul themselves to the summit of Alaska's precipitous Chilkoot Pass on their way to the Klondike in this 1898 drawing by Julius Price (to which color has been added). Thousands of Americans streamed through Alaska in search of gold, and many stayed to develop other riches of the huge territory. The gum-booted miners in the frontispiece photograph, for example, have a decidedly settled air as they assemble in 1902 before a butcher's cabin on Candle Creek in far western Alaska.

CORRESPONDENTS: Elisabeth Kraemer (Bonn); Margot Hapgood, Dorothy Bacon (London); Susan Jonas, Lucy T. Voulgaris (New York); Maria Vincenza Aloisi, Josephine du Brusle (Paris); Ann Natanson (Rome). Valuable assistance was also provided by Carolyn T. Chubet (New York).

Other Publications:

WORLD WAR II
THE GREAT CITIES
HOME REPAIR AND IMPROVEMENT
THE WORLD'S WILD PLACES
THE TIME-LIFE LIBRARY OF BOATING
HUMAN BEHAVIOR
THE ART OF SEWING
THE EMERGENCE OF MAN
THE AMERICAN WILDERNESS
THE TIME-LIFE ENCYCLOPEDIA OF GARDENING
LIFE LIBRARY OF PHOTOGRAPHY
THIS FABULOUS CENTURY
FOODS OF THE WORLD
TIME-LIFE LIBRARY OF AMERICA
TIME-LIFE LIBRARY OF ART
GREAT AGES OF MAN
LIFE SCIENCE LIBRARY
THE LIFE HISTORY OF THE UNITED STATES
TIME READING PROGRAM
LIFE NATURE LIBRARY
LIFE WORLD LIBRARY
FAMILY LIBRARY:
   HOW THINGS WORK IN YOUR HOME
   THE TIME-LIFE BOOK OF THE FAMILY CAR
   THE TIME-LIFE FAMILY LEGAL GUIDE
   THE TIME-LIFE BOOK OF FAMILY FINANCE

© 1977 Time-Life Books Inc. All rights reserved. No part of this book may be reproduced in any form or by any electronic or mechanical means, including information storage and retrieval devices or systems, without prior written permission from the publisher, except that brief passages may be quoted for reviews. First printing.
Published simultaneously in Canada.
Library of Congress catalogue card number 77-79673.

CONTENTS

1 | Newcomers in the "Great Land"

Americans, even with a century of westward expansion under their belts, found it hard at first to comprehend the huge chunk of wilderness they bought from Russia in 1867. Alaska was twice the size of Texas, with 34,000 miles of coastline and uncharted rivers that emptied into three seas.

Not until gold was found in 1880 did Americans in numbers invade this last frontier. The "Great Land," as it was called by the Aleuts who lived on islands off its coast, engaged the newcomers in a struggle against astonishing distances, mind-bending isolation and wild extremes of weather. Yet they probed the wilderness by foot, boat and dog sled *(below)*, and discovered that everything about it was colossal—from the mountains and glaciers to the moose and bears. Alaska's bonanzas were enormous, too: gold laced the sand at Nome, sleek salmon abounded in the bays and fur seals crowded the beaches.

By 1912 Alaska was a Territory, and the land that had seemed so forbidding was attracting holiday travelers who wanted only to soak up the scenery. One was so awed that he advised the young to stay away because "it is not well to dull one's capacity for enjoyment by seeing the finest first."

6

Yost's Roadhouse, a refuge on the wintry trail from Valdez to Fairbanks, offered "blankets, beans and biscuits" to weary dog sledders.

"Oh, what a carcass," exulted hunter Dall de Weese after shooting this stupendous moose in 1897 on Alaska's game-rich Kenai Peninsula. In a letter written home to Colorado, de Weese described his prize's 16-foot length and 69-inch antlers—wider than his outspread arms. He had this picture taken to back up his claim that Alaska must be "the home of the largest moose in the world."

9

A pipe-chewing sourdough flanked by kibitzers (one of them in a flowered hat) pans for gold particles on the beach at Nome. The discovery of these easy diggings in 1899 transformed the remote coast into a turbulent tent city of seasoned prospectors—and impatient novices who expected to find a beach of solid gold. One newly arrived tenderfoot ran sand through his fingers, exclaimed "I knew it was all a hoax!" and caught the next boat for home. But many others stayed on—and panned a fortune from the golden sands of Nome.

11

Juneau's fire wagon, photographed around 1890, advertises the reliability of its volunteer crew, the first in Alaska. Fire was a persistent threat to the 10-year-old town, which was still expanding up the stump-ridden hillside at rear. Thanks to its fire fighters, Juneau never burned down.

13

A puffing locomotive plows open the White Pass and Yukon railbed—"the toughest 110 miles of track in the world"—after an avalanche in about 1902. Alaskans built the railroad through terrain "too steep for a billy goat and too cold for a polar bear" to transport miners from the port of Skagway to the gold fields of the Klondike.

15

All Fairbanks turns out on April 30, 1907, to watch a spectacular annual event: the ice going out on the Chena River. Acre-sized chunks of ice crunched downstream, making a noise "like a million bones being crushed" and smashing everything in their path. The breakup marked spring's arrival, a time eagerly awaited and heavily wagered upon. Townspeople would bet on the moment the ice carried away the town's only bridge (as it always did).

17

Precarious foothold on a bountiful coast

By 1830, a full decade before American settlers began crossing the Mississippi River in strength, a little-known outpost of Russian civilization had reached its zenith in the most remote and unlikely part of the Old West. This was the Alaskan port of Sitka. Culture and commerce flourished here in the shadow of a strong hilltop fort and an exotic Russian Orthodox church, while a small group of elegant aristocrats honored visiting sea captains and traders with lavish formal entertainment—all this on the wooded shores of a hostile wilderness, 3,000 miles from Sitka's nearest source of supply in Siberia.

These fine Russians disproved the view of outsiders that Alaska was unfit for habitation by civilized man. The aristocrats had come to Sitka to supervise its lucrative fur trade; but many of them had learned to love Alaska's harsh grandeur and to call the secure little town their home.

Though Alaska was too remote for casual American visitors, bold New England merchants, who by the 1820s had become the colony's main trading partners, brought back glowing tales of Sitka's Russian elite. William Heath Davis, a Yankee trader who, in 1831, made his first call there as a boy aboard a merchant ship out of Boston, was astonished by the Russians' gentility and hospitality. Davis described the governor of Sitka and his officers as "highly educated, refined in manners, intelligent and courteous. Most of the gentlemen spoke French and English in addition to their own language."

These urbane officials opened their homes to Davis' party, entertaining the Yankees with formal dinners and balls. Young Davis was smitten by the beauty and accomplishments of his hosts' wives and daughters, particularly by "the wonderful transparency of their complexions and their rosy cheeks."

The Americans' accounts revealed, however, that for all its civility, Sitka had wilderness underpinnings. Aleut hunters from the outlying Aleutian Islands brought in luxurious pelts for export; they also supplied the name Alaska, their word for continent or mainland. Scores of Indians and people of mixed Indian, Aleut, Eskimo and Russian blood worked in Sitka's warehouses, shops, flour mill, bakery, tannery, arsenal and shipyard. But the frontier spirit of the rough pioneers who had clawed out Russia's foothold in Alaska by the 1750s had died when they had died. In any case the Russian population—no more than a few hundred in Sitka and several smaller coastal outposts—never was large enough to support the development of the immense Alaskan interior.

Sitka was quietly enjoying its golden age when suddenly an epoch-making event signaled the return of its pioneering heyday. In 1867 the second-largest real-estate deal in history, exceeded in size only by the Louisiana Purchase, converted Russian America into American Alaska. For a time Sitka served the same purposes as had gold-rush San Francisco: it became a port of entry and supply depot for rough-and-tumble wanderers from the United States who came streaming through to seek a variety of treasures in the uncharted wilderness to the north. The Alaska purchase, conducted in dark secrecy in far-off Washington, set the stage for a frontier epic unsurpassed in scope anywhere in the Old West.

In later years the Americans who pioneered Alaska would look back with incredulity at their adventures, their ordeals, their accomplishments. They had started out willy-nilly, looking for anything of value.

Early Russian explorers planted the insignia of the Romanov Dynasty, a double-headed eagle, at intervals along the coast of Alaska to claim it for their mother country.

Their American luck held: in addition to its renowned fur-bearing animals, Alaska offered timber, coal, copper, gold, oil and the richest salmon-fishing grounds in the world. The trouble was that these bonanzas were jealously guarded by Alaska's difficult climate and forbidding terrain, which gave the treasure hunters all the fight they could handle.

Just to get into the Alaskan landmass, pioneers had to struggle through dense forests and across glacier-ridden mountain ranges, mighty rivers and boundless tundra. On the way (and often after they reached their destination) their suffering almost defied description. The milder Panhandle region in the south was drenched with rain or cloaked in fog at least 200 days a year. Along the Yukon and Kuskokwim rivers, winter held sway for eight months a year, with temperatures bottoming out at $-70°$ F. In the summer mosquitoes and black flies were so numerous and so fierce that they killed pack animals on the hoof and drove strong men to the brink of insanity. If adversity is an ennobling experience, the Americans' last great Western frontier was their most ennobling one.

Not surprisingly, the pioneers persevered; after all, they were cast in the same mold as the brave, ambitious, stubborn men and women who had recently pressed beyond the Mississippi and Missouri. Indeed, a fair number of them were the very same people—veteran Westerners tired of taming old frontiers and longing for a promising new one. Some were grizzled prospectors whose digs had petered out or turned into boring big businesses. A few were gunslingers and Indian fighters who opted for Alaska because their former haunts no longer tolerated their kind. Others were explorers, eager to plumb the unknown. And there were the familiar characters in the predictable ranks of camp followers: whores, cardsharps, confidence men, land speculators and preachers aching to save the souls of the ungodly. But most of the pioneers were tenderfeet, barely qualified for a weekend of rabbit hunting, yet driven by a lust for adventure and a yearning for a fuller life. With some exceptions, they too persevered, and nearly all lived to tell the tale and to proudly assume the name Alaskans came to give those who made it: sourdough.

Separately and together, these motley adventurers worked wonders in Alaska in roughly five decades of

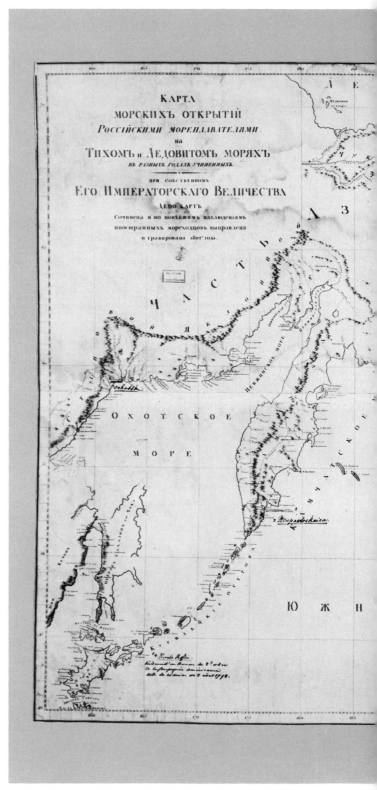

A Russian map of discoveries "in the Pacific and the Icy seas"

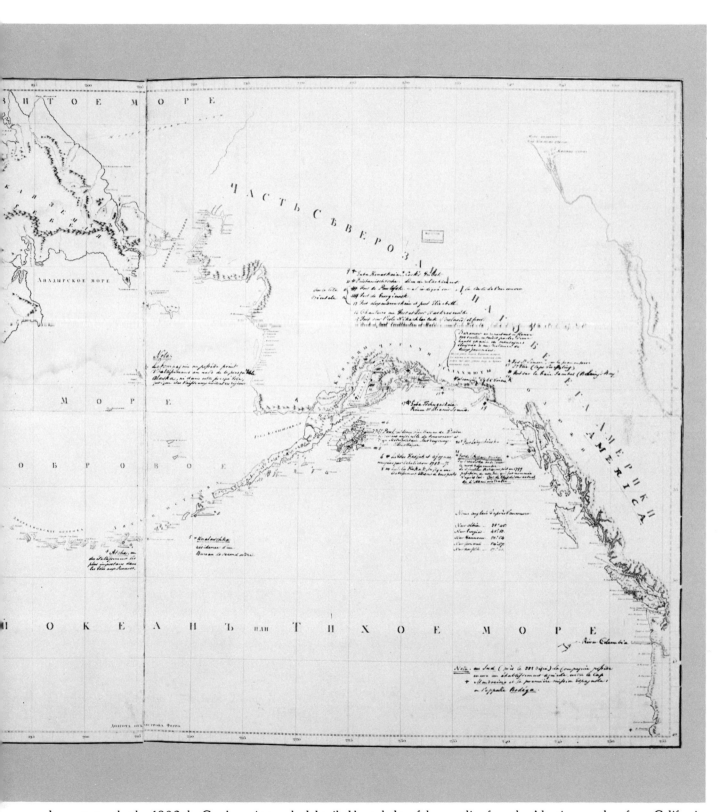

demonstrates that by 1802 the Czar's navigators had detailed knowledge of the coastline from the Aleutians south as far as California.

expanding American endeavor. They mapped the interior and even strung telegraph wires across it. They challenged the powerful Yukon River, running its rapids in rugged scows and using it for a frozen dog-sled highway in winter. In the Panhandle they built a stub railway over lofty White Pass on the way to the Klondike. To reach central Alaska from the port of Valdez they hacked out a dog-sled trail and later a wagon road, leading 376 miles north over mountain barricades to a broad valley where they flung up a town called Fairbanks.

The Americans wrested many fortunes from the intransigent land. Upstream on the glacier-fed Chitina River they found massive green cliffs of copper, with ore up to 70 per cent pure. They discovered gold lying on the beach at Nome—and were almost cheated out of their hoard by a great scalawag whose influence reached to the White House. They created the salmon industry and harvested furs with Yankee efficiency. And in 1912, when they finally won territorial status for Alaska, they could claim to have almost conquered their enormous domain.

Actually, Alaska was unconquerable; the pioneers had simply learned to cope with it, as the Russians had, then to love it and call it home. True, they had forced Alaska to yield its bounty on a grandiose scale. But, unlike the Russians before them, they had yet to realize that the sea otters and seals and whales would not last for very long unless they practiced prudent restraint in harvesting them. Such lessons were difficult for opportunists to learn in their zesty haste to make a future for themselves. But they could have learned them quite easily if they had paused in Sitka to inquire about Alaska's Russian past.

In June 1741 a two-ship expedition led by Vitus Bering, a Danish explorer in the employ of the Russian Navy, set out from the Siberian port of Petropavlovsk to find whatever lands and riches lay to the east. Bering's *St. Peter* and her sister ship *St. Paul* sailed due east into the northernmost Pacific, later to be called the Bering Sea. About 600 miles out the two brigs ran afoul of the Aleutian Islands, which curved down from the sharp chin of Alaska like a broken tusk 1,000 miles long. These strange islands, studded with dead or dying volcanoes, were bleak and treeless

little worlds, guarded by half-hidden reefs, battered by directionless tornadoes and gales that came to be known as williwaws. Here cold air from the arctic collided with the warm air accompanying the northbound Japan Current, brewing dense fogs that blotted out the islands and their perilous approaches.

The *St. Paul* and the *St. Peter* became separated passing through the fog-shrouded Aleutians; they never re-established contact. But by mid-July each had made an important landfall on a misty Alaskan shore.

On July 17 the captain of the *St. Paul,* Alexei Chirikov, was skirting the coast of an enormous island when he perceived, through a break in the mist, a great inviting bay flanked by wooded headlands. Chirikov dispatched his mate and 10 men to reconnoiter in a longboat. They disappeared around a headland and did not return. After several days of worried deck-pacing, Chirikov sent his boatswain and six more men to look for their missing comrades. Their boat rounded the same headland—and also vanished. Not one of the 18 men was ever seen again—at least by a white man. The only clue to their fate turned up much later in a legend of the local Indian tribe—the warlike Tlingits. It told of white men who had been led into a clever ambush by a warrior dressed in a bearskin. As for Chirikov, when his men failed to return he thought better of landing and set out for home. On the return journey to Siberia he lost 20 additional crewmen to scurvy.

Meanwhile, the *St. Peter* had sailed across a broad gulf, and on July 16, 1741, Bering sighted the Alaskan mainland. He took a sighting, at lat. 58° 14' N., on a lofty snow-capped peak, later named Mount St. Elias for the saint on whose day it was discovered.

Bering then began a long—and increasingly discouraging—cruise up the coast. The scouting parties he put ashore from time to time found nothing of value and very little food. By September the crew was weak from hunger and malnutrition; many took sick and one died. Bering himself had fallen ill, and in October the men voted to end the expedition and turned the *St. Peter* homeward.

After struggling westward through miserable weather, the explorers met disaster. On November 5 they neared an uninhabited island, later named after Bering, in the Komandorskiye group some 100 miles

The first treasure to attract white men to Alaska was the "soft gold" of the sea otter's pelt, hunted by Aleuts in kayaks (*below*) for their Russian overlords. An explorer-naturalist drew a specimen of the five-foot-long mammal in 1788 (*inset*).

from the easternmost coast of Siberia. While they were maneuvering close to shore, high seas and high winds drove the *St. Peter* onto the rocks. Then their real ordeal began, and it lasted nine months.

Through the long, dark, frigid winter, the castaways worked to build a small vessel out of the shivered timbers of the *St. Peter*. The weak and the sick died one by one. Bering died on December 8, and more than half his crew had perished from exhaustion and scurvy before the new boat was ready for sea. Besides hope, only one thing sustained the survivors. They discovered—and lived on—the creature that would make Alaska: the sea otter.

This dark brown, sportive creature abounded all the way down the Pacific Coast to California, and Spanish colonists undoubtedly had taken note of it by the 17th Century. But while the Spaniards disregarded the animal—they had little interest in the fur trade and no need for furs in California's warm climate— the survivors of the *St. Peter* owed their very lives to the sea otter. They ate its flesh (no easy task with their bleeding, toothless, scurvy-ridden gums) and

used its thick pelt to cover their freezing bodies. And, at last, when their new vessel was seaworthy, they sailed back to Siberia with all the otter skins they could load on board.

They arrived at Petropavlovsk in the late summer of 1742—just in time to solve two pressing Russian problems. In the course of the past 100 years, ruthless bands of professional hunters—the *promyshlenniki*—had ravaged the sable population of Asia from the Ural Mountains, 4,000 miles eastward, to the shores of the North Pacific. In the process they had conquered Siberia for Russia, and alarmed and alienated China with border raids. By 1742 the *promyshlenniki* needed a new source of income, and the Czar needed a way to divert the hunters' international barbarisms; both would be satisfied by the otter pelts that the *St. Peter's* survivors brought with them.

When the *promyshlenniki* saw those skins, their eyes lighted up with reverent greed. The pelts—up to five feet long and two feet wide, with dense, glossy black-brown fur three quarters of an inch deep— would surely be worth a great deal in trade. The

23

Alexander Baranov shaped Russian America's destiny and was its first governor. Washington Irving described him as a "rugged, hard-drinking old Russian; somewhat of a soldier, somewhat of a trader."

promyshlenniki immediately prepared to seek out the furry creatures in the fogbound islands to the east. Of course, these landlubbers knew next to nothing about seamanship or navigation, and they had no ships worthy of the name. But no matter; their bravery and ingenuity matched their ruthlessness. They rounded up green planks, bound them together with leather thongs, rigged them with sails made of reindeer skins and launched a mercantile navy such as the modern world had never seen.

Party after party set out into the Pacific in the uncertain craft. Many boats capsized in storms or ran onto hidden Aleutian reefs. Uncounted numbers of the *promyshlenniki* were drowned or marooned to die of starvation, scurvy or harpoon thrusts from Aleut hunters. But the *promyshlenniki* kept coming.

By 1745 the Russian hunters were established on Attu Island at the western end of the Aleutian chain. There, in addition to slaughtering sea otters, they slaughtered the male Aleuts for safety's sake and kept their women for comfort. The Russians' quickness with their muskets was commemorated by the name of Attu's harbor: Massacre Bay.

Island by island, the *promyshlenniki* advanced along the Aleutian chain toward the Alaskan mainland. By 1759 they had reached Unimak and Unalaska at the eastern end of the Aleutians, and they had again turned their muskets on the Aleuts. In reprisal for an uprising in which four Russian boats were sunk, the hunters butchered 3,000 Aleut men. They did their killing with calculated pleasure. According to one account, one Russian decided to see how many men could be killed by a single musket ball; he bound 12 Aleuts in a line and fired. The pellet stopped in the body of the ninth.

Presently, though, the Russians realized that genocide was impractical; they needed Aleuts to fetch the pelts. The otters retreated as the *promyshlenniki* approached them and would sink when shot in the water. And besides, otters were much too agile for club-wielding Russians in clumsy rowboats. It took Aleut hunters, armed with the tools of their ancestral trade, to outwit them.

The Aleut hunting canoe was a thin skeleton of driftwood and whalebone, covered with sewn and stretched sealskins, and weighed 30 pounds or less.

Its makers called it *ulluxtadag;* the Russians, not surprisingly, gave it their own name, *baidarka*. But the world eventually came to know the ingenious craft by the name the Aleuts' distant relatives, the Eskimos, gave to their version of it: kayak. By whatever name, the little vessel was marvelously well suited to the stormy waters of the Aleutians. Kayaks were designed to carry one, two or three men who wore rainproof seal-gut parkas that they lashed to the projecting rims of the craft's circular hatches to form a watertight pontoon. The boat was all but unsinkable with two Aleuts aboard; indeed, it rarely turned over even in the roughest weather. But when two Russians tried to hunt in a kayak, they often capsized it, even in calm waters, and occasionally a pair would drown while floating upside down.

The Aleuts' hunting weapon was a harpoon two feet long, tipped with stone and propelled with deadly accuracy from a slender hand-held throwing board. A group of kayaks, with one man paddling and a harpooner at the ready in each craft, would surround and harass an otter, keeping it diving until the animal was exhausted and in need of oxygen. Then, when it surfaced and lingered for air, they would harpoon it. The Aleuts successfully hunted other fur-bearing animals, including various seals and, on mainland hunting expeditions, red, blue, cross and black foxes. But the Russians' first priority was the luxuriant sea otter.

Once the Russians stopped massacring Aleut males, the Aleuts came to recognize the futility of pitting their harpoons against muskets. Gradually, the *promyshlenniki* and the Aleuts became not only interdependent but almost indistinguishable. They lived together in underground hovels, wore the same crude fur garments, suffered the same hardships with the same stoic calm. But for a long time the Russians' relations with the Aleuts produced little more than profits and children. In their first 40 years in the Aleutians and on the fringes of the Alaska Peninsula, the *promyshlenniki* built not a single house or warehouse, and they answered to not a single law.

This disorganized state of affairs began to change in 1784 when two well-equipped ships carrying more than 100 *promyshlenniki* arrived to set up a permanent colony. The leader of the expedition was Grigori Ivanovich Shelekhov, an ambitious merchant from the

Александръ Барановъ

Siberian town of Irkutsk. To mount the chancy venture Shelekhov had risked all his capital, taken on two partners to get more money and borrowed 50,000 rubles on top of that. To help secure his investment he brought along his wife, Natalia, who proved herself shrewd and aggressive in their business dealings. Natalia was the first—and for a long time the only—white woman to live in Alaska.

In late July, 1784, Shelekhov found just the right site for his settlement—on the grassy shores of Kodiak Island in a commodious harbor he named Three Saints Bay. Eighteen months later, the colony boasted a neat little village and a dozen outposts in the surrounding area, including one about 200 miles north in Cook Inlet—named for the British navigator

James Cook who had touched there in 1778. It was a remarkable piece of work, and all the more so because the people of Kodiak Island, an Eskimo group called the Koniag, soon became willing workers for the Russians—though they resisted at first. Just how Shelekhov enlisted the Koniags' aid remains unclear, but he was apparently scrupulous in this instance and paid them fairly for their labor.

By May 1786 the Shelekhovs had left their colony in the charge of an overseer and returned to Russia to put their enterprise on a sound legal footing. In St. Petersburg they appealed to the Empress, Catherine the Great, for an imperial charter and a fur-trading monopoly of the sort that the British Hudson's Bay

St. Paul, later known as Kodiak, was the second Russian settlement on Kodiak Island. Begun in 1792, after a tidal wave had devastated the first village at Three Saints Bay, it was a snug little town when the world voyager Urey Lisiansky visited it in 1804 and painted this watercolor.

Company had received in Canada. Catherine, preoccupied with waging war on Turkey and Sweden simultaneously, refused the grant but gave Shelekhov two consolation prizes: a gold medal and a sword.

Furious but undaunted by this rejection, Shelekhov tried to get his charter by devious means. He cultivated the friendship of the Empress' current lover and acquired another valuable ally by marrying off his daughter to a rising young courtier, Count Nikolai Petrovich Rezanov. Shelekhov continued to bombard Catherine's advisers and the leaders of the Orthodox Church with exaggerated tales of his achievements in North America. His colony was thriving, Shelekhov said; actually, it was near starvation. The natives were yearning for Christianity, and he himself had

converted many of them; more lies. But Shelekhov did offer to send missionaries to Kodiak Island at his own expense. And he soon made good the offer.

In 1790, with nothing settled at the court, Shelekhov hired a manager to replace the inept one he had left in charge at the colony. The new man was Alexander Baranov, and he was altogether unprepossessing in both appearance and background. Short and balding, the son of a shopkeeper in a village near the border of Finland, he had gone 10 years earlier to Siberia; there he had been a glassmaker in Irkutsk and, until hijackers ruined him, a fur trader. But Baranov was tough, resolute and known to be honest, responsible and enterprising. He would govern his wilderness bailiwick with an iron fist for 27 years and would

Count Nikolai Rezanov, chief officer of the Russian-American Company, had bold plans for a self-sufficient Alaska, with economic independence and its own army.

earn himself the unofficial title of "Lord of Alaska."

Baranov got off to an inauspicious start. On his way to Kodiak in October 1790, he was shipwrecked on Unalaska Island and was forced to spend the winter there. The following May he set out to cover the last 400 miles of his journey in an open boat with 16 men. He soon came down with pneumonia. But Baranov was unstoppable, and in mid-summer of 1791 his party at last reached the shelter of Three Saints Bay.

Recovering quickly on Kodiak Island, Baranov began his uphill battle against monumental odds. The hundred-odd Russians in the colony were threadbare, hungry and sick much of the time; everything was in short supply, from rigging and canvas for the repair of ships to tobacco for the soul. Baranov sent Shelekhov urgent demands for more supplies and men, but his letters took a year and more to reach St. Petersburg. Shelekhov, strapped for funds, rarely sent ships, and some of those he did send never made it.

Nevertheless, Baranov was in Alaska to get the furs out, and this he did with cold-blooded determination. Some said he enslaved the Aleuts in order to

mobilize more hunting teams; but, like Shelekhov, Baranov did pay them—when he had trade goods to pay them with. At times he could muster 1,000 Aleuts. In their kayaks they fetched Baranov's otter pelts, and they waged Baranov's wars against the hostile tribes encountered on the mainland.

Baranov had more than his share of personnel problems. Only the *promyshlenniki* were solidly behind him; at first they feared him, then they came to respect him and finally to revere him as their leader and friend. Baranov had annoying brushes with the aristocratic young naval officers who arrived on the infrequent supply ships. Because he lacked title or refinement, they sneered at him—until he faced them down by sheer force of will.

Baranov had more serious trouble with Russian poachers who made claims to his hunting grounds and terrorized Aleuts and other peoples under his protection. On one occasion he trapped a party of intruders on the mainland and put them in the stockade at Kodiak until they could be sent back to Siberia. But the Russians who really exasperated Baranov were the eight missionaries Shelekhov had sent to please the court and the Orthodox Church.

Baranov had many a bitter exchange with the priests, and the detestation was mutual. The clergymen, led by Archimandrite Ioassef, were accustomed to a comfortable life and the attentions of servants; they were appalled by the living conditions on Kodiak and were inclined from the start to blame Baranov for their hardships. They were appalled by his behavior as well: he roistered conspicuously and then attended church services as though he had done no wrong. One of the priests, a zealous Father Juvenal, noted in his journal that Baranov "stood there and listened and crossed himself and joined in the singing in the same hoarse voice with which he was shouting obscene songs the night before, when I saw him in the midst of a drunken carousal with a woman seated in his lap."

As Baranov saw it, the priests were plainly subversive; they stirred up confusion and discontent among his Aleuts by fulminating against polygamy and refusing to baptize more than one wife per hunter.

Baranov's fiercest quarrel with the priests arose over a matter involving his own household. Partly to improve relations with the local peoples and partly for

Russia's vain attempt to colonize California

In 1812 the Russians tried to establish a foothold in California; the effort was a disaster from its start. To begin with, the Russians were trespassing on Spanish territory, and they knew it. So they built their settlement, called Fort Ross, some 65 miles north of San Francisco, on high, impregnable tableland. The fort was bounded on the west by a 100-foot ocean cliff and on the east by rugged, wooded hills. This was fine for fending off hostile attacks — none ever came, as it turned out — but it left the colony without much arable land.

The settlers' avowed purpose was to till the soil and provide their hungry mother colony in Russian Alaska with tons of wheat, barley, fresh vegetables and beef. But instead of concentrating on farming, the first contingent of colonists devoted themselves to hunting the lucrative sea otter nearly to extinction.

When the Russians finally settled down to agriculture, their lack of expertise quickly became apparent. They forced the local Pomo Indians to work the fields for them. The Pomos thereupon stole their wheat and rustled their cattle. Stem rust, a disease caused by coastal fog, wiped out entire crops of grain. The vegetable yield was barely enough to feed Fort Ross, much less Alaska.

Fort Ross's first livestock consisted of 20 cattle and three horses, purchased from a Spaniard who had to teach the Russians how to milk the cows. As the herd grew, Aleuts in the colony were assigned to tend them, but these fearless sea hunters were hopeless with cattle. "Instead of driving in the animals," one colonist recalled, "they were often chased to the fort by wild bulls and steers."

The Russians thought they might build ships at Fort Ross. The plan became a debacle: four two-masters made of unseasoned oak rotted beyond repair within a few years. By 1838 the colony was losing 44,000 rubles a year, and Alaska was buying more food from Spanish California than it was growing in Russian California. In 1841 Russia's 29-year sojourn in California ended when the colonists were called back home and Fort Ross was sold for $30,000 to a Swiss rancher named John Sutter. (It was at Sutter's Mill, 120 miles to the east, that the great California gold rush began a few years later.)

By 1877 Fort Ross had passed through the hands of four private owners but still looked much as it had when the Russians built it.

Sitka, the capital of Russian America, is seen against the imposing background of Mount Verstovia in a watercolor done around 1860. The governor's mansion, also called Baranov's Castle, is the large building on the hillside at right, and spired St. Michael's Cathedral is at center. The Tlingit Indian village at left is separated from the town by a defensive stockade.

his own comfort, the 46-year-old manager—who had a wife at home—had taken as his woman the 18-year-old daughter of an Eskimo chief. Anna, he called her, bore him a son and a daughter. But another of Father Ioassef's priests, a Father Nektar, got Anna so distraught over her "sinful" state that she flung her infant son into the sea. Fortunately, the child was rescued in time, and he grew up to give his proud father the satisfaction of seeing him sponsored for appointment to the Russian naval academy. But Baranov never forgave the priests for what they did to his Anna, and nearly did to their son.

Baranov was by instinct an empire builder. In his very first year on Kodiak, when acute supply shortages would have kept a cautious man close to home base, he launched a campaign to expand his trade and terri-

tory at the expense of various Russian competitors. Rounding up a fleet of kayaks, Baranov set out for the mainland to appraise the potential otter harvest and to look for a wooded site on which to build a fort. During his scouting trip Baranov saw plenty of otters, plenty of timber—and the shape of things to come for Alaska. The future materialized in the form of a foreign schooner, which Baranov encountered at an island east of Cook Inlet in Prince William Sound. During a storm the ship had limped in with a broken mast and dropped anchor. Baranov, more curious than alarmed, paddled out to investigate.

The vessel was the British *Phoenix* under Captain Hugh Moore. The captain and his mate, a Boston Irishman who styled himself "Honest Joe" O'Cain, watched uneasily as Baranov, a grotesque figure in his seal-gut parka, came paddling alongside in his kayak.

It was not until Baranov removed his Aleut rain hat that the foreigners recognized him as a small, unintimidating white man.

Their shipboard conversation began with comical difficulty. Baranov's Russian evoked no response, and neither did Moore's English nor O'Cain's Boston version of it. The breakthrough came when Moore tried German, which Baranov knew well enough. Baranov offered to help the sailors fell a tall tree and step a new mast. In return the visitors passed on some distressing information. They told Baranov that British, American and even a few Spanish skippers had been trading for furs in Nootka Sound, about 1,100 miles to the south, on what would become Vancouver Island in British Columbia. The news of the encroaching competition reinforced Baranov's plan to expand down the coast. He realized that he had to head south to stop foreigners from coming north.

When the *Phoenix* was shipshape, Baranov gave the sailors some presents—silver-fox skins and Aleut waterproofs made of seal gut. Though they parted amicably, Baranov was far from pleased by the certainty that he would see others like them. O'Cain had already decided to return; he had recognized the potential of the otter industry on this grim coast.

Happily for Baranov, the next several years brought few foreign ships and, unhappily, few Russian ones. To make Baranov's supply problem worse, his employer, Shelekhov, died in 1795, and the colony's affairs passed to Shelekhov's widow and his son-in-law, Count Nikolai Rezanov, who had to fend off a series of challenges to their control.

Nevertheless, Baranov managed to strengthen his foothold on the mainland and even started a shipyard on the forested shore of an inlet he called Resurrection Bay. Baranov's Aleut and mixed-breed workers turned out a stout little vessel—the first of a number of boats with which he could compete with foreign interlopers and reduce his dependence on the unreliable supplies from home. With his modest fleet, Baranov got ready for a great leap to the south, there to plant a second colony.

In 1799 Baranov assembled 450 two-man kayaks and two small ships, one from his own shipyard. From Resurrection Bay he headed south along the mainland coast; his destination was an enormous wooded island, later named for him, that commanded the Panhandle coast of lower Alaska. Hugging the jagged, twisting shoreline, Baranov traveled about 600 miles; he could have saved 100 of them if he had dared to sail straight across the Gulf of Alaska.

On reaching the island, the men of the expedition quickly set to work building a stockaded settlement, which they named Fort St. Michael. There was good reason for haste. About six miles below St. Michael lay a stronghold of another kind, called Sitka by its Indian inhabitants, the Tlingits. They were obviously formidable and, though Baranov could not have known it, were descendants of the unfriendly folk who had ambushed Chirikov's landing parties during the Bering expedition of 1741. The tribe was numerous and far more culturally advanced than either the Aleuts or the Koniags. The Tlingits lived in well-built wooden houses, fashioned wooden boats, kept their wartime captives as slaves, carved totem poles in praise of their ancestors and worshipped a large pantheon of bird and animal gods. They were highly organized, wealthy and bloodthirsty.

The Tlingits raised no immediate objection to the Russian settlement up the coast, perhaps because Baranov paid them for the site in beads, brass and

SITKA FROM AN INDIAN'S POINT OF VIEW

An unknown Indian drew his own impression of Sitka at about the same time the traditional Russian watercolor on the previous pages was painted. The artist depicts many of the same buildings, but he does so with a freewheeling logic of his own and clearly without any knowledge of artistic perspective. The spired cathedral and the governor's "castle" on the hill *(upper right)* loom large. So do the parading Russian soldiers *(right center)* and the stockade that curves through the middle of the drawing, with its cannons perched menacingly above the Tlingit settlement *(lower left)*. In contrast, the rows of Indian houses in the village appear hopelessly small and defenseless.

33

bottles. With the Tlingits apparently neutralized, Baranov returned to Kodiak in 1801, and the 300-odd colonists he left behind grew carelessly confident. Then, in June 1802, a horde of Tlingits fell upon St. Michael while most of its men were off hunting. The Indians killed and beheaded the remaining men and carried off the women as slaves. Three Russian men, a few Aleut hunters and 18 Aleut women escaped the massacre by hiding in the forest.

The survivors were later picked up by a prowling British ship whose captain, one Henry Barber, had a piratical turn of mind. Barber ferried the survivors to Kodiak, held them captive aboard his ship and offered them to Baranov for ransom: fur pelts valued at 50,000 rubles—$25,000 at the prevailing rate of exchange. Baranov, staring at the muzzles of Barber's guns, paid with all the skins he felt he could part with—10,000 rubles worth.

Barber's larcenous visit brought Kodiak its first word of the catastrophe at St. Michael. Baranov received the news in grim silence, but he had no intention of letting the Tlingits get away with murder. At present, however, he was helpless, lacking the weapons or enough manpower to mount a punitive expedition. What he needed was a minor miracle, one that the sailor Honest Joe O'Cain would provide.

Honest Joe had arrived in Kodiak on his second visit in 1801, just after Baranov returned from St. Michael. At that juncture the Russians had not seen a supply ship for three years. When O'Cain showed up—this time as mate and part owner of the *Enterprise* out of New York under Captain Ezekial Hubbel—his ship was bulging with the very things Baranov needed most urgently: molasses, sugar, flour, canvas, tobacco and sundry manufactured goods. Honest Joe wanted to swap for otter pelts. Baranov had no authority to trade with foreigners, but he had to have supplies—and he had learned that the colony would not survive unless he made up his own rules.

Baranov told O'Cain that he would trade 2,000 red- and silver-fox pelts for the cargo. No, said Honest Joe, it had to be sea otter. To break the impasse, Baranov is said to have proposed a wager and offered two-to-one odds: if either O'Cain or Captain Hubbel could drink him under the table, the payment would

be made in otter, but if Baranov outlasted them both, it would be fox. Fox it was. This alcoholic showdown marked the start of a long and mutually profitable friendship between Baranov and O'Cain—and between Russians and Americans.

In 1803, while Baranov was aching to avenge the St. Michael massacre, O'Cain providentially showed up again, and again with what Baranov needed most. Honest Joe was now the owner of his own ship, which he had immodestly christened the *O'Cain,* and in its hold he carried muskets and even cannons left over from the American Revolution.

This time, Honest Joe is reported to have said, the trading would be done in otter skins and no drinking contest would fuddle the issue. Baranov eyed the weapons covetously, but he was forced to admit that the hunting had been light—most of his manpower had been tied up building the ill-fated fort at St. Michael—and there were few skins in his warehouse.

O'Cain then suggested a fascinating alternative that would, in effect, make him Baranov's subcontractor. The sea otter, said Honest Joe, was plentiful along the coast of California; the problem was catching it, and Baranov's Aleut hunters were clearly the experts in that field. If Baranov would lend him a force of Aleuts, he would go hunting outside Baranov's territory and would split the harvest with Baranov when he returned.

The proposition appealed to Baranov for more than the profits and weapons it promised; he wanted information about California, the next goal in his plan for expansion. Therefore, he told O'Cain that he would only consider the offer if a Russian overseer went along. Honest Joe readily agreed; he needed someone to handle the Aleuts. Baranov added another proviso: the Aleuts must be paid $2.50 for each otter they took. Again O'Cain agreed; the bounty was entirely reasonable since a prime otter skin fetched 10 times that much in trade. The deal was made, and Baranov sent a trusted lieutenant off with O'Cain to oversee the Aleuts and to do some scouting at the same time.

With O'Cain's ancient arsenal now in his possession, Baranov began mobilizing for the conquest of Sitka. Work was well under way when the glacier-slow mail from St. Petersburg brought good news.

Fully four years before, in 1799, Czar Paul I had finally granted the fur monopoly so long sought by the late Grigori Shelekhov. All Russian activities in Alaska were now consolidated under royal charter in a firm called the Russian-American Company. Czar Paul's successor, Alexander I, had appointed Shelekhov's son-in-law, Count Rezanov, High Chamberlain, giving the company a powerful friend at court. Moreover, in confirming Baranov as resident manager, Alexander had raised him to the rank of "collegiate councilor" and made him governor of Alaska. Baranov was unimpressed by the titles, and he doubted they would impress the Tlingits, either.

In the spring of 1804 Baranov set out for Sitka with an expeditionary force of 120 *promyshlenniki* in four small ships and 800 Aleuts in half as many kayaks. Months later the armada arrived at Sitka, and Baranov saw that help had preceded him. In the bay lay a warship flying the imperial Russian ensign—the first Russian fighting ship to appear in the Pacific. The vessel was the 450-ton frigate *Neva,* on an imperial cruise to inspect and protect Russian America; she had called at Kodiak after Baranov's departure with his slow fleet and, learning of his expedition against Sitka, had come to assist him.

Even with such formidable aid, the capture of Sitka turned out to be a grueling operation. It took a full day for the little kayaks to tow the *Neva* and its cannons into position to bombard the Tlingit stronghold, which was protected by a long gravel shoal and an arc of trees. Once the shelling commenced, it went on day after day and produced no practical results. Baranov, fed up with sitting and waiting, led an Aleut force ashore and tried to take Sitka by storm. But the Tlingits routed them, wounded Baranov in the arm and might well have wiped out the attackers but for covering fire from the *Neva's* guns and O'Cain's artillery on Baranov's four smaller ships. Finally, after they were kept awake many nights by the chanting of medicine men in Sitka, silence fell over the harbor. The Tlingits had abandoned their fortress, leaving Baranov little but ruins and a few corpses to show for his victory.

Baranov began building a new fort a mile west of the old one. He made it his headquarters and named it New Archangel, but in common usage it would be called Sitka. The move ended Baranov's worst struggles and ushered in a period of heady growth and profit—boom time for Russian America.

Baranov benefited by his transfer from Kodiak to Sitka; from 1805 he saw his varied, far-flung labors come together with spectacular results. The time he had spent organizing the Aleuts and Indian recruits into large hunting teams paid off in tens of thousands of pelts each year; one 1805 shipment alone returned $250,000. The chancy deal Baranov had made with Honest Joe O'Cain also returned increasing dividends. That upwardly mobile Irishman, whose borrowed Aleuts had brought Baranov 1,800 pelts from California, set up a syndicate with the Winships, a family of veteran traders based in Brighton, Massachusetts. On the next trip, Jonathan Winship showed up at Sitka as captain of the *O'Cain.* He took another batch of Aleuts south and harvested so many otter pelts that Baranov received $30,000 worth as the Russian-American Company's share.

Within a year the O'Cain-Winship combine had several ships putting in at Sitka. As an added bonus they brought Baranov a handful of American craftsmen—personnel he needed badly and had vainly petitioned St. Petersburg to send him.

More and more American ships dropped anchor in Sitka, which now became a regular stop on a Pacific trade route that Yankee skippers had been developing for two decades and more. The seagoing merchants arrived from Boston with foodstuffs and rum that they traded for Alaskan pelts. Then they stopped at Hawaii for a load of fragrant sandalwood and sailed on to China. In Canton and other Chinese ports they traded their pelts and sandalwood for silk, porcelain, jade and, most important, tea—all of which they finally marketed in Europe and on the American East Coast.

Baranov's plans for California, which had prompted him to send his own man south with O'Cain's Aleut hunters, gained support in 1805. Shortly after the capture of Sitka, Count Nikolai Rezanov arrived on an inspection trip, and Baranov opened their talks with his scout's report on California.

The 42-year-old Rezanov turned out to be shrewd and well informed. He conceded that Baranov lacked a reliable and inexpensive supply of foodstuffs for

A bedrock of lasting influence

The first handful of Russian Orthodox missionaries to arrive in Alaska in 1794 were ascetic monks, almost all of whom soon either died or returned home. But 30 years later when the Russian-American Company, seeking to train some of Alaska's natives for skilled jobs, called on the church for help, a rugged new breed of clergymen responded to the call. They schooled their pupils in reading, writing, arithmetic and religion, and trained the most promising as priests, thus establishing a local clergy that would remain a steadfast influence long after Alaska was sold to the United States.

Foremost among the missionaries was Father Ivan Veniaminov *(lower right)*, who was 27 when he arrived in Alaska with his family in 1824. On wind-scourged Unalaska Island he built a chapel, set up a meteorologic station and taught the indigenous Aleuts carpentry, blacksmithing and brickmaking. He learned their dialect, created an alphabet and translated the gospels for them. He spent four grueling months each year cramped for 14 to 16 hours a day in a kayak, traveling to the outlying islands in his parish. Ten years of this left Veniaminov with crippled feet and forced him to apply for an easier post at Sitka.

Over the next 16 years he built St. Michael's Cathedral *(right)*, started a seminary and even won the trust of the hostile Tlingit Indians when his inoculations saved them from a smallpox epidemic. In 1823 a traveler described Veniaminov as "quite herculean and very clever." Czar Nicholas I was equally impressed when he received Veniaminov in St. Petersburg two years later. Nicholas sponsored the energetic priest as Bishop of Alaska in 1840. In 1868 he was made Metropolitan of Moscow, Russian Orthodoxy's highest ranking office.

The flamelike copper cupola of St. Michael's Cathedral *(below)* reaches skyward as the congregation spills out onto Sitka's wooden sidewalks in the 1890s. A landmark of Russian Orthodox faith in Alaska, the frame church's gold and white interior *(right)* was adorned with brass candelabras, priceless icons and chalice covers embroidered by Russian nuns.

Described as "Paul Bunyan in a cassock," the indefatigable Father Veniaminov, shown here in his robes as Metropolitan of Moscow, commandeered dog sleds, kayaks and ships in order to spread the faith.

Russian missionaries built this humble wooden chapel with its tiny graveyard on windy Attu Island at the outermost tip of the Aleutians in 1830. Its sod roof was tied down with rope brought from Siberia.

Sitka, Kodiak and the several smaller Alaskan outposts. It cost the Russian-American Company $330 a ton to freight supplies from Siberia to Sitka. The provisions the Yankees brought were less expensive, but the Russians were reluctant to become too dependent on the ubiquitous Americans. The only alternative source was Spanish California, but the Spaniards were forbidden by royal edict from trading with foreigners. Therefore, Rezanov strongly favored planting a Russian agricultural colony on the coast north of San Francisco (then called Yuerba Buena).

Baranov was impressed by his employer's grasp of the problem, and Rezanov was delighted by his blunt, despotic little manager. "Wonderful man!" the Count wrote to Catherine's advisers in St. Petersburg. "I tell you, gentlemen, that Baranov is an original, and at the same time a very happy production of nature. His name is heard on the whole western coast, down to California. The Bostonians esteem him and respect him, and the savage tribes, in their dread of him, offer their friendship from the most distant regions."

Rezanov also reported that his cantankerous governor had made a request that would have been alarming if it were not so unthinkable: Baranov had asked to retire. The governor was now 60; he had spent 15 man-killing years in that arduous land and upon those brutal seas, and he complained of feeling ancient and used up. The Count expressed sincere concern—and so disarmed Baranov that he consented to stay.

Early in 1806 Rezanov boarded ship to inspect California for himself. Landing in San Francisco in the spring of 1806, the Count was cordially received by the port commandant, Don José Darío Argüello. Then the Count's heart betrayed his head: he fell in love with Don José's 16-year-old daughter, Doña Concepción, and she with him. Since the handsome and dashing Rezanov had been widowed two years earlier, an alliance might be possible—if the Russian Orthodox nobleman could get a special dispensation to wed a Roman Catholic. But it was not to be.

Rezanov, hurrying home to St. Petersburg to plead his case, caught pneumonia from a spill into an icy Siberian stream. Dangerously weakened, he nevertheless insisted on continuing his journey, and one morning fell from his saddle, was kicked in the head by his horse and died. Doña Concepción, waiting in California, finally learned the fate of her betrothed years later; heartbroken, she refused ever to marry and devoted the rest of her life to charitable works.

So Baranov was left to carry on alone, a circumstance he was long accustomed to. Not until 1812 was he able to act on the California scheme he had worked out with Rezanov. That March Baranov's most trusted lieutenant, Ivan Kuskov, landed on the coast of California, about 65 miles north of San Francisco, with a colonizing force of 25 Russians and 80 Aleuts. There Kuskov built a stockaded settlement and named it Fort Ross, after an old form of the word *Rossiia*—Russia. The Spaniards looked upon the interlopers with disfavor but lacked the strength to dislodge them. They grew darkly suspicious when, in 1813, Russians from Fort Ross brazenly established a satellite outpost just 25 miles from San Francisco. But that was the high watermark for Russian America; before long the tide would begin to recede.

In Sitka Baranov ruled on—but now he was getting truly old. Moreover, the sea otter—the passion that had kept him going for more than two decades—was growing noticeably scarcer. Periodically, Baranov petitioned St. Petersburg to be relieved. Each time his superiors put him off, and when they finally began to take him seriously, bad luck intervened to keep him on the job. One replacement fell sick and died en route to Sitka; a second was shipwrecked and drowned. Finally, in 1817 a live successor made it all the way to Alaska, and the next year Baranov, 72 and utterly worn out, was officially permitted to retire.

Yet Baranov could not quite bring himself to surrender his post. Though great honors awaited him in St. Petersburg, he dawdled aimlessly and took several months transferring the details of command. In the end he was summoned home; he bade farewell to Sitka and sailed for St. Petersburg by way of Europe. En route through the Orient, his ship stopped over at Batavia in the Dutch Indies where the tough old man was laid low by the unaccustomed languors of the tropics. Baranov died in Batavia on April 16, 1819, and the next day was buried at sea.

Thirteen governors followed Baranov in Sitka. They were men of rank and privilege, mostly naval officers, one a prince, another a baron. They and their aristocratic aides brought their wives, and those gentlewomen brought ball gowns, gilt-framed paintings, fine china, gleaming silver services and costly wines. And while the elite brightened their isolated existence with decorous parties and danced to the music of violins, Baranov's *promyshlenniki* faded into the background along with their seal-gut raincoats, rotgut rum and raucous song. The new administrators made Sitka ever more elegant, even as its importance declined with the diminishing haul of sea-otter pelts.

Baranov's successors were responsible men, and though none could match his exceptional drive, they did honor to his office in both of its functions— political and commercial. As civic leaders they showed a decent concern for the Aleuts and Indians. Three governors, among them a navy lieutenant who married Baranov's handsome daughter Irina, one of the children Anna had borne him, tried to improve relations with the troublesome Tlingits. For more amenable native Alaskans, the governors set up and maintained a school to teach trades and crafts—from navigation to clerking and engraving. Yet the cannons of Sitka were always trained on the Tlingit village, which grew up outside the town's stockaded walls, as a deterrent to the less amenable, and in 1857 they were used to put down a brief uprising.

In the governor's role as business administrator, Baranov's successors worked with diligence and imagination to develop new sources of income to make up for the shrinking fur trade. At the start of the California gold rush in 1849, one governor virtually stripped Sitka's warehouses to supply the boomtown of San Francisco. Another governor, working three years later with a group of San Francisco businessmen, started what then seemed a highly unlikely industry—supplying Californian coastal towns with Alaskan lake ice packed in sawdust. By the end of the decade more than 20,000 tons of Alaskan ice, at $35 a ton, had cooled the drinks of Californians.

The boldest and most constructive of the governors' innovations came in 1830, when Baron Ferdinand Wrangell took office as Baranov's fifth successor. The Baron put into effect the first comprehensive conservation program on the North American continent. He limited the hunting of fur seals by restricting the take to young males. To protect the endangered

sea otter, Wrangell divided the whole Alaskan coast, including the Aleutians, into strictly regulated hunting districts, each closed to hunters every other year. The sea otter gradually made a comeback—only to be hunted to the brink of extinction years later by the Russians' American successors. But between 1821 and 1862 the Russians shipped to Siberia only 51,000 sea-otter pelts—less than one third of what Baranov delivered during his 27-year tenure.

Through the post-Baranov period, events in the outside world were slowly but inexorably shaping the fate of Russian America. The Russian empire, overextended and bled white by a century of warfare with a half-dozen nations was badly in need of respite and retrenchment. After much soul-searching, St. Petersburg owned up to Russia's weakness and began to divest itself of its remote colonies.

One of the first properties to go was the struggling little outpost in California. The handful of Russian

Prince Dimitri Maksutov fought a losing battle to persuade his government to keep Alaska. After presiding over the transfer, he returned to Russia an embittered man.

farmers at Fort Ross could not grow enough wheat to make a dent in Alaska's need for bread. Since Fort Ross was otherwise useless, St. Petersburg in 1841 sold the colony for a token $30,000 to an ambitious Swiss named John Sutter. Oddly enough, the discovery of gold at Sutter's Mill seven years later caused more relief than regret in Russian circles. Clearly, St. Petersburg, 10,000 miles away, could not have controlled the mighty gold rush that ensued.

The idea of selling Alaska came into the open under bizarre circumstances in 1854. England was on the verge of entering the Crimean War against Russia. An official of the Russian-American Company, realizing that his nation was too weak to defend Alaska, concocted a scheme to "sell" the whole territory to the San Francisco company that imported Alaskan ice—his theory being that England would not dare lay hands on American real estate. The fur company

official, who was also the Russian vice consul in San Francisco, drew up a bill of sale, with blank spaces for the date and price, and a clause that would have returned Alaska to the Russian firm after three years. The ice company, convinced that its source of merchandise was in jeopardy, played along and signed the unusual document.

The bill of sale was then sent for approval to Edouard de Stoeckl, the Russian minister in Washington. Stoeckl, an urbane man who spoke fluent English, knew that St. Petersburg was not quite ready to authorize any sale of Alaska, much less this spurious one, but he shrewdly opened secret talks with American officials. The Americans were interested in Alaska but wanted no part of this particular deal, which was revealed as a fraud when England entered the Crimean War in March 1854. The British government, it turned out, had no designs whatsoever on Alaska, which it considered not worth even the modest effort required to capture the Russian outposts. In fact, England gladly signed a gentleman's agreement to leave Alaska alone in return for Russia's assurance that it would not invade the Canadian territories of the Hudson's Bay Company.

Then in 1856 came Russia's shattering Crimean defeat, and in the gloom that pervaded St. Petersburg, realistic officials recalled the aborted sale of Alaska and sent Ambassador Stoeckl orders to sound out Washington on a bona fide deal for the territory. The Russians needed money to pay their war debts, and they were well aware of the American passion for expansion. But the talks were interrupted again in 1860 by the overtures to another conflict—this time the American Civil War.

Late in 1866, with the Civil War over, St. Petersburg called Stoeckl home and instructed him to negotiate for the sale of Alaska, for a sum not less than five million dollars. The Russians never looked for another buyer; in fact, no other nation would have been interested.

Stoeckl returned to Washington in early March, 1867, and was greeted by the arrogant, brilliant, sometimes devious man with whom he would have to cross diplomatic swords: William H. Seward, Secretary of State under President Andrew Johnson. In the words of young Henry Adams, then in the diplomatic

service himself, Seward was "a slouching, slender figure" with "a head like a wise macaw; a beaked nose; shaggy eyebrows; unorderly hair and clothes; hoarse voice; offhand manner; free talk, and perpetual cigar." Seward, a New Yorker, had won the posts of governor and senator in his state's dog-eat-dog politics, and in the process, Adams concluded, "the politician had become nature, and no one could tell which was the mask and which the features." But Stoeckl knew Seward for an archexpansionist, determined to have Alaska for the United States, and the Russian envoy had orders to stand by passively and be courted profitably by his ardent, well-financed suitor.

Seward was more than ardent, he was in an all-fired nervous rush. He wanted to have the Alaska deal ready to present to Congress for ratification before that rebellious body adjourned at the end of March. He had no time for the nice proprieties that usually accompanied such negotiations between nations. President Johnson had been under increasing attack for his postwar Reconstruction policy. Though Seward could not have guessed that Congress would try to impeach Johnson only a year hence, he had good reason to suppose that Congressional resistance

to the purchase of Alaska—indeed to any administration bill—would grow stronger with the passing of time. So Seward began to discuss an Alaska purchase even before he was authorized by the President.

Seward began serious dickering on March 14 by offering Stoeckl five million dollars for Russian America. Then, to Stoeckl's amazement, Seward did not wait for an answer but immediately upped his own bid: "And we might even go to $5,500,000, but no more." Stoeckl was delighted by Seward's seeming naïveté. The Russian then availed himself of the recently laid transatlantic cable and advised St. Petersburg that he was going to try for six million dollars, or even 6.5 million.

Before his next encounter with Stoeckl, Seward attended a Cabinet meeting and casually asked for authority to offer seven million dollars for Alaska. Seward's fellow Secretaries were greatly surprised to learn of the negotiations; to that point Seward had confided in no one but President Johnson. But the Cabinet members cared little about Alaska, either way, and they did not object to Seward's request.

By March 23 the two negotiators had agreed on the main points of the sale. Stoeckl, with a gambler's

In Emanuel Leutze's 1867 painting the hectic 4 a.m. signing of the Alaska purchase becomes a staid gathering. Secretary of State Seward sits at left and Russian Ambassador Stoeckl stands at right.

sense of how far to push, had nudged the price up to the full seven million dollars that Seward had been authorized to bid. Stoeckl cabled the details to St. Petersburg and asked for authority to sign the treaty. He felt it necessary to apologize for his quick success; a transaction of such great importance should not have been rushed through in just two weeks. But, Stoeckl explained, "This whole affair has been managed in the go-ahead way of the Americans."

On March 29 Stoeckl received word from St. Petersburg that Czar Alexander had approved the treaty with minor provisos. That evening Stoeckl visited Seward at home to tell him the good news.

Seward was playing cards with his family when Stoeckl arrived, and word of the Czar's approval stopped the game instantly. Stoeckl said, "Tomorrow, if you like, I will come to the [State] Department, and we can enter upon the treaty."

"Why wait until tomorrow, Mr. Stoeckl?" asked Seward. "Let us make the treaty tonight."

At this Stoeckl turned vaguely suspicious and played for time to review his position. "But," he said, "your Department is closed. You have no clerks, and my secretaries are scattered about the town."

"Never mind that," Seward replied, "if you can muster your legation together before midnight, you will find me awaiting you at the Department, which will be open and ready for business."

Seward routed out his assistant secretary, William Hunter, and his chief clerk, Robert Chew. Preparing for the Congressional battle that surely lay in front of him, Seward dispatched his son Frederick to fetch Senator Charles Sumner of Massachusetts, the key to Congressional acceptance of the treaty. Sumner greeted the news coldly and departed without comment. (He did not attend the signing ceremony, though an imaginative artist portrayed him there.) Sumner happened to be burdened by democratic scruples: he did not believe that the Alaskan territory should change hands without a vote of approval from its inhabitants. But in the end he would suppress his misgivings and tell the Senate halfheartedly, "I regret very much to go for this treaty."

With Sumner forewarned, Seward hurried over to the State Department and made the Russian delegation welcome. Stoeckl, meanwhile, had decided to press for improvements on a few small treaty points. Seward refused to consider substantive changes at this late date, but he would not be denied while on the verge of what he considered a great personal triumph. To mollify Stoeckl he committed the United States to pay $200,000 more than the agreed price. So the final figure became $7.2 million. Alaska could have been had for considerably less if time was not of the essence. But as it was, Seward was about to acquire 586,400 square miles of territory — twice the size of Texas — for a little less than two cents an acre.

Two copies of the 27-page treaty, one in English and one in French, were properly engrossed. At about 4 a.m., Chief Clerk Chew brought the documents into Seward's gas-lighted office. The American Secretary of State and the Russian plenipotentiary then affixed their signatures.

This signing — this "dark deed done in the night," its critics soon reviled it — was hardly an auspicious beginning to the life of American Alaska. Indeed, it would not be a beginning at all until Congress acted, as it was called upon to do just six hours later. The struggle with Congress, first to approve the purchase and then to appropriate the money to pay for it, would be long and bitter. But Seward believed, with his usual arrogance, that he could ram Alaska down Congress' throat, and he was already planning which Congressional arms to twist first.

Seward's single-minded strategy would have impressed the tough old Russian who, more than anyone else, had paved the way for the Americans. Alexander Baranov might have recognized in Seward a man as determined as himself. Baranov never dreamed that Russia would ever part with his cruel, beloved land. But it might have consoled him to know that Alaska had fallen into the hands of a pioneering people whom he admired and to an aggressive government run by risk-taking men like William Seward. Sadly, though, Alaska would not capture the American imagination for nearly three decades.

But Seward sensed that, too. In 1870, when Seward was the butt of popular jokes for his Alaska purchase, a friend asked him what he considered the most significant act in his career. Without hesitation Seward declared, "The purchase of Alaska! But it will take the people a generation to find that out."

A colorful gallery of first Alaskans

In 1815 a Russian voyage of exploration set out to probe the Alaskan coastline for a sea passage to the North Atlantic with a 20-year-old artist named Louis Choris on board. In two years the expedition found no passage; its most lasting accomplishment may well have been Choris' detailed lithographs of the region's native inhabitants, the Aleuts and Eskimos.

Choris marveled at the success of these related Mongoloid peoples in adapting to their all-but-uninhabitable surroundings—the Aleuts living on the chain of barren islands stretching westward from the Alaska Peninsula and the Eskimos on Alaska's coast and offshore islands. Much of this land was volcanic rock or desolate tundra with scant vegetation in summer, and winter temperatures that reached $-65°$ F.

The Aleuts and Eskimos lived by hunting, chiefly seals, though some groups depended on caribou or whales and walruses. They used the flesh, blubber, hides, sinew, bones and teeth of these animals to supply almost everything they needed: food, shelter, boats, sleds, warm waterproof clothing, and hunting and household tools.

They dwelled in mobile skin tents in summer, in snow-insulated sod and skin houses in winter. So ingenious were these structures, and the smokeless seal-oil lamps that heated them, that even in the coldest weather temperatures on the sleeping platforms inside ranged upward of $80°$ F.

Sadly, the native Alaskans' skill in dealing with their environment did not prepare them for white men's firearms and infectious diseases. When the Americans bought Alaska in 1867, the Eskimos Choris had sketched had been reduced by almost half, and the Aleuts had declined to less than a tenth of their original population.

dess: et Lith. par Choris

At pains to record the Eskimo's material culture, Choris depicted a group from Kotzebue Sound in which two men wear ivory lip plugs through holes at the corners of their mouths and a woman in a finely ornamented parka has vertical lines tatooed on her chin. One man carries a sinew-reinforced bow and a quiver of ivory-tipped arrows.

Lith. de Langlumé

itans du Golfe de Kotzebue.

An Aleut couple stands by the shore as otter hunters set off in the background. The man, leaning on a double-bladed paddle, wears a visor of molded wood designed to protect a hunter from both sun and spray. The shape of the woman's elaborately trimmed dress of skins is a sign of the Russians' pervasive influence on the islanders.

The woman above has tied her hair in the traditional Aleut braids, but her dress is clearly Western and the cross she wears indicates that she is one of the many Aleuts who were baptized into the Russian church. The man sports a visor embellished with sea-lion whiskers and a waterproof *kamleika,* a paper-thin rain parka of seal gut.

In a skin-covered house on St. Lawrence Island, one Eskimo listens as another beats the only musical instrument known to his people — a tambourine made of skin stretched over a driftwood frame. Choris wrote in his journal that the huts "stank horribly from the whale meat, cleaned and dried intestines, and birds skins" stored in them *(left)*.

Dutch Harbor stretches beyond the village of Oululuk (now Unalaska), the principal Russian settlement in the Aleutians at the time of Choris' visit in 1817. The village had four houses of wood and 30 of sod, with a population of 150 Aleuts and 16 Russians, most of whom, wrote the artist, had "lost hope of returning to their country."

2|A rich harvest for the taking

An American-led killing gang of Aleuts wielding five-foot clubs methodically slaughters a pod of seals on St. Paul Island in the Pribilofs.

Even before Congress voted funds to buy Alaska in 1868, Yankee freebooters began tramping northward in search of an icy El Dorado. Most of them, having found no overnight bonanzas, went home empty-handed in a year or two. Some did stay, however, to exploit one of Alaska's few recognized resources: furs.

The fur traders soon saw their business revolutionized by a simple invention. The new machine removed in one stroke the outer layer of bristly guard hairs from the skin of the fur seal, exposing the dense, downy pelt beneath. The cost of doing this by hand had formerly ruled out the fur seal as a luxury pelt everywhere but in China.

The dehairing machine and the markets it opened up had a devastating effect on the seal herd. Since 1834 the Russian-American Company and the United States monopoly that succeeded it had restricted the harvesting of fur seals to their breeding grounds on the remote Pribilof Islands, killing only young bachelor males *(below).*

But by the 1870s demand for the trimmed pelts reached such heights that reckless freelance hunters began killing seals — including pregnant females — on the open sea. The fur seals' numbers plummeted from about four million to a low of 110,000 in 1911, when an international treaty finally ended the indiscriminate slaughter.

53

Learning to cope with "Seward's Icebox"

At Sitka on the cool, misty afternoon of October 18, 1867, Russian and American cannons fired a salute into a cotton-colored sky, and the Imperial flag came down. Then, to the continuing thud of the cannons, the Stars and Stripes was raised. Alaska, though not paid for (even as Old Glory ascended the 90-foot pole, Congress and the nation at large were taking sides on the question of whether to pay for it at all), had passed into the hands of the United States. And the enterprising Yankee nomads who had scrambled from one infant and flourishing settlement to another across the Old West now stood on the last frontier, below their country's ensign, eager to turn a dime.

Although Alaska was now officially American territory, nearly half a century would pass before it would acquire full legal status and be able to send a representative to Congress. The intervening years would be a time of turmoil, largely as a result of Congress' neglect. During that difficult period, two types of Americans were to play crucial roles in the development of Alaska.

One group was made up of sober-minded citizens who wanted law and order for the territory and agitated persistently for self-government, for representation in Washington, for property rights and for better education. Their spokesman was a short, muscular Presbyterian missionary who came to Alaska to have a look at the untamed land and fell passionately in love with it. The other group comprised those who headed north solely for the purpose of quick gain. Some ar-

rived with financial backing, and a few of them were very successful; one industrious fellow took over the interests of the Russian-American Company and earned millions of dollars for himself and his partners—and the U.S. Treasury as well—harvesting the fur seals of the Pribilof Islands.

Other fortune seekers had hard times, and soon turned back and headed for home. But a scattering, for whom gold was the attraction, hung on, scrambling from one creek to another, each of them sure of hitting pay dirt somewhere down the line—and often perishing in the attempt.

But in Sitka, on that autumn day when the flag went up, Alaska's future seemed bright. The sun set on a stake-dotted town. Homesteads had been plotted as rapidly as sticks could be driven into the soil. Shanties were thrown up. A restaurant, two tenpin alleys and a row of saloons were being built. Existing stores were changing hands overnight, and the new owners were hastily erecting new signs. The Yankees named the main thoroughfare Lincoln (Russian maps had left it unnamed); two cross streets were christened Russia and America. In no time, it seemed, the newcomers had gained a toe hold on the best-known part of Alaska, the Panhandle.

To the south along the coast of California, other bold optimists prepared to sail north toward prosperity. "Among the civilians on the way to Sitka," one newspaper correspondent reported, "is a California forty-niner with an outfit of whiskey and tobacco, the proceeds of which he will invest in lands about the promising town. He has an undoubted faith that in a dozen years Sitka will contain 50,000 inhabitants." This kind of grandiose projection was commonplace in Alaska during the autumn of 1867 as bumptious American speculators strode ashore at Sitka with squatters, gamblers, cooks, promoters, businessmen,

U.S. revenue cutters *Bear (foreground)* and *Corwin,* photographed lying in the ice off Nome, patrolled the Bering Sea in the 1880s and 1890s, hounding seal poachers and rescuing shipwrecked whalers.

barbers and would-be politicians in search of sinecure.

Unfortunately, the attitude of the United States Congress was quite the contrary. Congress had been extremely reluctant to purchase Alaska in the first place. Many of President Johnson's opponents saw it as one more arbitrary act by a Chief Executive who they would soon try unsuccessfully to remove from office. The Senate had begrudgingly ratified Secretary Seward's treaty only after being warned that rejection would be viewed as an offensive act by Russia, the Union's great friend. By the time the debate turned to appropriation, in the summer of 1868, the impeached President had avoided conviction, but the wounds of his trial were still raw and Alaska became a handy target for Congressional vitriol.

Massachusetts Congressman Benjamin F. Butler said caustically that he did not object to paying for the Czar's friendship "if we could only get rid of the land — or ice, rather — which we are to get by paying for it." The halls of the Capitol reverberated with sarcastic epithets for the newly acquired territory: Walrus-sia, Icebergia, Polaria, Seward's Icebox and, of course, Seward's Folly.

But the outcry was not restricted only to Washington. The *New York Tribune* editorialized: "We may make a treaty with Russia but we cannot make a treaty with the North Wind or the Snow King. Ninety-nine hundredths of Russian America are absolutely useless. To Russia it was an encumbrance, to us it would be an embarrassment." The New York *World* summed up its position more pithily: "Russia has sold us a sucked orange."

The dissidents kept insisting that Alaska was unusable, uninhabitable and unworthy of purchase. In fact, Alaska was only unusual. To be sure, 17,000 square miles were permanently under ice. But in Alaska, enormous Alaska, 17,000 square miles was but a plug in the melon, a mere 3 per cent of a territory that, as it turned out, contained enough wealth, both animal and mineral, to repay the purchase price many times over. Royalty income from the fur-seal harvest alone — an industry restricted to two tiny specks in the Bering Sea, St. George (27 square miles) and St. Paul (35 square miles), collectively called the Pribilof Islands — would, over the next 20 years, feed into the national treasury almost

as much as had been expended for all of Alaska. For more than three decades the Russians had hunted the fur seals under a program of careful conservation initiated by Baron Ferdinand Wrangell, and included in the territorial package Seward had accepted was a seal herd estimated to number four million.

But Congress, at least in the beginning, gave little thought to such resources. The legislators saw Alaska as a remote and noncontiguous territory, a long-term investment in no need of immediate development. Already at hand were the much more pressing problems of Southern reconstruction, Northern industrialization and the occupation of the West. So, perhaps understandably, Congress developed a blind spot when the frontier was suddenly moved even farther westward and, worse, north of the 49th parallel to the Arctic Circle and beyond. As Representative Benjamin F. Loan of Missouri put it, "to suppose that anyone would leave the United States to seek a home in the regions of perpetual snow is simply to suppose such a person insane."

The Congressman was expressing a feeling widely held in the United States at the time. The result was that a handful of Yankees, men and women with strengths as extraordinary and rough-edged as the climate and geography of the land they clung to, would have to develop the territory with almost no help from home. Their fellow Americans might think of Alaska as too big, too cold, too inaccessible and too much, but these pioneers never would.

Congress, with more important concerns and aware that there were few Americans — and still fewer voters — in Alaska, paid them scant attention. It was not until gold was discovered in large amounts that the Alaskan pioneers were joined by a substantial part of the nation's population. Gold would win Alaska recognition as a possession of merit. But gold in substantial quantities was a long time in the finding; in the 30 years between Seward's purchase and the highly publicized gold strikes of the late 1890s, the largest peninsula in the Western hemisphere would have to fend for itself.

When the Stars and Stripes was raised for the first time above Sitka, a newspaper correspondent from San Francisco observed: "Democratic institutions

An 1867 cartoon portrays Alaska as a block of ice purchased by President Andrew "King Andy" Johnson and Secretary of State Seward to placate Congress.

PREPARING FOR THE HEATED TERM.

King Andy and his man Billy lay in a great stock of Russian ice in order to cool down the Congressional majority.

now extend over an area hitherto the possession of a despotic government. The occasion inspired the soul of every American present and, as the officers retired, three mighty cheers were given and we all rejoiced that we now stood on American soil."

Somewhat less inspired were the Russians; the several hundred employees of the Russian-American Company faced imminent unemployment. Under the treaty they were given a three-year option on whether to go to Russia or remain in Alaska and become American citizens. The employees had grown used to a slow-paced, paternalistic pattern of living. But now a vivacious American commercialism consumed their capital. Within weeks almost all of the Russians had sailed for home. Most of the workers of mixed Russian and Eskimo, Aleut or Indian ancestry—called Creoles by the newcomers—stayed in Alaska and coped with the culture shock of American occupation as best they could.

The Russians' departure left Alaska with a population of approximately 30,000 indigenous peoples, who lived in isolated places scattered here and there throughout the territory, and 900 Americans. The majority of the latter were concentrated at Sitka—and they asserted themselves immediately. Less than a

month after the takeover they held a convention, elected a mayor, five councilmen, a recorder, a surveyor and a marshal, and framed a city charter.

The charter, like just about everything else done in Sitka at the time, was drafted in haste. "Upon inquiry," one of its authors recalled, "it was found that not a single copy of the Constitution of the United States, nor a single state, not a copy of any municipal charter or ordinance, not a law book, nor a statute of any kind, save one, which Murphy the tailor had—*Wharton's Criminal Practice*—was obtainable."

As it turned out, lack of reference material was the least of the problems facing the town's new stepfathers. Among the larger issues to be dealt with was the awkward fact that as inhabitants of a place that was neither a state nor a territory they could not legally govern as a town council. In fact, they could not even incorporate a town—or buy or sell town lots. All those stakes they had driven on the day of transfer signified nothing; the land laws of the United States did not embrace Alaska—and would not for several years—and, consequently, no one could take possession of land with any hope of clear title. Nor could Alaskans legally impanel a jury, for United States law provided that only taxpayers could serve on a jury. Alaska had no taxes and thus no taxpayers. And if a person died, he or she could not leave a will—because there was no probate court.

Typically, the Americans refused to allow any of these obstacles to stand for long in the way of civil government for Sitka. Instead, they applied basic frontier logic, which held that they had a right to make their own rules when the law made no provision otherwise. They established a "mayor's court" and gave the mayor authority to impanel juries. The court would be funded from fines that ranged from as little as three dollars for being drunk and disorderly ($50 for being *extremely* drunk and disorderly) to $100 for assault. To meet other city expenses, such as sanding the sidewalks in winter and purchasing paper and pens, they established a two-dollar poll tax, a two-dollar dog license fee and business taxes that ran from $25 quarterly for brewers to $75 quarterly for dealers in lottery tickets.

On July 4, 1868, the citizens of Sitka turned out to celebrate their first Independence Day. With

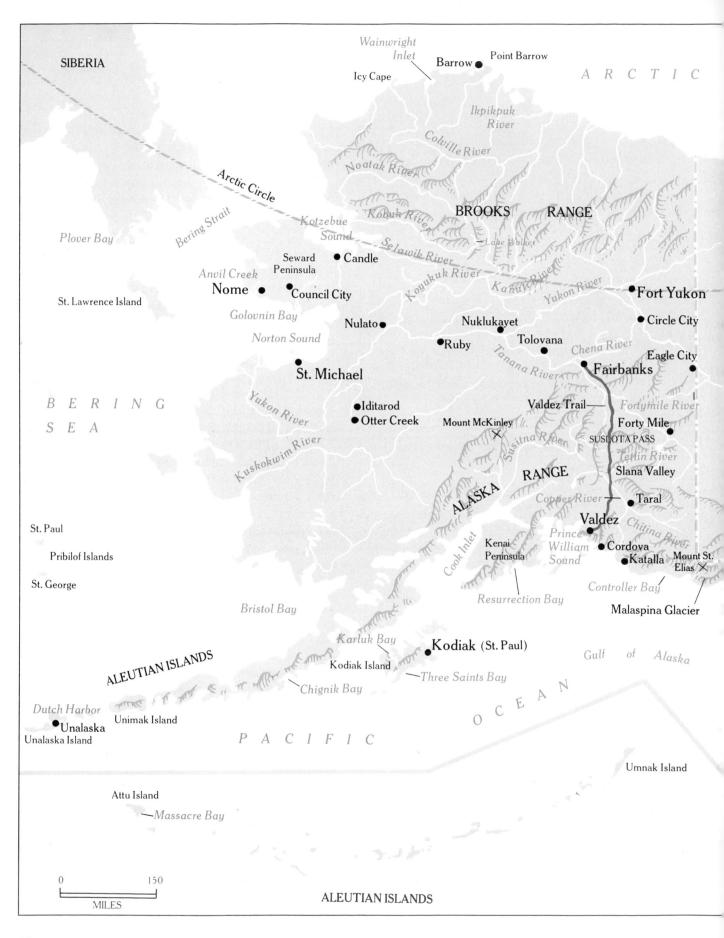

SIBERIA

Wainwright Inlet   Barrow ●   Point Barrow

Icy Cape

A R C T I C

Ikpikpuk River

Colville River

Noatak River

Arctic Circle

Bering Strait

Plover Bay

Kotzebue Sound

Kobuk River

BROOKS   RANGE

—*Lake Walker*

Selawik River

Koyukuk River

Kanuti River

Yukon River

Seward Peninsula   ● Candle

Anvil Creek

Nome ●   ● Council City

St. Lawrence Island

Golovnin Bay

● Fort Yukon

● Circle City

Nulato ●

Nuklukayet ●

Tolovana ●

Chena River

Eagle City ●

Norton Sound

Ruby ●

Tanana River

Fairbanks ●

St. Michael ●

B E R I N G

S E A

Yukon River

● Iditarod
● Otter Creek

Mount McKinley ✕

Susitna River

Valdez Trail—

Fortymile River

Forty Mile ●

SUSLOTA PASS

Tetlin River

Slana Valley

ALASKA   RANGE

Copper River

Kuskokwim River

St. Paul

Pribilof Islands

St. George

Taral ●

Valdez ●

Chitina River

Prince William Sound

Kenai Peninsula

● Cordova

Mount St. Elias ✕

Cook Inlet

Katalla ●

Controller Bay

Resurrection Bay

Malaspina Glacier

Bristol Bay

Karluk Bay

Kodiak ● (St. Paul)

Gulf   of   Alaska

ALEUTIAN ISLANDS

Kodiak Island

—*Three Saints Bay*

Chignik Bay

Dutch Harbor

Unimak Island

● Unalaska

Unalaska Island

P A C I F I C

Umnak Island

Attu Island

—*Massacre Bay*

O C E A N

0   150

MILES

ALEUTIAN ISLANDS

Superimposed on a map of the United States, Alaska spans the 2,300 miles from Georgia to the California coast.

KON
RRITORY

rt Reliance

—Klondike River

wson City

A NEARLY IMPENETRABLE LAND

Alaska did not permit easy access to those who wished to penetrate it. Mountains discouraged entry from the east, and the 34,000 miles of coastline were, on the whole, harsh and inhospitable. A few rivers offered highways to the interior. The greatest of these was the Yukon, which rose in Canada, flowed north to the Arctic Circle, then swerved west and south to the Bering Sea. Despite the obstacles, by 1912 much of the wilderness was dotted with towns and smaller settlements, as the large map demonstrates.

● Whitehorse

Lake
Lindeman
CHILKOOT PASS

WHITE PASS

Dyea
Taiya Inlet
kagway

uir Glacier
Juneau

cier
Bay
Douglas
Treadwell
Stikine River

CANADA

Sitka

ranov Island

Kasaan Bay
● Wrangell

'rince of Wales Island
● Ketchikan
Klawock
● Tongass

$150 collected by private subscription and with a $385 subsidy received from the city council, they held a parade. All dogs, children, civilians and soldiers participated, according to one enthusiastic account. There was even a wagon, "decorated and seated full of young ladies dressed in white, representing the States and Territories, while an infant child, supported among the others portrayed Alaska as the youngest of the sisters, the weakest and most dependent upon the grand cordon of States."

The day was rounded out with stirring speeches that called forth the thrilling prospects just beyond their present sacrifices. Sitka's mayor, William Sumner Dodge, expounded on the same hopeful message he had already dispatched to the Treasury Department in Washington. Alaska, he said, "is full of wealth and under proper management bands of hardy adventurers, the pioneers of our civilization, will rapidly develop its resources and in a few years repay tenfold the cost of the purchase."

In Washington, 23 days following the Independence Day celebration in Sitka, Congress finally approved the appropriation for the purchase of Alaska, though no suspender-snapping oratory accompanied the action. On the contrary, Representative Hiram Price of Iowa spoke for many of his colleagues by casting his vote with this lament: "Now that we have got it and cannot give it away or lose it, I hope we will keep it under military rule and get along with as little expense as possible."

That was exactly what was done. Congress decreed Alaska a military and customs district and put the whole half million square miles of it under the jurisdiction of one customs officer with four deputies and the commandant of the American garrison. About 250 soldiers had been there since the transfer; for the protection of the inhabitants the military force was soon increased to 500.

Federal law enforcement was dependent upon the whim of the troop commander. The first one of these, Brevet Major General Jefferson Columbus Davis, seems to have been extraordinarily lax, at least in so far as the discipline of his officers and men was concerned. Most of the troops were stationed at Sitka and at Wrangell, a former trading post near the mouth of the Stikine River. Both were located far down the

Brigadier General Lovell Rousseau formally received Alaska for the United States on October 18, 1867. He believed the Russians would stay and become U.S. citizens "if treated kindly." But they were abused and most left Alaska.

Alaska Panhandle, and both were situated on heavily forested islands.

For soldiers on liberty there was very little to do. Worse, liquor was forbidden in the district. This put quite a strain on the soldiers' ingenuity, but they proved themselves equal to the challenge. The Indians had been brewing an innocuous beverage made with bark and berries for generations; now the soldiers taught them how to beef up this bland stuff with molasses and yeast and then to distill it. The result was a skull-splitting concoction that was called hoochinoo (a shortened form of which soon attained a place in American slang).

The soldiers' behavior promptly took a turn for the worse. In 1869 Mayor Dodge, who was also serving as U.S. customs officer, complained that the military's conduct "has been bad and demoralizing in the extreme. Many is the night I have been called upon after midnight, by men and women, Russian and Aleutian in their night-clothes, to protect them against the malice of the soldiers."

Another witness, a Russian holdover named Stephen Ushin, reported sorrowfully: "Before the arrival of the American soldiers there was at least some kind of order, but with the raising of the American flag, all life of Sitka changed to the detriment of the entire population."

At about the same time Sitka was experiencing its decline in morality, its economy also began to slide. The hopeful speculators who had arrived at the time of transfer were still in town, but many were now disheartened and were starting to think of pulling out. And while they pondered leaving, they stopped paying their taxes, creating a financial crisis that forced the fledgling city council to slacken city services. It took but a few months for Sitka to fall into serious disrepair: swine wallowed in the streets, the boardwalks worked loose and became hazardous to pedestrians, and a public-health officer described overriding filth. In the fall of 1869 the desperate townspeople dispatched a plea to Washington: "The Citizens of Alaska, having for two years past been deprived of any voice in the making of laws, ask from Congress the formation of a territorial government." But Congress did not act.

People began departing and the town's economy sagged further. By now, even the military payroll could not generate enough commercial activity to sustain Sitka's merchants. On Independence Day in 1870, the city council could not muster enough money or interest to hold a parade.

In less than three years of American control, Sitka, where the Russians had lived in colonial elegance, had wilted. An era brief as a daydream was over. One of those who left was William S. Dodge, the customs collector and mayor who abandoned the thankless posts to practice law in San Diego.

Dodge's successor in the nonpaying mayor's chair was John Kinkead, who had also steamed north with dreams of power and had served as postmaster, councilman and keeper of the town's trading post. "The accumulation of honors," he later commented solemnly, "was distressing." Kinkead kept the job of mayor for less than a year, then disillusioned, he drifted back to the States.

But while failed men packed their broken aspirations and prepared to flee Alaska, there did emerge in 1870 a single shining success. Hayward M. Hutchinson had been in Sitka in 1867 when the Russian-

American Company shut down. For $350,000 he and his San Francisco partners bought all the assets of that fur-trading firm: steamers, sailing vessels, wharves, salt, furs, and warehouses at Sitka, Kodiak, Unalaska and the Pribilof Islands. Also included in the package were a number of remote northwest trading posts. Thus was Hutchinson launched into the fur-sealing industry, backed by a coterie of powerful West Coast investors.

In 1868 the firm organized itself as the Alaska Commercial Company, with some new investors and assets of $1.8 million, and began a major lobbying drive in Washington. Hutchinson and his friends were concerned over stiff competition among other American concerns for the skins from around the Pribilofs, which made rapid depletion of the seal herds a strong possibility—and, of course, compelled the Alaska Company to share its profits.

In 1870 Congress passed an act making the Pribilof Islands a protected federal reserve. The law limited the annual harvest to 100,000 sealskins, permitted only male animals one year or older to be killed and forbade the use of firearms to kill them. Sealing rights on the Pribilofs were put up for lease to the highest bidder—and the lease was awarded to the Alaska Commercial Company.

Under the contract the company agreed to pay an annual rent of $55,000 plus a royalty of $2.625 on each sealskin taken. It also undertook to establish schools for the 400 or so Aleuts who were living in the Pribilofs and to provide their sustenance by furnishing free of charge each year 25,000 dried salmon, 60 cords of firewood, and salt and barrels for preserving seal meat. After accomplishing that, the company began its work—and Congress, having taken one of the very few reasoned and farsighted actions that any administration or any Congress would take with regard to American Alaska in its first 45 years, lapsed again into indifference.

The nature of the sealing contract was attuned to the 30-million-year-old rhythms of the yearly seal migration. For seven or eight months through winter and spring, the seals were away from the Pribilofs, feeding and sleeping on the open Pacific. In the summer, back from their 6,000-mile journey, they assembled on the Pribilofs in numbers so great that one observer crouching on a cliff top above a rookery counted tens of thousands, and then quit.

Harvesting the annual toll of 100,000 skins was a carefully orchestrated ritual. At dawn a dozen hunters would dodge among the rocks and the grassy hummocks, trying to get between the open sea and the enormous bands of young males and old bull bachelors that were all sleeping together far from the breeding grounds (cows and calves were spared). Rising to full height, the hunters would shout, "Hai! Hai!" In moments a few startled seals would head inland toward the tundra plateau. That was usually all it took to set off a fin-slapping stampede.

The seals were herded toward the killing ground a mile or two away, in effect carrying their own skins to the salthouses. There the hunters moved in, armed with hickory bludgeons five feet long, stabbing knives, skinning knives and whetstones. The chosen foreman stepped among the herd and drove out 100 to 150 seals, which the butchers rounded up into a group. Then the foreman looked them over and culled the old bulls and the young that had shabby or thin fur;

61

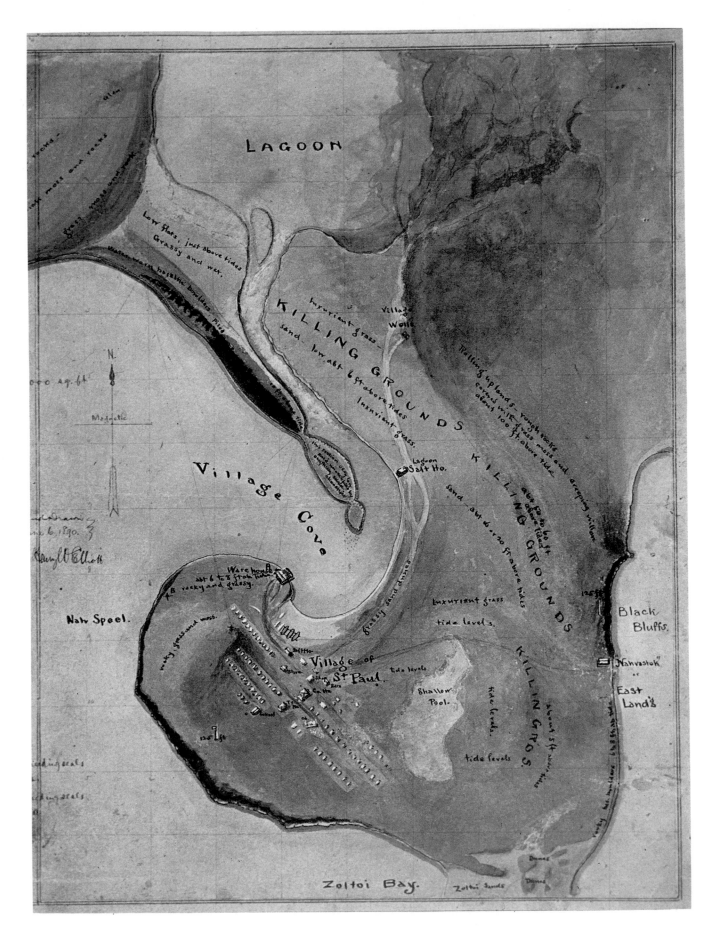

LAGOON

Low flats, just above tides.
Grassy and wet.

Luxurient grass –

Village
Wells

KILLING GROUNDS

sand low abt 6 ft above tides

Luxurient grass.

Rolling uplands – rough rocks
covered with grass moss and
about 100 ft above tide.

KILLING GROUNDS

N.

Magnetic

Village Cove

Lagoon
Salt Ho.

sand – out 6 or 20 ft above tides

abt 40 to 60 ft
above tides

Naw Speel.

Ware house
abt 6 to 8 from tide
rocky and grassy.

grassy sand dunes

Luxurient grass

tide levels.

KILLING GRDS.

Black
Bluffs.

Nahvastok
or
East
Land's

Village of
St. Paul.

Shallow
Pool.

tide levels

tide levels.

tide levels.

About 5 ft above tide

125 ft.

Zoltoi Bay.

Zoltoi Sands

these were left to make their way back to the beach.

No such luck for the full furred. At the signal "Strike!" from the foreman, the hunters crushed the seals' skulls with blows from the hickory bludgeons. The skinning was done quickly, for sealing men believed that skin left on the carcass for much over an hour—even less if it was a hot day—was irremediably spoiled. The skins were then piled on top of each other—"hair to fat"—packed in salt and left to "pickle" for about three weeks before being shipped to San Francisco. Most of the best sealskins eventually were sent to London, where furriers had perfected the arts of curing and dyeing pelts.

The seal harvest went on year by year, paying into the U.S. Treasury an annual average of $317,000,

---

A 40-YEAR CRUSADE TO SAVE THE SEAL

Conservationist Henry W. Elliott made several trips to the fur-seal breeding grounds on the Pribilof Islands and campaigned for 40 years to curtail the slaughter of the seals. In 1872, when the seal population was at its height, he painted himself amid a sea of pups (above). Eighteen years later he drew the map at left of the southern tip of St. Paul Island for a report to Washington. It shows the extensive killing grounds where seals were slaughtered and illustrates how their breeding grounds had shrunk from 1872 (dark shaded coast) to 1890 (in red). Under pressure from sealing interests, the government suppressed the report.

by itself a fair rate of interest on the original Alaskan investment. At about the time the contract was made with the Alaska Commercial Company in 1870, a fur-seal skin was worth three to four dollars delivered in London. Six years later the same skin fetched $15 or more, and by 1881 the price had climbed to $20. Alaska Commercial's take averaged 92,811 skins a year, and in the first 20 years the concession paid its 14 owners a net profit of $18 million.

With breeding bulls and females protected by law, the herd increased by appreciable numbers through the 1870s, when the rising price of skins attracted less careful hunters to the northern Pacific. These were pelagic—open sea—sealers, who killed with rifles and shotguns loaded with buckshot. The practice was devastating. Thousands of pregnant females were slain, as well as nursing mothers whose orphaned pups were left to starve ashore. Moreover, since a dead seal sank underwater quickly, more than half the kill was never recovered.

As more and more independent schooners, both American and Canadian, entered the business, Alaska Commercial saw its monopoly falling to pieces and pressured the federal government for help. What happened as a result of the company's pleas was good for the fur seals and nearly disastrous for American foreign policy. In 1886 the Revenue Marine cutter *Corwin* seized one American and three Canadian ships engaged in sealing in the Bering Sea. The schooners were escorted to Unalaska and stripped of their rigging to prevent flight. The skippers, though justifiably protesting that they had been beyond the three-mile limit and thus were legally sealing in international waters, were hauled to Sitka and consigned to a month in jail. The next year, the U.S. seized a dozen sealing ships in Bering waters.

These police actions brought a threat of war with Great Britain, which on behalf of the Canadians, asserted the right of freedom of the seas. Eventually, the case went to an international tribunal where the verdict was mixed: the United States was ordered to restore the captured vessels and pay $473,151 in reparations to Canada, but the tribunal also prohibited pelagic sealing anywhere within 60 miles of the Pribilof Islands. At last, in 1911 an international treaty was signed providing that seals could be taken only on land and under strict controls.

While the sealing industry fell into capable hands almost at the outset of American control, the rest of Alaska was faring poorly. In 1873 Sitka's city council collapsed. The last meeting was held on February 18, and there is no indication in the minutes that it would be the last. The councilmen simply did not meet again. Though the record does not say why, it is easy to guess: Sitka was going broke. The number of prostitutes in town, perhaps the best barometer of economic decline, had fallen from a high of 34 in 1870 to a low of 18 two years later. Maritime traffic at the port was so sparse that full receipts at the Customs House for 1873 came to a paltry $155.25. "It may as well be confessed," one official wrote after departing, "that most of us thought political greatness would be thrust upon us, and we were prepared to submit gracefully."

The Army pulled out in 1877; the men were needed to help put down the Nez Percé Indian uprising in Idaho and Montana. The only officials left in all of Alaska were Montgomery P. Berry, the customs collector at Sitka, his deputies, three postmasters and a few Treasury agents in the remote Pribilofs. And the only tools Berry possessed with which to enforce his rule over the 586,400-square-mile territory were two cases of rifles and two cases of ammunition that were somehow shipped to him by mistake. And he

alone was authorized to load and fire the weapons.

As Alaska's top lawman, Berry's responsibilities included making sure no liquor was smuggled into the territory. For years smugglers all over the globe had enjoyed a lively trade along Alaska's coast. The Army had been unable—at times, it seemed, unwilling—to enforce prohibition. Now Berry was expected to police 34,000 miles of ragged coastline as well as unnumbered islands. The customs collector did not even have a rowboat.

On another front, the Tlingits, who had once overwhelmed a Russian garrison and who had been demonstrably unhappy during the 10 years of military rule, were believed to be aching for revenge. As much as the small white population at Sitka had disliked the Army's obstreperous regime, it was even more alarmed by the soldiers' withdrawal.

With the blue-coated show of authority gone, hard types in both the white and Indian communities drank large quantities of alcohol, argued, fought and threatened to cause serious trouble. Early in 1879 one witness reported that a "gang of rowdies and bummers" got an Indian woman drunk, then burned her alive in her cabin. As tempers flared and street fights broke out daily, good citizens sent an anxious plea for help to Washington. As a result, the U.S. gunboat *Alaska* was dispatched from San Francisco to protect Sitka from the Tlingits.

But the episode turned out to be humiliating because the British Navy got there first. The Sitkans, understandably convinced by their past experiences that they would never hear from Washington, had also sent a message for help by mail steamer to Victoria, British Columbia. Answering the call, Captain H. Holmes A'Court took Her Majesty's man-of-war *Osprey* to Sitka, arriving on March 1, 1879. Captain A'Court trained his guns on the Tlingit village and announced that he would stay until the United States did something about protecting its own citizens. A day later the revenue cutter *Wolcott* arrived on a regular patrol.

But the H.M.S. *Osprey* remained until April 3, when the much better-armed *Alaska* finally pulled into port. In June the U.S.S. *Jamestown,* under Commander Lester A. Beardslee, came on the scene, and for the next five years the government of Alaska, such as it was, remained in the hands of Navy officers.

The Navy's administration did not operate under any more legality than had the Army's regime, and Beardslee complained that "acts be performed by us which could not be justified by any law except the natural law by which might becomes right." His successor, Commander Henry Glass, who assumed command in 1881, asked for instructions on what to do about three civilians who were charged with attempted murder. The Secretary of the Navy advised him that "in the absence of any legally constituted judicial tribunal," he could "keep these men in confinement as long as, in your judgment, the interest of peace and good order may require."

What Alaska desperately needed all along was an effective lobbyist, an informed spokesman in Washington, D.C. Just one person working full time in the best interest of the territory would be one more than Alaska now had. Providentially, in 1877, the year the Army left, just such a man arrived. His name was Dr. Sheldon Jackson, and like John Calvin, he despised sin and loved work.

Dr. Jackson, then 43 years old and only five feet tall, had had the desire to serve the Lord ever since the first time he had read the Scriptures as a boy. In early manhood he had founded churches and schools from the Canadian boundary to the Rio Grande. He had visited the Alaskan territory just to have a look at the raw new land; he went away so fired with enthusiasm that for the next three decades he was Alaska's most energetic, vocal and persuasive champion back in the United States.

Dr. Jackson returned south determined to awaken his nation to the needs of Alaska; from Denver to Boston and back he bounced, appealing to hundreds of groups with a standard impassioned speech: "In all that country there is no law—there can be no restraint—and the lowest animal passions of the rough miners, trappers, hunters, soldiers, and sailors rage unchecked. The Indian woman is considered the lawful spoil of those men!"

To women's auxiliaries throughout the nation he told the compelling story of a ne'er-do-well from Wrangell named John Boyd who drank too much, killed a man and was sentenced—even though Alaska had no judicial system—to be "jerked to Jesus" posthaste. "Twice in the night he sent for me," Jackson was quoted as saying. "He was then in great distress. He had not heard a prayer for 20 years until I prayed with him." But Jackson, heeding the call, reacquainted the doomed fellow with the Deity, and when John Boyd swung from the gallows the next day, he died a saved man.

This was powerful stuff, delivered with histrionic zeal, and it evoked just the response the feisty little preacher desired. Sunday-school children everywhere soon became familiar with the plight of the Godforsaken creatures up there in the cold Northwest; their mothers packed and mailed packages of goods, and whole families forewent new Sunday shoes in order to support an "Alaskan seeking Christ."

For six years Jackson electrified Christian opinion and magnetized the country's humanitarians to join his cause. Then, in 1883, he moved to Washington and did the job that most needed to be done on Alaska's behalf. Senator Benjamin Harrison of Ohio, a fellow Presbyterian, was already pushing for a legislative act for Alaska that would bring law and order to the territory, and Jackson became Senator Harrison's formidable ally.

In a superb display of pressure politics, the preacher managed to get the combined Presbyterian, Baptist, Methodist and Episcopalian armies to bombard Congress with appeals for an appropriation for Alaskan schools. Jackson swung the National Education Assembly to his side, then the National Education Association, followed with petitions from the teachers' associations of a dozen states. He had more than 100,000 circulars printed, urging "friends of education to rally and flood their congressmen with petitions asking special attention to the claims of Alaska." By the spring of 1884, Congress was awash in petitions from 25 states.

On May 17, the Organic Act of Alaska was passed. While not ideal, it was a start. The Organic Act placed the territory under the civil and criminal laws of Oregon. It created a governor and a district court with a judge and a district attorney, a marshal, four deputies and a clerk, and four commisioners to handle minor legal matters. It also provided $25,000 for education in the territory. As for administering the

Presbyterian missionary Sheldon Jackson, shown here dressed for a summer in Alaska, spent his winters lobbying in Washington, D.C., where his influence extended to the appointment of territorial governors.

Two Eskimo families in southwestern Alaska—one in furs, the other in calicoes and frock coats—were photographed by missionaries in 1884 to demonstrate the supposed advantages of civilization.

ESKIMO FAMILY ON THE KUSKOKWIM RIVER, ALASKA
(UNCIVILIZED).

PHOTO-GRAVURE CO., N. Y.

ESKIMO FAMILY ON KUSKOKWIM RIVER, ALASKA.
(CIVILIZED).
From Photographs by Messrs. Hartmann & Weinland.

money, that job fell to Sheldon Jackson, who became Alaska's first general agent of education.

In more ways than one it was an impossible assignment. Jackson's mandate required him to visit each school in the territory at least once a year. But if, for example, he proposed to visit the school at Nulato in the Yukon basin, he would have to travel from Sitka on the monthly mail steamer to Juneau, 166 miles away, and from there hire native paddlers to take him by canoe to Taiya Inlet at the foot of the Chilkoot Pass, 100 miles to the north, then walk 25 miles over the pass to the headwaters of the Yukon. At this juncture he would have been obliged to build a raft and float downstream through the Yukon's shoals and rapids another 1,600 miles. Alternatively, he could have started the journey by traveling back to San Francisco, catching a steamer to St. Michael on the Bering coast at Norton Sound, then a riverboat from the mouth of the Yukon and up another 769 miles to Nulato, a total of 5,663 miles.

Prudently, Jackson did not make many such trips, but he did the best he could to staff the schools. In the autumn of 1886, when several mission schools were scheduled to open at scattered points in the territory, he chartered a schooner to carry the teachers to their jobs; no other transport was available since regular shipping had shut down for the winter. The schoolma'am schooner spent 104 days at sea, battered by gales and once marooned on a reef—but all of the teachers survived to greet their students, most of whom were Indians and Eskimos. By the winter of 1887-1888 there were 16 American schools in operation and Alaska at least had the skeleton of an educational system.

In the early 1890s Jackson, who was never one to scorn a good idea simply because it had occurred first to somebody else, became the founder of a new industry in the territory. From Captain Michael Healy, commanding the revenue cutter Corwin, and a zoologist traveling with Healy, Jackson learned that the Eskimo villagers around the Bering Sea coastline above the Aleutian Islands were starving, victims of the indiscriminate slaughter of walruses and whales by Yankee whalers. Healy was familiar with Siberian ports on the other side of the Bering Sea and informed Jackson that the people living there depended on domesticated reindeer as their principal source of food.

Jackson, who still divided his time between his duties in Sitka and lobbying in Washington, headed off to Washington to obtain money to purchase reindeer. Congress, as was often the case, turned a deaf ear to this suggestion. But Jackson was a hard man to daunt; he raised $2,146 from private sources, bought 16 reindeer in Siberia and shipped them to Unalaska Island in the Aleutians.

This turned out to be a mistake. The animals, unaccustomed to the perennially wet islands and unable to find the reindeer moss they habitually ate, all died in the first winter.

Unfazed, the preacher went back to Congress and again asked for reindeer money. This time, after some delay, the legislators reluctantly came through with $6,000. But while he was waiting, Jackson raised more private funds, and by the time the first federal money arrived he had a thriving herd of 300 animals comfortably grazing on the cold but more hospitable Seward Peninsula. There they were tended by Lap-

67

Reverend S. H. King *(center)* and part of his flock inspect a miner's cabin converted in 1891 into the second Presbyterian church of Juneau. Logs of the new bell tower at right were numbered with chalk to guide the Indians who built it.

landers recruited by Jackson because of their long experience in dealing with reindeer. The animals prospered, and thereafter the money came more easily. Within a decade Jackson had inveigled $222,000 out of Congress; by 1905 the Alaskan herd had increased to 10,000 reindeer.

However successful, the reindeer project became the eventual cause of Jackson's downfall. Almost from the first he had been a controversial figure. Other missionaries accused him, probably correctly, of favoring Presbyterian missions in his disbursement of public money. Whites accused him of favoring education for Eskimo, Aleut and Indian children while neglecting their own. By 1905 the criticism focused on his management of the reindeer herds.

In an investigation authorized by President Theodore Roosevelt, it was learned that Jackson had turned over less than 40 per cent of the deer to the Eskimos, for whom they had originally been intended. Instead, he had parceled out the largest share to the denominational missions to distribute when and how each saw fit. Jackson was accused of misusing his authority and was dismissed from office.

But though his exit was made with some accompanying disgrace, no one ever questioned that Jackson, the clerical mover and shaker, had accomplished more than any other person or agency to further the cause of education in Alaska. He had also founded a viable, if somewhat exotic, cattle industry suited to the Far North. By the time he was dismissed he had prodded $1,112,000 out of Congress for schools and reindeer herding and had raised as much as that or more by eloquent private appeals through church organizations. After 28 years of strenuous activity, he left Alaska for good—"a short, bewhiskered and bespectacled man," in the words of one who knew him, but "by inside measurement a giant."

Throughout the 1870s and 1880s, while Sheldon Jackson had been commuting back and forth between Alaska and Washington, D.C., men in search of gold were continuing to straggle into the North. Most were miners out of the Old West, seasoned by the diggings in California, Colorado, Montana and British Columbia. No power on earth could have kept them away once it was assumed, as it had to be, that if the

southern Rocky Mountains held gold, their frozen sister peaks to the north almost certainly did as well.

The veteran prospectors who arrived in Alaska to conduct the search for gold were ideally suited to the task. They knew the gold pan, the pick and the long-handled shovel; their back and leg muscles had long been inured to squatting in creek beds, slowly washing the dross over the edge of the pan with expert swishes while they waited for the rich sheen to show itself on the bottom.

Two of the first arrivals on the Alaskan side of the Canadian border were Leroy Napoleon McQuesten and Arthur Harper. McQuesten, New England born, had been a prospector all his adult life, having begun in the California gold rush and then following word of gold north in 1858 to the Fraser River country of Canada. Harper, born in Ireland, had immigrated to the United States as a youth and thereafter had followed essentially the same trail as McQuesten. At the time the two began panning for wealth in the Far North in 1873, there were not more than half a dozen white men along the whole, looping 2,000-mile length of the Yukon River.

Neither McQuesten nor Harper found any considerable traces of gold in their first Alaskan years, but being mortally sure the stuff was there somewhere, they stuck with it. They may not have been striking it rich but they and the few others like them and the gradually increasing trickle of fur traders were performing a higher service. They were opening up the wilderness, learning the great Yukon River and its tributaries, cutting the opening wedge into the untapped and little-known interior.

McQuesten took a job with the Alaska Commercial Company in order to support the continuing search. In 1874 he opened a fur-trading post, Fort Reliance, on the Yukon, well into Canadian territory. Harper became his partner; after that it was Harper who did most of the prospecting for the pair.

The first strike of any consequence on the Alaskan side of the Yukon basin came in the autumn of 1886 on Fortymile River, a Yukon tributary named by prospectors because its mouth was approximately 40 miles from Fort Reliance. Hearing the news, Harper, who was tending the store while McQuesten was in San Francisco ordering the next year's supplies,

moved downriver and set up a branch store almost on the Alaska boundary.

Nuggets worth only about 50 cents apiece were reported, but the strike seemed promising enough to lure prospectors from both up- and downriver come springtime. Harper wished he could get word to McQuesten to buy more heavily for the next season—the store was certain to be a gold mine if nothing else was—but winter had set in and the possibility seemed almost nil. He hired a prospector named Tom Williams to travel upriver and through the mountains and glaciers down to open water in the Panhandle—and in the process Williams became responsible for

one of the legendary endurance stories of the Yukon.

Williams set out on December 1 with an 18-year-old Indian named Bob, whose main function was to walk ahead in his snowshoes and break trail for Williams' dogs. Eleven days later Williams wrote in his diary: "Traveled all day through heavy pack ice, making only about 10 miles. If the ice continues in our road, we will have a long, weary trip."

Day by day his entries in the diary describe the pair's slow, painful progress southward in heavy snow. Occasionally they broke through the ice and had to crawl out of frigid water, the dogs faring no better than the humans. January 3: "All tired today,

A transplanted herd of Siberian reindeer blankets the Alaskan tundra. These arctic cattle provided milk, fresh meat and fine skins and even hauled the U.S. mail.

both men and dogs." January 13: "Left one of our dogs behind as it could not follow us, through fatigue. After traveling about 2 miles we had to camp on account of snow storm."

There the diary ends. After 44 days on the trail, the exhausted men had reached the Chilkoot Pass and had walked into a blizzard. Their dogs had died off one by one until all were gone. Half frozen, the men built a snowhouse three miles below the summit of the pass. For five days Tom Williams and the Indian, Bob, lived without fire or food. When the sky cleared on the sixth day, they crawled out of the hut, abandoned everything they had and started walking. But Williams had no strength. He made it only a few yards, then collapsed in the snow. The youth lifted Williams and slogged along for five more days before he came upon some Chilkat Indians, who helped him

build a sled and pull it to a place called Healy's Post on Taiya Inlet, about 150 miles north of Sitka.

Williams roused himself from the sled just long enough to mention gold and to say that the details were in a letter from Harper. Then he died. The letter, however, was back up the pass, in the snow hut he and Bob had built. A search party found it a few days later, and soon hundreds of men were on their way to Forty Mile. For his efforts the young Indian was given a sled worth eight dollars, and grateful prospectors collected $102.25 to give him for clothing and medication. Bob went back home, Williams was buried, and word of the strike reached McQuesten in time for him to order more supplies. (Some of the prospectors rather wished he had not gotten the chance. "The bacon was in slabs three feet long, all of which was yellow," one man reported. "We called it

the 'Yard Bacon.' The flour was moldy, the rice was lumpy, the fruit was green and in the beans were plenty of rocks and gravel.")

In 1893 a considerable find on Birch Creek, a tributary that joined the Yukon at its northernmost reach, brought in additional miners. By 1896 more than 1,000 prospectors, including some women, were in the Yukon basin on the Alaskan side of the border. The great river and its tributaries had become a familiar highway network, allowing travel by raft or steamer in summer, by dog sled or snowshoes in winter. The mystery of Alaska's interior was unfolding, and even a scant fabric of civilization began to form— that is if an occasional rude cabin roadhouse or trading post along the river could be called civilization.

A year later the Klondike discovery in Canada brought the first of 100,000 gold-crazed fortune hunters storming through Alaska. Most of the prospectors struggled through the Chilkoot Pass, rising from Taiya Inlet 225 miles northwest of Wrangell, on which Tom Williams had spent his last energy. Long before the gold played out, the Chilkoot, 25 miles in length and steeper than a schoolyard slide, had become the most famous strip of up-and-down real estate in the world.

The Klondike rushers, unlike the veterans who had been prowling Alaskan creeks for a generation, were mostly cheechakos, as newcomers were known in Chinook, the hybrid jargon of the Pacific Northwest. They had little qualification beyond an ardent desire to get rich. Many chose to bypass the crowded and toilsome Chilkoot and blaze their own trails— sometimes to their regret. Of all the tenderfeet, surely the worst advised were 18 New Yorkers, who were assembled and led by one Arthur Dietz, a YMCA physical-education director. Among their number were several office clerks, a postman and two policemen. Nobody has ever explained why this misled group of men attempted to reach the interior by crossing the biggest glacier in Alaska, the 50-mile-long Malaspina, which slides down from the flanks of majestic Mount St. Elias, first sighted by Vitus Bering a century and a half earlier.

The New York party started up the glacier in April 1898, carrying 1,000 pounds of food and gear per man in addition to an 800-pound hoisting engine. Their journey soon became a nightmare. A continuous wind swept down the glacier into their faces. The sun, reflecting off the ice, burned their skin and impaired their vision. A blizzard left their gear covered with two feet of snow.

The first to die was the party's doctor, who fell into a crevasse and vanished, taking with him a sled, dogs and all his medicines. Two more men with sleds and dogs disappeared before the party reached the summit and could make their way down to firm ground in early June. Through the summer they wandered into the interior, panning unmapped streams with little success. One more died of a mysterious fever. Then winter set in. Three men went to look for an Indian village and were not seen again. The remaining members hastily constructed a rude cabin and holed up for the rest of the winter, spending most of their time in sleeping bags trying to keep warm.

When spring came another man died, of scurvy, and three others were buried under an avalanche. In April 1899—one year after the party had started up the Malaspina—the remaining seven members, subsisting on the flesh of their dogs, returned to the coast by a different route. Three more died of starvation and exhaustion. By the time a revenue cutter spotted their signal fire and picked them up, two of the four survivors were blind and the sight of the others had been permanently damaged.

A wise traveler in Alaska learned to depend on a hardy ally, the sometimes temperamental dogs that pulled his sled. On the trail in winter a man prudently prepared his dogs' dinners and fed them before he fed himself. Usually man and dog ate the same fare: dried

A row of weathered totem poles stands before a long-deserted

Wearing face paint, nose rings and costumes of Western and

The good life of a prodigal people

When the United States Army announced it was evacuating Sitka in 1877, the town's white inhabitants worried about the reaction of the neighboring village of several hundred Tlingit Indians. The tribe had fiercely resisted the Russians 75 years earlier, and Sitkans feared the once-formidable warriors might try to re-establish their dominance.

The Tlingit domain had once encompassed the whole Alaska Panhandle. From the fish abounding in those waters and the forests covering the land, they supplied themselves almost effortlessly with food. With their needs provided for, the Tlingit and related tribes had the leisure to develop one of the New World's most sophisticated native cultures.

Their most striking material accomplishments were wrought with trees. They built gabled lodges that could house a dozen families, hollowed out canoes that held up to 60 men and shaped 50-foot totem poles, each with magnificent carvings describing a family's real and mythical history. Most of the tangible wealth belonged to nobles who affirmed their hereditary status by feting one another with opulent feasts known as potlatches. At these affairs the host would lavish gifts on his guests; sometimes, in a show of prodigality, he might even kill a couple of slaves for use as rollers in beaching the canoe of the visiting chief.

The Tlingits prospered through the early days of the fur trade, but eventually the white man's liquor and diseases exacted a heavy toll. Despite the Sitkans' fears, the Tlingits were in no condition to fight. When the Army left, the feared uprising came to little more than a few drunken forays in the white part of town.

Tlingit village, photographed in 1899. Each pole bears the emblems of a particular clan.

tribal origins, a group of Tlingit dancers gathers to perform at a trading post in 1895.

Partners Arthur Harper *(above)* and Leroy Napoleon McQuesten were among the first Americans to prospect in Alaska. They eventually made their fortunes, but not in gold. Instead, they built and operated trading posts along the Yukon River at which they profitably dispensed grub, mining tools and advice to newcomers.

salmon, bacon and rice. If camp was made in a shelter, the lead dog was often invited to share the man's bed; both then slept more warmly.

The payload on the dog sled was lashed down under a tarpaulin on the light wooden frame and weighed about 100 pounds per dog. Except for tools, it consisted mainly of food, weapons and blankets. Driving a team was hard work. On a typical one-man sled, the driver, commanding the lead dog with a whip and his voice, ran straddling the rope that hitched the team to the sled. He also had to manage the gee pole, which was attached to the right front of the sled and served to steer it. On a clear trail he ran in back of the sled and guided it with the handlebars, or on a run across the side of a hill, used the handlebars to prevent the vehicle from turning over. If there were two men and the snow was fresh and deep, one went

ahead on snowshoes, breaking trail for the dogs.

The point of peril for both men and dogs was the condition of their feet. For the dogs the gear always included sets of caribou-hide moccasins, soft and pliable yet tough and insulating, to be worn when the trail led over flinty ice that could cut their pads. The worst hazard came in spring when the ice, out of sight under the snow, was beginning to rot—to go to pieces. When men or animals broke through into this treacherous footing they were in serious trouble. Unless a man could get out of the slush and into dry footgear in a hurry, his feet could freeze in minutes— and then he was just as good as dead. It was a simpler problem for the Malemute. As soon as the dog was out of the slush, he flopped down and went to work on his feet gnawing the ice from between his pads and then meticulously licking them dry. Dogs brought up

Richard Harris (*above*) and Joseph Juneau discovered the first big gold field in Alaska in 1880 and laid out a town site on nearby Gastineau Channel. Harris, the better educated of the two, named the place Harrisburg. But in 1881 other miners, angry with Harris for staking multiple claims, renamed it for his partner Juneau.

from below the 49th parallel, although they were often better trained and more companionable with men, lacked this elementary first-aid know-how inherited from a wolf ancestry. Such dogs often froze and died in a short time.

To communicate with his team, the prospector-driver found himself using terms already familiar from his earlier days in the Old West—with one exception. "Gee" meant turn right, "haw" meant left and "whoa," of course, meant whoa. The exception was "mush" or "mush on," a bastardization of *marchons*, meaning "let's go," which the Malemutes had first learned from French Canadian trappers.

If a prospector could not afford dogs, the only alternative was to "neck" his load: he would pull his own sled, using a harness with a strap across the forehead, so that he took most of the strain on his neck muscles.

After a year or so of such demanding effort, these fellows were standouts in any Alaskan barroom, for their necks were as large as the average man's thigh.

The gold hunters who restricted their prospecting to the Alaska Panhandle had a somewhat easier time of it. Nothing so huge as Alaska could be all glaciers or all Yukon basin permafrost. A land mass that ran through a full 17° of latitude, from Barrow above the Arctic Circle south to Tongass on the Canadian border, had to offer some milder climate somewhere. The Panhandle, though warmed by the Japan Current, was no tropic idyl; it had fog, torrential rains and gales strong enough to stop a running man in his tracks, and it also was subject to occasional earthquakes.

It was to the Panhandle that chance brought an unlikely pair of men who seemed predestined to stum-

Juneau, the first boomtown of the Alaskan gold rush, sprouted beside a deep-water channel beneath mountains where miners sluiced $25 worth of gold a day in 1881.

ble onto gold. Their names were Joseph Juneau and Richard Harris; both were hapless fellows who had within them little more than the ability to sit up and take nourishment, usually liquid. Harris was, in the words of one of his employers, "an inveterate drunkard." As for Juneau, "between hooch and squaws he never had a cent to get away on." Late in 1879 the two stepped unsteadily off a ship at the dock in Sitka. They still owed the fare for their passage, and they had to find work.

At the time a cantankerous German mining engineer named George Pilz was grubstaking prospectors and paying them four dollars a day to fan out over the 400-mile-long archipelago. Pilz's return, should there be any, was his choice of two claims from every three his men might stake. With this understanding, Joe Juneau and Dick Harris, both about 45 years old and fresh from the mines of British Columbia and the American Northwest, signed up with George Pilz. They set forth in July 1880 with a boat, three months' provisions and two or three Indians of the

Auk tribe who had signed on as guides for a dollar a day and a ration of hardtack and tea.

Seven weeks later Juneau and Harris were back at Sitka, their supplies exhausted, their boat lost, their Indian guides disgusted. Sinful was the word for the way they had spent their days, and Pilz's goods. Away from Sitka less than two weeks, having done only light prospecting here and there on their northeasterly route, they put in at an Auk village. There they bought hooch and the companionship of Indian women, then more of the same, paying for their pleasures first with food, then with equipment. Finally, before they could offer their boat in trade, it floated away with the tide. Boatless, penniless and hung over, they paid the Indians a rifle to take them back to Sitka, 150 miles away.

As they traveled homeward, Cowee, principal chief of the Auks, proposed they make one stop. Earlier, Pilz had promised Cowee 100 blankets and steady employment if he would lead the way to any field that held gold in considerable quantities; Cowee thought he knew such a place. He led the two miners a short way down the Gastineau Channel to the mouth of a small stream, then up the stream. Juneau and Harris did a bit of panning along the way and got what Harris later described as "very good float gold quartz." But the underbrush was thick and they were tired and unsteady so, in spite of Cowee's objections, they split company and turned back.

The protesting chief followed the two miners back to Sitka, and while they were engaged in explaining, with great prevarication, their misfortunes of the previous weeks, Cowee showed George Pilz some of the rich gold quartz. There was much more farther upstream, he said.

Pilz now confronted a monumental dilemma. With fall coming on and the season running short, he looked around Sitka and found to his dismay that the only men available for hire were Harris and Juneau. The decision was painful, but there was no alternative: Pilz gave Harris and Juneau fresh money and supplies, including a new canoe. In mid-September, after grandly naming their vessel the *Alaska Chief of Gold Creek,* the two paddled off with Chief Cowee and some of his tribesmen.

This time they made it to the headwaters of the stream, climbing a mountain to skirt the thick brush, and came upon a gulch where thousands of years of erosion had deposited gravel veined with gold. "I broke some with a hammer and Juneau and myself could hardly believe our eyes," Harris later wrote. "We knew it was gold, but so much and not in particles, streaks running through the rock and little lumps as large as peas or beans." This time they staked claims, as well as a townsite of 160 acres beside the Gastineau Channel.

It was a fabulous strike. Soon dozens of prospectors poured into the region, spreading out in every direction around the Juneau-Harris find, which Harris named the Silver Bow after a mining district in Montana. Some of the newcomers became very rich. One claim on nearby Douglas Island, which was bought by a California man named John Treadwell, yielded more than $66 million in the 35 years that it was worked *(pages 80-91)*. Not quite so fortunate was Dick Harris, who with various partners took out gold worth $75,000, spent it, lived until 1907 and died

broke in an Oregon sanitarium. Juneau, who made about $18,000, had nothing left within two years. After he died in Dawson City in 1899, Juneau's colleagues honored his wish and raised $400 to ship his body for burial to the town that fellow prospectors named for him after he and Dick Harris had discovered the Silver Bow.

A collateral benefit of the human stampede inspired by the great gold finds—large strikes were also made later at Nome, far to the northwest of Juneau—was that, for the first time, the federal government bestirred itself to endow Alaska with a little more of something it badly needed: the machinery of law. Since the Organic Act of 1884, the monster territory had been forced to struggle along with a single federal judge. But in 1900 a blizzard of lawsuits over mining claims—at Nome, up and down the Yukon and in the Panhandle—forced the passage of a new act that provided three U.S. district judges for the Alaskan territory.

Gold also moved Washington to grant Alaska one more concession. In 1906 Congress granted the area limited representation in the person of a nonvoting delegate in the House of Representatives. Not until 1912, four and a half decades after the purchase, did Alaska get territorial government with an elected legislature. Even then Congress retained the power to veto any local legislation that it might not approve.

During those 45 years of limbo, a small collection of tough Americans had met challenges even greater than had confronted the rugged pioneers below the 49th parallel: challenges of climate, isolation, distance, of almost total lack of communication with the rest of the world. They had learned to cope with Malemutes instead of mules, and reindeer instead of longhorns. They had searched for gold and, discovering a little, persisted until they had opened up the riches of an immense wilderness that so many at home had said was worthless.

Gold was never the principal element of Alaska's enormous natural wealth, but it was beyond question the catalyst that brought the huge, hitherto almost forsaken territory to the attention of the world outside and, most particularly, to the belated attention of the U.S. Congress, on whom its development depended.

The gold mine that grew into a company town

The Alaska-Treadwell Gold Mining Company was the first large-scale mining operation in Alaska, and one of the most bountiful. Between 1882 and 1917 when a cave-in and flood finally put it out of business, the Treadwell alone produced gold worth nearly 10 times the $7.2 million purchase price of Alaska. Its stamp mills—which extracted gold particles from ore brought up from depths of 2,000 feet and more—were the largest in the world.

The Treadwell was more than a conglomerate of four mines: it was a town in itself, with 2,000 workers at its peak. Most employees were single men who, by rule, had to live in company-run boardinghouses. But the company liked to project itself as a benevolent despot, providing the men with a gym, reading room, bowling alleys, heated swimming pool and, on occasion, lavish banquets that individual sourdoughs could only dream of.

The Treadwell's smokestacks, stamp mills, aerial tramways and wharves sprawl along Douglas Island, across the channel from Juneau.

Some begrimed Treadwell miners gather around a white-collar boss *(seated, center)* for this photograph in 1908.

The Treadwell mines were not noted for their safety standards and had the grim, if exaggerated, reputation of averaging one accidental death every day. The first diggings were made in the open cut below, known as the Glory Hole because it had sent so many workers on the road to glory.

85

Bookkeeping for the Treadwell mines was handled in the general office, which boasted electric lights and even a wall telephone. Miners were paid $90 and up per month, but clubhouse and other fees were deducted, and bachelors were charged a third of their salaries for bed and board. These policies led to miners' strikes in 1907 and 1908.

The Treadwell butcher shop offered rib roast, rabbit, fowl and deer—and stools for its customers.

Treadwell ran its own well-stocked and neatly organized company grocery, with a wide assortment of teas (top shelf), sweets (in and on the display case, left) and fresh fruit, including such tropical imports as ripe bananas.

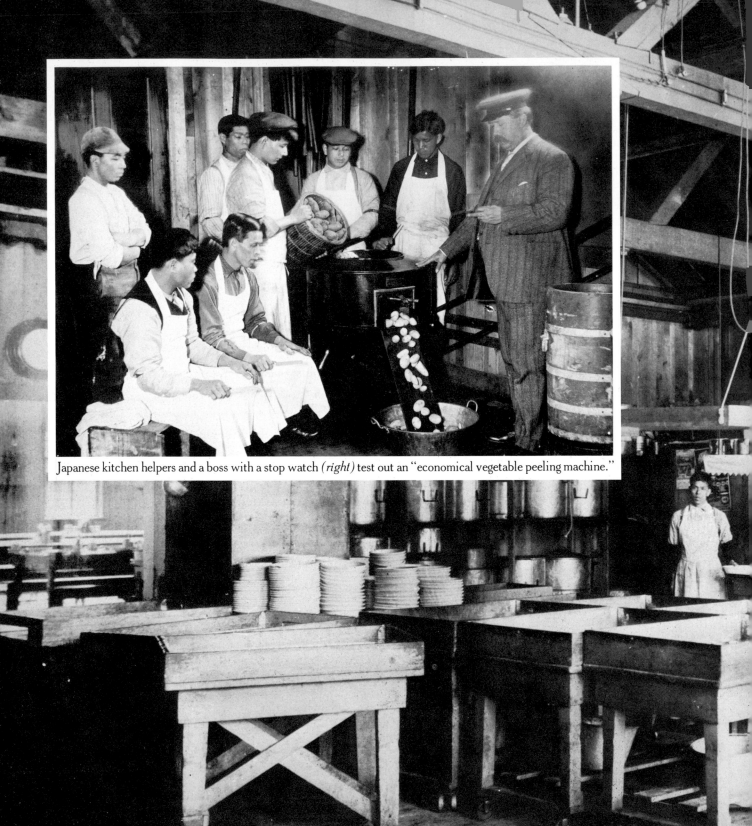

Japanese kitchen helpers and a boss with a stop watch *(right)* test out an "economical vegetable peeling machine."

"In the kitchens and preparation rooms," declared a brochure issued by the company in 1909, "all is shining and methodical. Vegetable steamers, percolating coffee urns and dozens of similar conveniences aid in the task of preparing and serving the food for the relays of hungry men."

Dressed in their best, more than 300 company employees sit down to a hearty banquet at the Treadwell Boarding House in 1908. Rolled napkins and bouquets of fresh flowers add a festive touch to tables covered in oilcloth.

91

3 | Probing the unknown interior

Alaska was a great unknown when the U.S. bought it in 1867. Years earlier the Russian government had instructed its agents to explore the interior and to "note down where anything may be found in the entrails of the earth, and where beasts and birds and curious seashells" might be encountered. But limited manpower restricted Russian expeditions mostly to the coast.

The first American probes began shortly before the purchase, when Western Union undertook to lay a telegraph line across Alaska to Siberia as part of an ambitious project that would link the United States to Europe. In the picture shown here, Frederick Whymper, an artist traveling with the Western Union expedition, recorded the breathtaking moment when, after two weeks of sledding overland from the Bering Sea, the party "broke from the woods, shot down a steep bank, and stood on an immense snow-clad field of ice— the mighty Yukon!"

The telegraph project was abandoned far short of completion. But under American ownership, the exploration of Alaska began to pick up pace in the hands of hardy individuals as different as the motives that drove them: they were prospectors and missionaries, map-making soldiers, inland sailors and seekers of scientific knowledge. By 1900, thanks to their efforts, much of the great land was no longer a mystery.

The Western Union wire-laying expedition gets its first glimpse of the frozen Yukon River in November 1866.

The epic task of exploring the wilderness

In Alaska, as elsewhere in the Old West, professional explorers were preceded for the most part by handfuls of self-reliant amateurs. Too impatient to wait for maps and information, they plunged right into the new land. By the early 1870s hunters, traders and prospectors were making inroads into Alaska's vast interior, traveling up the Yukon and Kuskokwim rivers in Indian canoes and aboard small steamboats operated by companies trading in the territory. A few hundred miles upriver they left the known world behind; the Russians before them had explored no farther (map, pages 20-21). Only then, surrounded by Alaska's uncharted immensity, did they realize that this wilderness was simply too remote, too big and too perilously changeable from one season to the next to yield easily to the frontiering savvy that had sufficed in the trans-Mississippi West.

Once a person left the major rivers and headed cross-country in any direction, he had nothing to go on but his compass, the uncertain help of local Indian guides and his own hand-drawn reminders of the route he had taken. More than a few veteran pioneers got lost and perished in the jumbled mountains of the coastal ranges with their enormous glaciers and in the stony northern extensions of the Rockies. Others learned to their dismay that many streams in the enormous central plateau followed unpredictable courses, determined by the imperceptible rising and falling of the land or by mountain barriers. For example, one party of prospectors, hiking north from the Yukon, came upon a northward-flowing stream and embarked on rafts; they failed to notice that the stream was gently swinging around to the south—until it deposited them back on the Yukon, less than a dozen miles from their point of departure three months before.

These early pioneers yearned for much more than just maps. They wanted at least rudimentary geological guidance, even if it was no more than what kind of mineral deposits might be found in which broad areas. And with their own survival in mind, they wanted to know how much game inhabited the deep interior. Denied supply shipments for as long as nine months each year while the rivers were locked in ice, they needed information on the character and customs of the region's Indians with whom they had to trade for food and furs. Early pioneers worried unduly about the native inhabitants; friendly Indians often alleged that distant bands were bloodthirsty raiders—warnings that usually turned out to be greatly overblown.

Of course, all this data could eventually be gathered the hard way—by inexperienced people poking and prying through Alaska's half a million square miles of wildly varied terrain. But most knew that trained explorers—geologists, naturalists, ethnologists and, above all, surveyors and map makers—could do the epic job far better and much faster. The question was: how soon?

The new Alaskans, assuming the federal government would gladly relieve their unique plight, appealed confidently to Washington for experts to map the territory and supply solid data on its resources. But Congress refused such a crash program for the same reason it had ignored the Alaskans' demands for a territorial government of their own: the cost would be excessive for so vast a realm of uncertain value that harbored only a few hundred Americans.

The Alaskans grew angrier as each year of lost opportunities passed. They agreed with one of their

---

Explorer Frederick Schwatka, an articulate Army lieutenant, mapped the upper Yukon in 1883 and wrote popular books about his expedition that spurred American interest in the 2,000-mile river.

Naturalist Robert Kennicott led a party of surveyors and scientists who set out in 1865 to string a telegraph line across Alaska. The project had only begun when he died of heart failure beside the Yukon.

we have learned more of Alaska's geography and topography, its people and resources, in 25 years than Russia learned in 126 years of possession."

The American exploration of Alaska began a few years before the purchase, with private enterprise taking the lead as it so often did. The author of the ambitious first project was a businessman named Perry McDonough Collins, who was touring Russia in 1856 when an inspiration struck him. Collins conceived the idea of running a telegraph wire from the western United States through Canada and Russian Alaska to the Bering Strait, linking up there with a Russian line to Europe. Since the Bering Strait was only 56 miles wide, Collins figured his plan stood a much better chance for success than that of a fellow American, manufacturer Cyrus Field, who hoped to lay an undersea cable all the way across the Atlantic Ocean to England.

Sure enough, Field's first try failed in 1857, prompting Collins to act on his own plan. He obtained both a Russian charter and permission from the British to string his line northward across Canada from the Washington Territory. William H. Seward, then a senator from New York and already an ardent expansionist, supported the project in Congress, which approved it readily enough since no government financing was required. The Western Union Telegraph Company, fresh from its triumphant completion of the first transcontinental line to California in 1861, became entranced by the project. It estimated grandly that the line would gross nine million dollars a year by handling 1,000 international messages a day at $25 each. But not until 1864, when Cyrus Field obligingly failed in his fifth transatlantic attempt, did Western Union organize three field parties, one each for Russia, Canada and Alaska.

Command of the Alaskan sector was awarded to one of the few Americans who had actually set foot in the territory. He was Robert Kennicott, a nervous, moody naturalist from Northwestern University, who had qualified for the post by spending the winter of 1860-1861 along the ill-defined Alaska-Canada border collecting animal specimens on a grant from the Smithsonian Institution and the Chicago Academy of Sciences. Kennicott's primary duty was to keep the

number who exclaimed bitterly, "If those Senators and Congressmen don't know any more about the tariff than they know about Alaska, the Lord help the rest of the United States!"

So it was that professional exploration of Alaska in the first decades of American ownership went slowly, carried forward haphazardly and usually on a shoestring by a variety of adventurous individuals—military men, customs agents and specialists employed by businesses or subsidized by scientific societies. These brave men traveled thousands of arduous miles and filled in the blanks on the map bit by bit. As early as 1892 one explorer could justly say that "at a comparatively insignificant expense to the Government,

From this Russian fort, St. Michael, located on Norton Sound, a telegraph line was to run overland to the Bering Strait and then 56 miles underwater to Siberia.

The telegraph's intended Siberian terminal was Plover Bay, where an American construction crew built an outpost and blithely raised their own flag and the flag of Western Union. After the successful laying of a transatlantic cable in 1866, the Russian-American project was dropped.

Alaskan surveyors and wire-stringing crews working on a brisk schedule. At his insistence, he was also authorized to form a separate corps of scientists who would conduct research unrelated to the actual building of the telegraph line.

In recruiting his scientific corps, Kennicott could offer only minute salaries, but six young men joined him in San Francisco, eager for the chance to study virgin territory. Five of the six would become well-known scientists, and one of the five, a young Bostonian named William Dall, would spend most of his life in the territory and become recognized as the "dean" of Alaskan naturalists.

In August 1865 Kennicott brought his expedition to St. Michael, near the broad delta of the Yukon River. At that point the six scientists broke off, each to pursue his separate studies wherever he pleased. Plans called for the rest of the Western Union men to proceed to Nulato, a Russian outpost 550 miles from the Yukon's mouth, and then to split into two parties of explorers, surveyors and wire-stringing crews. One party would stretch a line across the Seward Peninsula to the Bering Strait, where it was to link up with the wire from Siberia. The main party, under Kennicott's command, would continue upriver to the headwaters of the Yukon, laying a line to meet the wire that the Canadian expedition was bringing north across British Columbia.

It was autumn before Kennicott's men started up the Yukon, and their progress was disappointingly slow. To complicate matters Kennicott showed disturbing signs of strain. At each new camp along the way he struggled resentfully with his many administrative duties, which left him little time for his own studies. All through the winter he complained obsessively that various company men were inefficient, insubordinate and were conspiring to make a reputation at his expense. In turn, his irascible behavior affected his men's morale.

By May 1866, when the main party reached Nulato, Robert Kennicott was a desperate man on the brink of a breakdown. Then on May 13 he went for a walk along the river and did not come back. A group of searchers found him dead of a heart attack. William Dall, who succeeded Kennicott as leader of the scientific corps at the age of 20, was independently studying fish and mollusks along the coast when he was advised of the death of his friend. Dall wrote that "he was murdered, not by the merciful knife but by slow torture of the mind."

The expedition carried on grimly. Chief surveyor Frank Ketchum, Kennicott's successor as head of Western Union telegraph operations, set out from Nulato with his aide, Michael Lebarge, to reconnoiter the river as far as Fort Yukon, a Canadian trading post about 1,000 miles upstream. Traveling by kayak, they had no trouble reaching the fort, and they returned to Nulato before the Yukon froze solid. By now, however, the wire-stringing crews were lagging far behind schedule, delayed by shortages of supplies, sled dogs and Indian packers.

William Dall also spent the winter of 1866-1867 at Nulato, sharing his quarters with another member of the expedition, a footloose English artist named Frederick Whymper. In their bitter-cold hut Whymper sketched and painted. "Between every five strokes of the pencil I ran about to exercise myself," he later wrote. "I mixed some colors with water that

had stood near the oven and, wetting a small brush, commenced to apply it to my drawing block. Before it reached the paper, it was covered with a skin of ice." In spite of temperatures hovering around 30° below zero, Dall kept busy collecting and preparing almost everything he could lay his hands on for shipment home, including specimens of Alaskan woodpeckers and titmice. He even went so far as to steal a skull from an Indian burial ground, discreetly executing the foray on a day when his tracks were quickly covered by a heavy layer of new snow.

In March 1867 Ketchum and Lebarge headed up the Yukon again, this time to map its twists, turns and tributaries. They started out traveling with four sleds, 14 dogs and four Indian packers. On the way they mushed through a blinding 18-day blizzard. By the time they reached Fort Yukon the ice was breaking up, and they were able to canoe upriver into Canada. Dall followed the Western Union party in a skin canoe. En route, he paused to examine a seam of coal that Ketchum's men had discovered near the juncture of the Tanana River and to add to his growing catalogue of Alaskan fauna. Nothing was too small or unimportant to escape his notice. He identified four kinds of mosquitoes, all of them merciless; he observed that only buckskin "defied their art."

Ketchum's group and Dall were reunited at Fort Yukon, and on their return to Nulato they received orders to come to the coast. The party reached St. Michael in July. There they got some good news and some bad. On learning the good news—that Russia had sold Alaska to the United States—Dall excitedly ran the Stars and Stripes up the post's flagpole. But first came word that Cyrus Field had succeeded the previous year in his sixth attempt to lay a transatlantic cable. The Alaskan telegraph project was dead and the expedition disbanded.

Dall's final estimation of the venture was appropriately cautious. The Western Union expedition had strung only 80 miles of wire in all. Still, the earliest American effort to explore Alaska had achieved a great deal. It produced the first map of the entire 2,000-mile Yukon, and the scientists had gathered enough information to fill scholarly papers in a dozen specialized areas, from anthropology and botany to meteorology and zoology. But so much more had yet

Naturalist William Dall was only 20 when he became Western Union's chief scientist in Alaska in 1866. After the United States bought Alaska, he stayed on to become a prolific authority on its wilderness.

to be done. "The field now open for exploration and discovery is grand," Dall wrote. "The interior everywhere needs exploration."

The opportunity Dall described so enthusiastically was ignored until 1869, two years after the purchase, when the United States government made a first feeble attempt to plumb the interior. Suspecting that the Canadians' Fort Yukon was really in Alaskan territory, the War Department told the Army at Sitka to determine once and for all the exact location of the trading post. The soldier named to command the mission was Captain Charles Raymond of the Corps of Engineers. In early July, 1869, Raymond and two assistants hitched a ride up the Yukon on a steamboat used to supply the scattered traders of the Alaska Commercial Company, which, in addition to its virtual monopoly in fur sealing, was beginning to establish a network of small trading posts in the interior.

At Fort Yukon the engineers set up their transit instrument and telescope in two wall tents with slits in the roof to sight through. After a week of foul weather, Raymond finally got a clear shot at the sun, and his calculations proved that Fort Yukon was not just slightly inside Alaska but 121 miles from the border. Raymond did not know it, but the Canadian fur traders who used the post were under orders from their government to avoid an international incident if their presence was challenged. So when Raymond informed the sole Canadian occupying the fort at the time that he was trespassing, the man simply packed up his gear and left.

Raymond's mission turned out to be the Army's only act of exploration for more than a decade. Paradoxically, not until after 1877, when the troops assigned to protect Alaska were shifted from Sitka to Fort Vancouver in the Washington Territory some 1,300 miles south, did the Army become seriously involved in the exploration of the territory. This new interest in Alaska came about through the efforts of one man who had never even been there, General Nelson A. Miles.

In 1880 Miles took over Fort Vancouver as commanding officer of the Northwest Department of the Columbia, Division of the Pacific—a huge but lightly populated jurisdiction of which Alaska was a

part. Miles was an ambitious field soldier abruptly stuck in what he considered a dull command. In his distinguished career as an Indian fighter, he had defeated the Cheyennes and Comanches, Sitting Bull's Sioux and Chief Joseph's Nez Percé, and would tackle Geronimo's Apaches before long. Various military men had pronounced him fearless, too blunt for his own good and rather like the glory-seeking rival whom he had admired, General George Custer. Now, with no one to fight but the War Department and Congress, Miles sought a new challenge. In spite of orders to keep out of Alaska unless his troops were needed for its defense, he saw exploration as his main chance for excitement and further recognition.

In 1882 Miles proposed to officials in Washington that he make a tour of military inspection. In order to get permission he had to state in writing that he would not meddle in Alaskan affairs, which the Navy had been adminstering in an offhand way since the Army's departure. Miles took his trip, but the officers

These brave soldier-explorers—Frederick Fickett, Henry Allen and Cady Robertson—blazed a trail to the Yukon and beyond.

who accompanied him were obliged to do so on leave time and at their own expense.

Miles's journey was a modest one; he did little more than visit Sitka and inspect portions of the heavily wooded southeastern coast. Yet he returned fascinated by Alaska's wilderness and eager to learn more about it. In 1883, looking for an excuse to begin proper exploration of the territory, Miles ordered his aide, First Lieutenant Frederick Schwatka, to probe the Yukon country, count the native population and their weapons and determine whether they harbored militant intentions against the whites who were beginning to press in on them.

Lieutenant Schwatka, a versatile and enthusiastic young fellow who was licensed to practice both law and medicine, assembled a party of six men including a topographer. Miles doled out a small amount of expense money from his meager departmental funds, and in April the party sailed from Seattle under strict orders to keep a low profile. Schwatka wrote that he felt "like a thief in the night."

But Schwatka was much too ebullient to stay inconspicuous. Starting up the Yukon, he began renaming landmarks, already known by their Indian names, after friends in the international scientific community. He also staged an impromptu invasion of Canada, following and mapping the waters that flowed into the Yukon. At Lake Lindeman the expedition built a 40-foot raft equipped with a sail made from a tent. Embarking on this exotic craft, Schwatka drifted 1,300 miles downstream through 100° summer heat that, he noted, "made one feel as though he were floating on the Nile, Congo or Amazon." At the village of Nuklukayet, Schwatka swapped his raft for a trader's small boat and, with a tow part of the way from an Alaska Commercial Company steamer, got to St. Michael safe and sound. In August, four months after he started, Schwatka reported back to General Miles at Fort Vancouver.

The expedition succeeded in its unstated purpose, getting Miles's foot more firmly planted in Alaska, and it soon proved valuable in another, unexpected way. Schwatka turned out to be an energetic press agent for Alaska. He published short accounts of his journey in *Century* and other periodicals and wrote about it again in a book, *Along Alaska's Great Riv-*

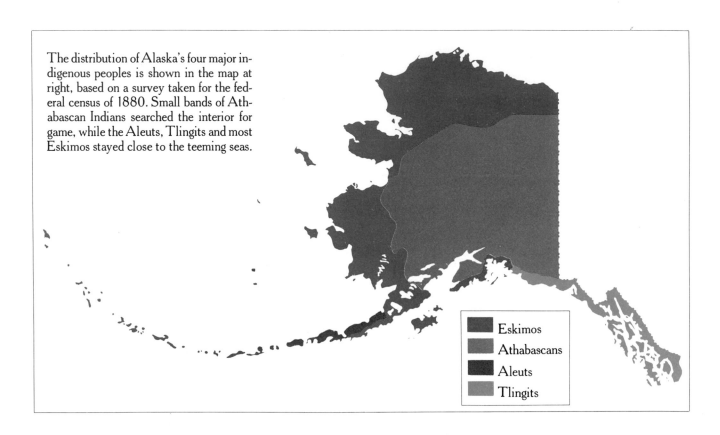

The distribution of Alaska's four major indigenous peoples is shown in the map at right, based on a survey taken for the federal census of 1880. Small bands of Athabascan Indians searched the interior for game, while the Aleuts, Tlingits and most Eskimos stayed close to the teeming seas.

Eskimos
Athabascans
Aleuts
Tlingits

er, which ran through numerous editions. Readers were enthralled by Schwatka's romantic word picture of the entrance to a spectacular gorge on the Yukon: "Through this narrow chute of corrugated rock the wild waters of the great river rush in a perfect mass of milk-like foam, the roar being intensified by the rocky walls which act like so many sounding boards. Huge spruce in somber files overshadow the dark canyon, and it resembled a deep black thoroughfare paved with the whitest of marble."

Schwatka took pleasure in demolishing the myth that Alaska was no more than a giant icebox. "In whatever direction the eye might look," he wrote of an upland excursion at Chilkoot Inlet, "wild flowers were growing in greatest profusion. Dandelions as big as asters, buttercups twice the usual size, and violets rivaling the products of cultivation were visible around. Berries and berry blossoms grew in a profusion and variety which I have never seen equaled in lower altitudes."

Schwatka's Alaskan writings helped focus attention on the last American frontier, but they were, at

best, superficial. General Miles, who had sent the author north, did not appreciate the publicity Schwatka attracted, his odd new place names, his Canadian invasion or his sketchy exploration. Miles was determined to get more substantial results; his next plan was for a two-pronged assault on the Copper River. The Copper was a tempting target for two reasons. It seemed likely to lead to an overland shortcut to the Yukon basin, and the Indians claimed that somewhere upstream its banks were rich in copper ore—hence its Indian name Atna, meaning "copper."

In 1884 Miles sent Lieutenant William Abercrombie to ascend the Copper from its delta on the Gulf of Alaska, and he dispatched a civilian scout, Willis Everette, to explore a route over the Chilkoot Pass, down the Yukon past the mouth of the White River, then cross-country to the Copper. Neither party made it. Everette got as far as Fort Reliance, Jack McQuesten's trading post on the upper Yukon, where he settled in with an Indian woman and could not be budged, even by prospectors who offered to guide him. Abercrombie proved to be no more diligent. He tinkered around the delta, surveyed a route to the river mouth and invented excuses for going only a short distance upriver.

This double fiasco nearly exhausted Miles's reserves of soldierly determination. Yet in 1885 he was ready to make another attempt, his last. This time he struck pure gold in his choice of a leader and was rewarded with what was undoubtedly the greatest single journey of Alaskan exploration.

The new leader was Henry Trueman Allen, a 25-year-old junior lieutenant who at first glance seemed too soft for the rigors of the wilderness or even for the responsibilities of command. Allen was a tall, handsome, pleasant Kentuckian who had been earmarked as a ladies' man and chronic party goer since his days at West Point. But Allen had unsuspected enterprise and drive. He had requested duty on Miles's staff, and as he wrote to the woman he later married, "I am willing to forego almost any benefit for an attempt at exploration in Alaska." Moreover, he had developed a plan for a journey deep into the northern interior, and he had some strong ideas on how to go about it.

A large expedition, Allen told Miles, was bound to bog down of its own weight; besides himself, he wanted no more than two Army men in his party. Miles, on the other hand, felt he ought to take anywhere from four to nine. The issue was settled indirectly in Allen's favor by General Philip Sheridan, commanding officer of the U.S. Army, who had been embarrassed by Miles's Alaskan failures at a time when critics were saying that the Army had no business exploring anywhere. Sheridan wanted the smallest, cheapest expedition possible. Even then Allen had a good deal of trouble drawing $2,000 in advance pay for himself and two companions, plus $1,500 for subsistence and transportation.

Allen had planned to start up the Copper River in mid-March, while the weather was moderating but the river ice still frozen solid enough to serve as a level roadway. But the difficulties he encountered drawing money delayed his departure from Fort Vancouver. It was late March and the ice was already crumbling when the little gunboat *Pinta* delivered him to the Copper Delta with his hand-picked men, Sergeant Cady Robertson and Private Frederick Fickett.

Though Allen had tried to restrict their equipment and supplies to a minimum, the bare essentials added up to a considerable load. In addition to several hundred pounds of grub, they carried weapons, a tent, waterproofed sleeping bags, and a number of instruments: two sextants, a barometer, a camera with glass plates, some compasses and thermometers, and a psychrometer for measuring relative humidity.

At a village on the delta, Allen tried to hire Athabascan Indians to help with the hauling and to serve as guides and interpreters. Finding them reluctant, he appealed to their pride and gambling instinct. He suggested that they draw lots for the honor of accompanying this important expedition. The ploy worked. Six Indians drew, and Allen pronounced five of them winners. It was the first example of Allen's knack for dealing with the native peoples, even those who were generally considered hostile.

On March 29 the party headed upstream in rented canoes. For a while the men paddled and dodged floating chunks of ice, portaged stretches still frozen solid and returned to the river whenever they could. But with conditions worsening as they went along, Allen ordered two canoes cut in half and used as sleds to carry the supplies and equipment. However, the men could drag no more than 150 pounds on each unwieldy sled, and Allen was forced to admit that his definition of traveling light was not light enough.

The next day Allen applied a painful remedy. As he wrote, "We abandoned about one half of our ammunition, cooking outfit, food, clothing, etc. A few hours later we abandoned our tent and more clothing and food, and then had with us about 150 pounds of flour, 100 pounds of beans, 40 pounds of rice, two sides of bacon, 15 pounds of tea, some Liebig's extract of beef, deviled ham and chocolate. A pack of 50 pounds on the back was, under the circumstances, as much as the strongest man could carry."

On the third day of the journey, the explorers reached two great glaciers flanking the river. Allen spied "a high wall of ice, visible as far back as the eye (aided with a field glass) could see. To the north and almost joining the glacier on the northeast, we saw another monster." To avoid the risks of crossing the two glaciers, they took to their remaining canoes and paddled hastily between the crumbling ice cliffs. ◉

An impoverished race of nomads

The Athabascan Indians encountered by explorers as they traveled up Alaska's rivers bore little cultural resemblance to the coastal peoples with whom white fur traders and seamen had been dealing for more than a century. These inlanders had none of the material wealth and elaborate social order of the Tlingits, nor did their artifacts exhibit the degree of ingenuity that made the Eskimos and the Aleuts such masters of their inhospitable environs. By contrast, the inhabitants of Alaska's interior—linguistic cousins of the powerful Apaches and Navajos of the American Southwest—led lives of bare simplicity and often of dire scarcity.

They lived in small nomadic bands and moved with the seasons in search of game. Their usual quarry were caribou, moose and smaller animals like rabbits, which provided most of their food and clothing as well as shelter; the big hides were used to cover their tents. The Athabascans cut tanned caribou hide into narrow strips called babiche, which they utilized for all forms of binding and to make nets, snares and the webbing of their greatest material creation, the snowshoe.

When hunting caribou, they would drive part of a migrating herd into a babiche corral. There they used lances and arrows—the best of them acquired in trade from the Eskimos—to kill their prey. No part of the dead animals was wasted, and surplus meat was stored in protected caches. But game populations fluctuated, and when it was scarce, many Athabascans faced prolonged periods of famine. Sometimes the pursuit of elusive prey became so desperate that anyone too old or weak to keep up was left to die, and on rare occasions—with no relief in sight—these poorest of native Alaskans were even driven to cannibalism.

A top-hatted Athabascan turns out with his band in assorted Western clothing near a

Copper River village in 1906. White traders discouraged the wearing of traditional furs and skins so as to increase their haul of pelts.

A shabby summer wickiup of canvas offers scant shelter to a group of Copper River Athabascans. A winter hut might be covered

with as many as 40 caribou hides sewn together with snow packed on for insulation, but even the best was probably cold and drafty.

A woebegone Athabascan mother nurses her youngest in this 1903 photograph. Beside her are snowshoes of birch and hide.

Having safely reached the ice fields beyond the glaciers, Lieutenant Allen's party ran into a new problem: snow blindness. Even under leaden skies, with rain and snow darkening the days, the glare of light on the ice was torture for their squinted eyes. Several of the men discovered that they awoke with eyes puffed shut, and they could not see until they treated their eyes with warm water, tea and ointments.

On April 10, 1885, the explorers reached Taral, a large Athabascan village at the confluence of the Copper River and its tributary, the Chitina. Caching most of his remaining grub there, Allen took four days' rations for his party and set out on a side trip to explore the Chitina. The food was nearly gone by April 13, Allen's 26th birthday, and he celebrated by dining on the flesh of a decaying moose carcass that one of his Indians found on the trail. By the next day the food was gone, and Private Fickett informed his diary that "rotten moose meat would be a delicacy now." The men, he added, were "so weak from hunger that we had to stop at noon to hunt. All so weak that we were dizzy and would stagger like drunken men." Fortunately, Allen could soon write, "An old woman brought into camp a small piece of meat and a moose's nose, which, with the rabbits we killed, considerably strengthened us."

Hungry again two days later, Allen decided to make a short portage northwest to an Indian village at the headwaters of the Chitistone River. The party was greeted by the *tyone,* or chief, one Nicolai, whose name, besides being Russian, was a synonym for dastardly despotism among the region's Indians. But Allen's friendly approach won over Nicolai, who proved to be an openhanded host. He had his women stew a five-gallon kettle of moose meat, beaver, lynx and rabbits cooked whole with their entrails still inside. Allen guessed that each of his men consumed five pounds of meat and broth, yet the next day they all woke up famished.

Having eaten Nicolai out of hut and home, the adventurers left his village on April 26 in a sturdy 27-foot boat that they and Nicolai's people had fashioned of willow branches bound together with rawhide strips and covered with moose skins. The trip down the Chitina was easy enough, but Allen knew they would have to battle a swift current, flowing seven to nine miles per hour, once they resumed their journey up the Copper. To prepare for the ordeal Allen gave his men a day of rest and picture-taking at Taral. His personnel was now radically changed. The Indians from the Copper Delta had gone home, and Allen had replaced them—as he would do again from time to time—with local men who were familiar with the country ahead.

Retrieving their food cache, the explorers returned to the Copper on April 27. They traveled by cordelling: two men stayed in the loaded boat, one to steer and one to pole, while the rest of the party struggled along the rugged shoreline, dragging the clumsy craft with a 150-foot tow rope. This slow, back-breaking toil continued day after day for more than a month. But by May 15 Allen's expedition had passed the mouth of the Tazlina River and entered territory that, as far as anyone knew, had never been seen by a white man before.

Most of the time the men went hungry. Game was scarce; the only good hunt yielded six *tebays*—small mountain sheep—that were quickly consumed with the remaining Army grub. Occasionally the party came upon an Indian who shared his meager fare. One dished out boiled meat, which Fickett found tasty, "maggots and all." Another gave them wormy meat and rotten goose eggs—meals that Fickett judged to be "about one quarter of what we needed." On May 28 he wrote tersely, "Party nearly played out for want of food. Can just crawl."

On May 30 Lieutenant Allen decided to abandon their battered boat. He broke out his instruments and determined that they were at 62° 54' N.—approximately 285 miles south of the Arctic Circle. Then, using a compass, he plotted a course to the northeast, away from the Copper River. His men shouldered their packs and headed overland in a single file. Leading the way was an old, crippled Indian, who had joined Allen's party uninvited but had proved himself indispensable by digging up edible roots and serving as their interpreter.

For more than a week the explorers trekked through Slana Valley toward a great pallisade of towering mountains—the Alaska Range. They found the valley crisscrossed by a multitude of streams and

Lieutenant George Stoney pushed the Navy's exploration of northern Alaska to the Arctic Ocean. He urged deerskin as the best winter wear and devised a wire mask against the mosquitoes of summer.

streamlets that flowed south to form the Copper River. Here they were treated to an awesome Alaskan phenomenon—the run of salmon to their upstream spawning grounds. To shouts of joy from the half-starved party, one man scooped a lone salmon from a fast-flowing freshet. Soon there were dozens of salmon, then hundreds, then thousands. In some channels, Allen noted, "There was so little water that the fish actually shoved themselves out of the brook and onto the land." For once the men had a chance to gorge themselves, and they did. Allen reported that "one of the party ate three salmon including the heads of all and the roe from one." He also made a mental note that future expeditions should be timed for the salmon run. If his own departure had not been delayed, his party might have arrived at the spot two weeks ahead of the salmon—and might have starved to death before the fish arrived.

On June 9 Allen reached the mountain chain and found a low pass through snow-clad peaks 11,000 to 16,000 feet high. At 1:30 a.m., as the sun was rising, the explorers climbed to the crest of the pass—Suslota, the Indians called it. "We had nearly reached the 'land of the midnight sun' to find in our front the 'promised land,'" Allen wrote. "The views in advance and rear were both grand, the former showing the extensive Tanana Valley with numerous lakes and the low, unbroken range of mountains between the Tanana and Yukon rivers." For one of the few times on the journey, the reserved Allen recorded his feelings: "On this pass, with both white and yellow buttercups around me and snow within a few feet, I sat proud of the grand sight which no visitor save an Atnatana or Tanana Indian had ever seen."

Emerging from Suslota Pass, the party hiked down the Tetlin River for three days and came to another Indian village. Since they were now on the other side of the watershed formed by the Alaska Range, they could travel downstream on a north-flowing river. Allen set his men to work building a boat for the journey. All were in a sadly debilitated condition. Sergeant Robertson's body was covered with ugly black splotches—a telltale sign of scurvy. It was high time to run for the Yukon and look for medical help.

As soon as the new boat was waterproofed with a covering of sewn caribou hides, Allen's party clambered aboard and made the short trip down the Tetlin to the Tanana River. Embarking on the Tanana, they discovered that at times it could carry them 50 miles a day, but many impassable rapids often erased any gains, forcing them to make difficult portages to navigable waters downstream. But there were compensations. They passed a dazzling variety of scenery: hot springs, long sandspits, low mountains, lofty bluffs of yellow granite, stretches of riverbank ablaze with thousands of wild roses, stretches of dense spruce forest, sometimes overhung with smoke from Indian signal fires announcing the approach of the explorers. Since the sun was up 21 hours a day at this time of the year, the waters of the muddy river became surprisingly warm to the touch. Allen wished he could take the temperature of the river, but by now his thermometers and most of his other instruments had been lost or broken.

On June 25 the party reached the broad Yukon and the tiny community of Nuklukayet. The men—who were now barefoot because they had discarded their worn-out shoes—made for the trading post, which was run by a man of Russian and Indian blood named Androosky. They were bitterly disappointed by its meager stock: three dozen hard crackers, three quarts of canned beans, 20 pounds of flour, a little salt

Stoney's rival in Alaskan exploration was Lieutenant John Cantwell of the Revenue Marine (later the U.S. Coast Guard). In 1884 Cantwell located a "green mountain" of jade on the Kobuk River.

and investigate the Koyukuk River in the hunting grounds of the Koyukon Indians.

Allen hired as guides seven Koyukons who had come to Nuklukayet to trade and established sound working relations straightway, announcing that they would get their rations only after traveling a satisfactory distance each day. Allen bought provisions and five dogs. Each of the dogs carried a 25-pound load, while each man strapped on a 50-pound pack. The party set out north on July 28. "Our start," Allen wrote, "was just at the zenith of the 'sand fly' season." He was puzzled "why this gnat, which exists where there is not now or ever was any sand, should be so called," and soon learned to his misery "why some consider the gnats worse than the mosquitoes."

After hiking about 120 miles across marshy, lake-studded terrain, the party reached an Indian village on the Kanuti River. There Allen acquired two birchbark canoes and embarked on the swift, erratic stream. Although it came out of the north and at first zig-zagged southward, it was flowing almost due north when it finally emptied into the Koyukuk River. At this confluence Allen could have headed down the Koyukuk to rejoin the Yukon, but he had not had enough. Instead, he headed upstream, northeastward. He crossed the Arctic Circle and came to three southward-flowing streams that formed the Koyukuk. Still farther Allen went, up the main fork of the Koyukuk, into a bleak windswept region of dwarfed trees and low granite mountains, the southern edge of a snow-clad barrier across the northern tier of Alaska. Finally, on August 9, unsated but practical, Allen decided to start homeward in time to beat the early onrush of winter.

It had been an astounding journey. Allen and his men had justified the stubborn persistence of their commanding officer, General Miles. In less than six months they had cut a new trail well over 1,500 miles long, not counting doubling back and detours. In the process they had discovered the vital Suslota Pass through the Alaska Range, had found encouraging signs of mineral wealth and had made the first complete maps of three major river systems—the Copper, the Tanana and the Koyukuk. Allen's maps opened up the Alaskan heartland for exploitation and further exploration. They were perhaps his crowning achieve-

and some machine oil. They dined on salmon fried in the machine oil, found it tolerable and ate very little else while they waited for the first steamboat of the season to arrive.

During their two-week vigil, the explorers were joined by groups of Indians who trailed in from all over the region to await the steamer and trade for goods. Soon the station was crowded with festive Indians who, Allen wrote, "indulged in jumping and wrestling and a game of ball peculiar to themselves," and on the Fourth of July celebrated with "a grand firing of guns."

Several days later the steamer arrived, and Allen's expedition began to break up. The Indians who had most recently joined departed first; they drew their pay and, without ceremony, began to retrace hundreds of miles of the trail they had just blazed. Allen sent the scurvy-ridden Sergeant Robertson down the Yukon by steamer to St. Michael and then home. Now he and Fickett were alone.

Allen should have been satisfied and exhausted by his momentous travail, but he could not call it quits in the middle of the traveling season and in the heart of Alaska's beckoning wilderness. He proposed a new journey to Private Fickett, who, being a man much like Allen, said he was game. They would hike north

A magnificent "solitude of ice and new-born rocks"

"I've been wandering through a thousand rooms in God's crystal temple," exulted John Muir, the naturalist, in 1879 on descending from the Alaskan glacier that would bear his name. "Solomon's marble and ivory palaces were nothing like this."

If boyhood hours spent memorizing Bible verses in his native Scotland had shaped Muir's rhetorical style, years of clambering around the High Sierra in California had made him fit to explore one of Alaska's great wonders, the glacier-lined shores of 40-mile-long Glacier Bay.

Muir was not the first white man to see the awesome bay (an Army lieutenant had glimpsed it from a distance two years before him), but he was the first one to explore and map it. He arrived at the place partly by accident. In the summer of 1879 he had been glacier-prowling in the Stikine River canyon near Alaska's southeastern coast, and in October set out to see the Fairweather Mountain Range before winter closed in.

Sailing from Wrangell with four Indians and a missionary named S. Hall Young, Muir was deflected toward Icy Strait, which led into Glacier Bay, by reports of "whiskey quarrels" and shoot ups among the Chilkat Indians farther on. After a fifth Indian—a Hoonah seal hunter encountered en route—came aboard as a guide, Muir's party sailed into Sit-a-da-Kay, or Ice Bay, as the Hoonahs then called Glacier Bay.

"A solitude of ice and snow and new-born rocks, dim, dreary, mysterious" is how the glacier-swept landscape first appeared to Muir. Its magnificence overwhelmed him, and a vivid crimson sunrise behind the distant Fairweather Range with "every mountain apparently glowing from the heart like molten metal fresh from a furnace" gave him a religious experience surpassing even those he had known in the mountains of California. "The white, rayless light of the morning, seen when I was alone amid the silent peaks of the Sierra, had always seemed to be the most telling of the terrestrial manifestations of God. But here the mountains themselves were made divine."

Deteriorating weather and the Indians' fear of being caught in their canoes in the ice forced Muir to return to Wrangell without fully exploring the bay's biggest glacier, the one that would be named after him. But the next year he came back to gauge its huge bulk: 50 miles from the frontal wall to the mountain spring from which it descended and 25 miles across its widest point. "As much ice as all the 1,100 Swiss glaciers combined," Muir reckoned.

Muir became best known for exploring and writing about California's Yosemite Valley, but he also had a profound effect on the development of Alaska. He wrote so glowingly of "the nightless days of that beautiful Northland" that readers by the thousands were longing to share his experiences. Within four years of Muir's initial expedition into Glacier Bay, regular excursion steamers were chugging up it to the same fjords that the naturalist had explored in a canoe.

During two decades, John Muir made six trips to Alaska. Only his commitments in California prevented him from going more often. The battle "between landscape righteousness and the devil," as Muir saw it, was already raging, and he had become leader of the forest conservation movement. From California Muir thought of Alaska. When Reverend Young, his missionary canoemate, told him he was leaving Alaska, Muir responded: "Your heart will cry every day for the North like a lost child; and in your sleep the snowbanners of your white peaks will beckon to you."

Naturalist John Muir wrote vividly of his discovery, Glacier Bay.

The "broad, undulating prairie" of Muir Glacier, though apparently motionless, actually moves forward five to 10 feet each day.

Muir Glacier's front wall extends 300 feet above the water and another 720 feet below, and spews off up to a dozen icebergs an hour.

ment in what was to be a long and distinguished career. Allen rose to the rank of general and, four decades after his epic trek, would be considered as a nominee of the Democratic Party for the Vice Presidency of the United States.

Praise for Allen's journey came from many quarters. Even cautious scientists waxed enthusiastic. Typical was the accolade of geologist Alfred Hulse Brooks, whose name later honored a mighty mountain range even farther north than Allen had ventured. Brooks declared, "No man through his own individual efforts has added more to our knowledge of Alaska than Lieutenant Allen."

In addition to Allen's triumph, the decade of the 1880s witnessed an encouraging increase in Alaskan exploration by scientific organizations. Scholars with various special interests began arriving in appreciable numbers. In the field of ethnology, for example, two representatives of a German geographical society, the brothers Arthur and Aural Krause, came to Sitka in 1881 to launch a major study of the Tlingit Indians. The next year a Berlin museum sent an experienced explorer, J. Adrian Jacobsen, to collect Indian materials on a long trip that coincidentally opened up unknown portions of the Seward Peninsula. Soon German ethnologists were challenging the Smithsonian's early lead in the field, which Dall had initiated. Such competition made for general progress.

However, competition of a wasteful sort was also on the rise. No less than three federal services were vying for the job of improving on the Russians' charts of Alaska's coastal waters: the United States Navy; the Coast and Geodetic Survey, an agency of the Treasury Department; and the Revenue Marine (later renamed the Coast Guard), which acted principally as a customs police collecting duty for the Treasury Department. There was plenty of coastline for all three to map, but in the absence of overall control or any interservice planning, they often duplicated each other's work, with confusing results.

The Navy and Revenue Marine were soon engaged in a more or less good-natured race to investigate the unknown interior far to the north, this time with worthwhile results. The seaman who started the competition was Navy Lieutenant George Stoney, a studious, sobersided fellow with a secret yen for exploration. In 1883 the Navy chose Stoney for a routine public-relations errand, sending him far up the Pacific Coast to distribute rewards to Indians and Eskimos who had rescued survivors from two ships lost at sea. As the Navy had no vessel available for the trip north, Stoney hitched a ride aboard the Revenue Marine cutter *Corwin,* which was commanded by Captain Michael Healy.

With Healy ferrying him around, Stoney finished his assignment and then expressed an interest in the unexplored rivers of the Far North. Healy had become accustomed to the aggressive curiosity of his passengers, many of whom were scientists making coastal surveys, and he obligingly put Stoney ashore with a crewman to look around the coast of Kotzebue Sound, just above the Arctic Circle.

Stoney soon found the mouth of the Kobuk River, whose location had virtually been forgotten since its discovery by a British sea captain in 1845. From the marshy willow groves of the delta, the curious lieutenant wandered about 40 miles up the Kobuk and came back excited by two tales he had heard from local people: one of a green mountain of jade far upstream and another of a river, even farther inland, that flowed north into "the frozen sea"—the Arctic Ocean. Stoney began lobbying his Navy superiors to launch an exploration of the Kobuk.

Meanwhile, Captain Healy himself became curious about the stories that had excited Stoney. Returning to Kotzebue Sound in the summer of 1884, Healy put Lieutenant John C. Cantwell over the side with a steam-powered launch, a crew of Revenue Marines and orders to find that jade mountain. Cantwell pressed up the broad Kobuk, whose banks were gouged by ice and littered with trees uprooted by the spring floods. About 300 miles upriver he discovered the mountain, and it did contain jade—more precisely, the mineral jadeite. In the process Cantwell made the much more important discovery of extensive coal deposits, which he mined as needed to fuel his launch's boiler.

Cantwell was heading back when he met Lieutenant Stoney coming upstream with a party of sailors. Having appealed successfully to Navy pride, Stoney had been given the schooner *Ounalaska* to explore the Kobuk, preferably before the Revenue Marine.

Though Cantwell had beaten him, Stoney felt sure that this disappointment would "only prompt us to make our work more thorough, if such was possible." He did go farther upstream than Cantwell and brought back samples of the jade mountain. On the deficit side, he ran his launch aground in shallow water and had to finish the journey in skin canoes acquired from the natives.

In 1885 Healy brought Cantwell back for another try at the Kobuk. In the upper reaches of the river the swift current plunged through a dangerous rock-strewn channel, forcing the party to make frequent portages. Some 600 miles upstream, Cantwell finally reached the source of the Kobuk, Lake Walker.

At the same time, Cantwell's second in command, assistant engineer S. B. McLenegan, was exploring a river still farther north, the Noatak. McLenegan and his men spent a rainy month struggling up the swollen Noatak, making portages around roaring rapids. As they penetrated deep into the wet wilderness, McLenegan reported, "The sense of utter desolation and loneliness which took possession of the mind was indeed difficult to dispel. No trace of human habitation could be found, and even the hardy waterfowl seemed to have forsaken the region, leaving nothing to remind us of the great and busy world thousands of miles below."

The party crossed the timber line and pressed 200 miles beyond to the headwaters of the Noatak. There, McLenegan wrote, "In every direction, as far as the eye could see, the dreary expanse of the tundra, covered with small lakes and half-frozen marshes, stretched away in the distance. Not a vestige of life was to be seen." Only then did he finally decide to call it quits. The explorations of McLenegan and Cantwell resulted in maps that would remain authoritative for a generation.

Cantwell was heading down the Kobuk when, once again, he met Lieutenant Stoney coming upstream. This time Stoney had come equipped for a major effort. He had a party of 18 men, enough provisions for 20 months and a portable sawmill that, powered by his boat's boiler, would turn out finished lumber to be used for building a solid winter camp. Stoney had also done something about one of the

hazards of summer, bringing along mosquito-proof wire-mesh masks of his own invention.

From his camp, which he named Fort Cosmos after a scientific club in Washington, D.C., Stoney sent out well-disciplined exploring teams all through the winter. One crossed the frozen tundra southward to the frozen Koyukuk. Stoney himself explored the Selawik River and probed north until he found a tributary of the Colville, the great river that emptied into the Arctic Ocean. He dispatched his boldest expedition in April 1887, when the arctic cold began to abate and a little more light glimmered around the edges of the black winter sky. Under the leadership of Ensign William Lauriston Howard, the five-man party located the Colville River, tracked it northeastward for a short distance, then veered north to the headwaters of the Ikpikpuk River. Howard was able to follow that river almost due north to its mouth on the Arctic Ocean, not far from the northernmost tip of Alaska, Point Barrow.

Howard's 600-mile trek to land's end closed the contest between the Navy and the Revenue Marine. In spite of their claims to the contrary, neither service had measurably outdone the other. Between them, however, they had achieved much. They had spun a web of survey trails through Alaska's mysterious northeastern regions and had transformed the remote Kobuk basin into one of the most thoroughly explored sections of the territory.

In the wake of Stoney's and Cantwell's efforts, however, Alaskan exploration by military or other government personnel slid into a 10-year relapse. Federal funds continued to be meager. Whenever a special appropriation was made, there was often accompanying confusion over which service or scientific group should get it. Fortunately, $5,000 voted by Congress in 1895 for a study of Alaska's gold and coal resources did go immediately to the right service, the United States Geological Survey—and with gratifying results.

The Geological Survey, founded in 1872 as an adjunct of the Interior Department, had a franchise broader than its name suggested: it was charged to explore, map and classify all public lands, and to study and recommend the development of all resources therein. The Survey had done important work in the trans-Mississippi West and was just getting its feet wet in Alaska when an epoch-making emergency thrust it to the forefront.

Full-scale exploration became an urgent need late in the 1890s when the rich gold strikes along the Klondike and the Yukon rivers and on the beach at Nome brought tens of thousands of Americans rushing into and through Alaska. With so many citizens in the suddenly attractive territory, Congress at last had to abandon its wait-and-see attitude. Money and trained manpower had to be thrown into the breach, and quickly, or the government would be counting casualties instead of pennies.

The Geological Survey, working under the supervision of the Smithsonian Institution, immediately began outperforming the other services by a wide margin. In 1898 alone the Survey sent four parties to Alaska on major explorations. One went into the gold country around Fortymile River and made detailed relief-and-contour maps of 2,000 square miles of terrain. The region just to the south, between the White and Tanana rivers, was surveyed by geologist Alfred Brooks, whose party covered 600 miles in 66 days. A third party swept in a 1,300-mile arc up the Susitna River and down the Kuskokwim. The fourth party surveyed its way up the Susitna River to the area of Mt. McKinley, at 20,320 feet the highest peak in North America.

In 1900 Congress increased the Survey's annual budget from $25,000 to the generous sum of $60,000. Congress also created order out of what had been a chaotic situation by assigning the various services of the government definite roles in exploration. The Geological Survey took over as the sole official explorer on land, and the Army was restricted to the kind of heavy work suited to its numbers and matériel: building roads and communications lines. The Navy, the Revenue Marine, and the Coast and Geodetic Survey were restricted to their nautical beats and to charting Alaska's coastline.

In spite of the gigantic strides made, the exploration of the deep interior was far from complete; roughly four fifths of Alaskan territory still appeared as blank spots on the map. But the size and shape of the job remaining were clearly understood, and trained cadres stood ready and efficiently organized to pursue the task.

As a new phase of exploration began, the Army, settling into its limited role, undertook the job that the Western Union explorers had begun in the 1860s: the laying of an Alaskan telegraph line. Adopting roughly the route blazed by Lieutenant Allen in 1885, men of the Signal Corps under General Adolphus Greeley started from the vicinity of the Copper Delta and headed northeast, bound for Eagle City about 700 miles distant.

In 1901, after nearly a year's work, General Greeley was fed up with his corps' slow progress. Looking for a troubleshooter, he picked an energetic 21-year-old, Lieutenant William Mitchell. Despite his youth and the boyish nickname Billy, Mitchell had seen service in Cuba, the Philippines and the Orient.

Young Mitchell returned from his first inspection tour with a transparently simple suggestion. The surveyors and wire-laying crews had tried to work in the summer, as they thought the winter too brutal for outdoor labor. Draft horses bogged down in the soggy tundra and were good for no more than 20 miles a day under maximum loads of 200 pounds. But, Mitchell added, "In winter these same animals could pull 1,000 to 2,000 pounds over the frozen snow."

Impressed, Greeley sent Mitchell back to take charge of the work himself. As Billy headed north again, he carried along as his only extra baggage a few books on the esoteric new science of aeronautics; he was an eager acolyte of General Greeley, who had been assigned by the Signal Corps to investigate the potential of flight. A quarter of a century later, Billy Mitchell would get himself court-martialed for zealously insisting that airplanes could win wars.

Lieutenant Mitchell soon had his wire-laying crews moving ahead at a faster clip. Besides switching the season of heavy labor, he added a bit of Old West wisdom by substituting "indestructible" mules for the injury-prone horses. Thereafter, work on the telegraph line proceeded smoothly.

The line opened for traffic on June 27, 1903. "I made the last connection myself," Billy Mitchell wrote. "Then from St. Michael and Nome on the Bering Sea, clear through to New York and Washington, the current transmitted out messages with the speed of light. Alaska was open to civilization."

Intrepid whale hunters of the arctic seas

Daring Eskimos had hunted whales before white men came to Alaska, and in the late 1880s American whaling companies began hiring Eskimo crews to kill the great bowheads that migrated each spring past Alaska's arctic coast. Using the traditional skin-covered craft called umiaks or small wooden boats provided by the Americans, the Eskimos pursued whales that weighed 50 to 75 tons. The whale-hunting scenes shown here were colored in crayon in about 1890 by an unknown Eskimo in a mission school.

Members of a boat's crew hang on to the line as a har-
pooned whale pulls them across the icy waters of the
Arctic Ocean. In the bow an Eskimo rifleman takes aim at
the spouting whale, while the American skipper, steering
from the stern, tries to avoid the whale's smacking flukes.

To signal that a kill has been made, an Eskimo runs the whaling company's American flag to the top of the boat's mast. The Eskimo sharpshooter standing in the bow fires an exploding projectile into the dying whale, while three other Eskimo crewmen prepare to hoist the craft's sail.

Against a horizon of icebergs, Eskimos in four umiaks paddle in unison toward shore with their kill in tow. Below, two American supervisors help the Eskimos hoist the whale onto the ice with the aid of a double block and tackle, a laborsaving device introduced by the Americans.

A tired but proud whaling team and their American supervisors *(right)* stand beside their rich prize. Several of the Eskimos hold the long-handled spades and hooks they will use to cut up the whale for its blubber and bone. A typical bowhead yielded 2,000 pounds of ivory-like baleen bone and enough meat to feed an Eskimo village for weeks.

VIEWS TAKEN at NOME AND OTHER PLACES IN ALASKA BY W.H.POTTER. WITH THE LOS ANGELES and CAPE NOME MINING Co.

Above the five dots shown along the rail are members of our party.

F.G.French
F.M.De Mange
E.P.Jeanes
H.Goodwin
Mrs Goodwin
G.W.Scarberry.

THE OHIO COMING IN TO SEATTLE MAY 18-1900 FROM FRISCO

S.S.OHIO IN OF N.Y.

LIFE 1900 BUOY

THE OHIO LEAVING SEATTLE FOR NOME, 3.45 P.M. MAY 24TH 1900 — 706 PASSENGERS. I am sitting on the point of the anchor crane just over the "H" in "OHIO". Scarberry stands above me.

A more desolate setting for a great gold rush can hardly be imagined than Nome, a featureless strip of sand wedged between the ice-strewn Bering Sea and the barren tundra of Alaska's northwest coast. But the bedrock in Nome's creeks was seamed with gold-rich quartz; on the beach itself, thousands of years of erosion had deposited a fabulous treasure—"the most exten- sive and phenomenal gold find in histo- ry," proclaimed the November 25, 1899, *Nome News*.

Of the 30,000 gold-smitten for- tune seekers who rushed to Nome, few were so well equipped and organized as the 9 men and one woman below, sponsored by the Los Angeles and Cape Nome Mining Company, who left Seattle on the steamer *Ohio* in May 1900. Led by Walter Patrick Butler of Minnesota, they successfully worked claims on creeks near the fa- mous beach. Butler kept a diary of the expedition and later assembled a 37- page, elaborately decorated album, it- self a treasure despite his inexperience as a photographer (noted at bottom right) and the film's underdevelop- ment by a darkroom amateur in Nome.

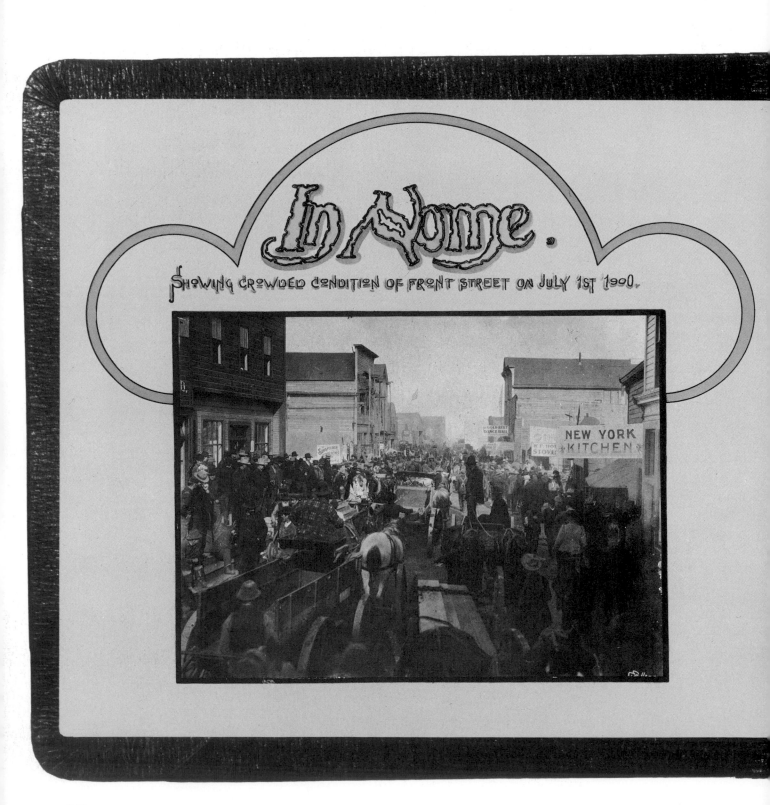

In Nome.

Showing crowded condition of Front Street on July 1st 1900.

neg # 74-362

View: LOKING EAST FROM LANE'S DERRICK, SHOWING THE SAND-SPIT OR WEST END OF NOME, THE POINT NORTH OF SNAKE RIVER & THE TENT TOWN ON THE TUNDRA IN THE BACKGROUND ACROSS DRY CR. MOUTH OF R. BEYOND DREDGE

VIEW OF NOME, FROM THE SPIT.

See Map. P. 11.   JULY 11th   From point 3

Cape Nome 12 M. IN THE DISTANCE. OUR OFFICE AT X ON THE BANK OF SNAKE RIVER. MAIN PART OF NOME IS IN THE DISTANCE. THE "RED ELEPHANT" PORTLAND DREDGER BEING BUILT ON THE BEACH, & A LIGHTER IN THE FOREGROUND NEAR GASOLINE TANKS.

129

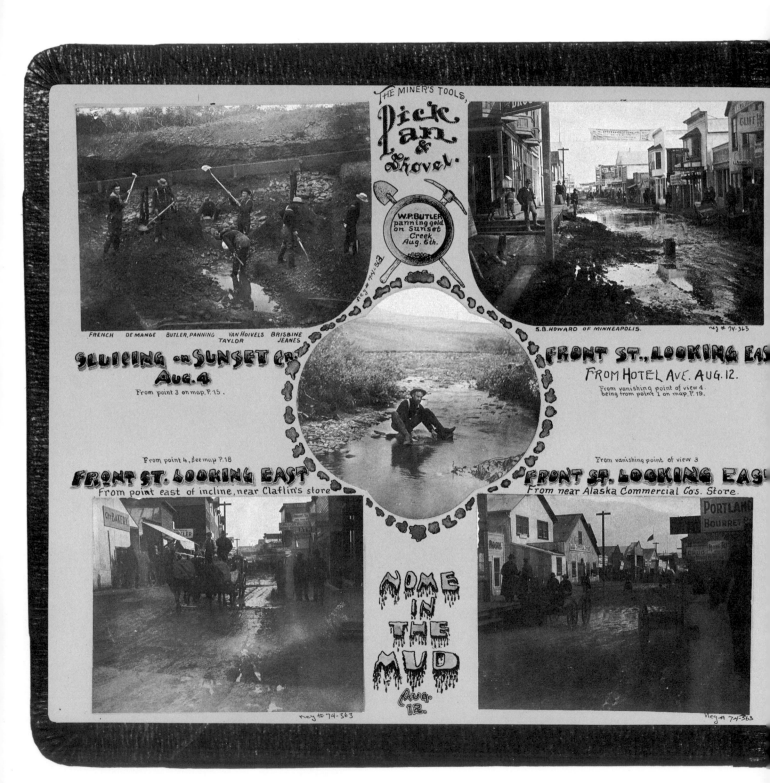

THE MINER'S TOOLS,
Pick, Pan & Shovel.

W.P. BUTLER
panning gold
on Sunset
Creek
Aug. 6th.

FRENCH   DE MANGE   BUTLER, PANNING   VAN HOIVELS   BRISBINE
                              TAYLOR   JEANES

S.B. HOWARD OF MINNEAPOLIS.   neg # 74-363

SLUICING on SUNSET CREEK
AUG. 4
From point 3 on map, P. 15.

FRONT ST., LOOKING EAST
FROM HOTEL AVE. AUG. 12.
From vanishing point of view 4.
being from point 1 on map, P. 19.

From point 4, See map P. 18

FRONT ST. LOOKING EAST
From point east of incline, near Claflin's store

From vanishing point of view 3

FRONT ST. LOOKING EAST
From near Alaska Commercial Co's. Store.

NOME
IN
THE
MUD
AUG.
12.

neg # 74-363   neg # 74-363

130

VIEW ON PAGE 10 WAS TAKEN FROM POINT 4

VIEW ON THIS PAGE FROM POINT 1

VIEW ON PAGE 12 WAS TAKEN FROM POINT 2

VIEW ON PAGE 13 FROM POINT 3.

Tundra
Cemetery
DEPOT
P.OFFICE
FRONT ST.
ANCHORAGE

WASHING THE "GOLDEN SANDS OF NOME" SHOWING ROCKERS AND SLUICE-BOXES IN OPERATION.

BEACH MINING

LOOKING S.E. FROM THE TUNDRA JUST WEST OF THE CEMETERY, AUG. 1900. ANCHORAGE IN DISTANCE

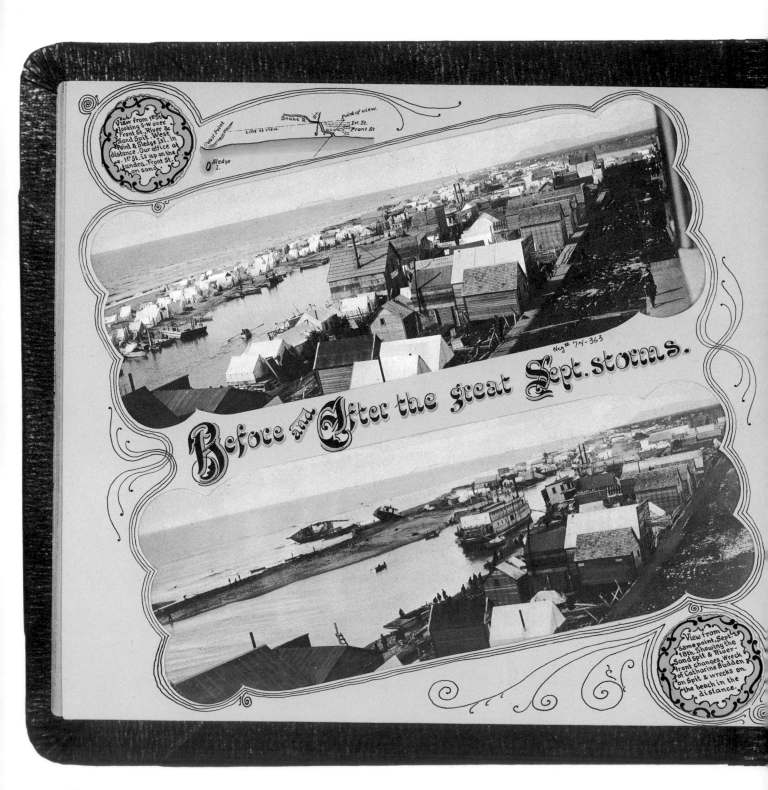

Before and After the great Sept. storms.

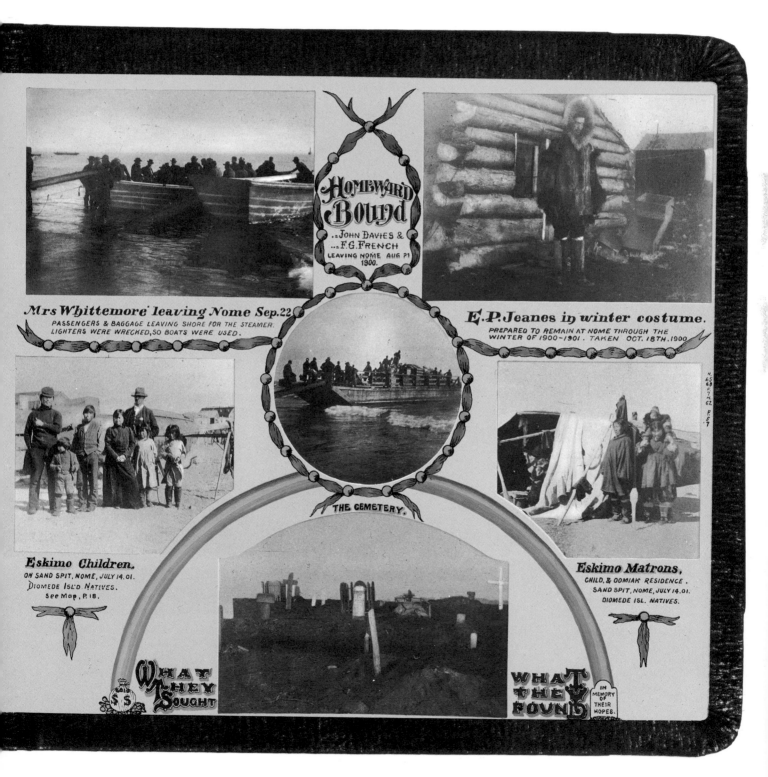

Homeward
Bound
..John Davies &
...F.G. French
LEAVING NOME AUG 21
1900.

Mrs Whittemore leaving Nome Sep.22
PASSENGERS & BAGGAGE LEAVING SHORE FOR THE STEAMER.
LIGHTERS WERE WRECKED, SO BOATS WERE USED.

E.P. Jeanes in winter costume.
PREPARED TO REMAIN AT NOME THROUGH THE
WINTER OF 1900~1901. TAKEN OCT. 18TH. 1900.

THE CEMETERY.

Eskimo Children.
ON SAND SPIT, NOME, JULY 14.01.
DIOMEDE ISL'D NATIVES.
See Map, P.18.

Eskimo Matrons,
CHILD. & OOMIAK RESIDENCE.
SAND SPIT, NOME, JULY 14.01.
DIOMEDE ISL. NATIVES.

WHAT THEY SOUGHT

WHAT THEY FOUND
IN MEMORY OF THEIR HOPES.

A bonanza on the beach that inspired villainy

One day in the last winter of the 19th Century, an Indian at a village near Fort Yukon looked out over the frozen trail that ran by his tent and gaped at the sight that met his eyes. Whisking down the rutted, icy dog-sled paths was a man bundled up in furs, his legs furiously pumping a bicycle. "White man," the Indian later explained, "he set down, walk like hell!"

The bike rider's name was Ed Jesson, and the reason for his hurry, and thus for his unorthodox mode of transportation, was gold. Jesson was a prospector who had been in the North since 1896 without ever striking it rich. He was working in the Klondike region of Canada as a contract supplier of caribou meat when word arrived that good-sized finds had been made on the far side of Alaska, at a place on the Seward Peninsula called Cape Nome. By the time Jesson was able to make his way to the nearby town of Dawson, it was emptying almost as quickly as it had filled during its own hectic gold rush two years earlier. "I'm telling you," Jesson wrote in a diary, "my fever was up to the breaking point."

Once more the stampede was on. Hundreds of seasoned sourdoughs, not the sort of men to wait for warm weather and the breakup of ice in the Yukon, deserted their campsites and started immediately down the 2,000-mile frozen river toward Nome. Many had to walk. Those who had dogs—few did since good sled dogs were scarce enough to fetch $350 a head or more—mushed.

One man named Archie Burns lit out on an old white mare. Things went well for him at first, but there was little feed along the trail, and by the time he reached Fort Yukon, about 240 miles from Dawson, his nag was starving. After permitting a group of Indians to inspect the horse, the first they had ever seen, Burns asked them to feed it. But the horse refused to eat what was offered, and the next day, after making barely a mile, it keeled over and died. Burns trudged back to Fort Yukon, where he found the Indians still speculating about the strange beast. "What's the matter?" one of the Indians asked him. "Big white dog no eat salmon?"

A week or so later Ed Jesson arrived on his two-wheeler and gave the Indians their second surprise. Jesson had spotted the bike in an Alaska Commercial Company store in Dawson, which was stocked with all manner of exotic merchandise bearing inflated price tags because of the Klondike boom. Jesson bought the vehicle for $150 and spent eight days teaching himself to operate it on ice. With great forethought he bought some recent stateside newspapers that had been brought over the Chilkoot Pass, then he strapped on his gear and pedaled off down the Yukon for Nome. The day Jesson left Dawson the temperature was − 20° F.

By the time night fell he had covered nearly 50 miles. Roadhouses along the river were situated about 25 miles apart, so Jesson calculated that he could bed down and breakfast in one, come up to another for dinner at midday and reach a third in time for supper. The plan failed on his second day out when the mercury dropped to − 48° F. "The rubber tires on my wheel were frozen hard and stiff as gas pipe," Jesson recorded in his diary. "The oil in the bearings was frozen and I could scarcely ride it and my nose was freezing and I had to hold the handlebars with both hands, not being able to ride yet with one hand and rub my nose with the other." Both the bike and the

A sourdough relaxes amid his possessions outside his shanty home, near the gold-laden beach at Nome. He used the boxlike rocker at left to sift the sands for gold.

biker reached Eagle, just over the border into Alaska, after hitching a ride on a dog sled.

"It looked like a white elephant on my hands," Jesson wrote about his bicycle. "But one good thing, it didn't eat anything, and I didn't have to cook dogfeed for it."

When the temperature rose a few degrees he set out again, and one day, riding on a smooth stretch of river ice and pedaling hard to keep warm, he made 50 miles before lunch. On another good day he overtook and left behind a big Norwegian prospector who was making the journey to Nome on ice skates. Jesson concluded that he had chosen the superior mode of transportation; the Norwegian conceded that the best he could do on skates was 40 miles a day.

Strong winds nearly put Jesson out of business about halfway down the serpentine trail. "I was back-peddling to keep from going too fast and at times the wind picked me up and landed me where it pleased, into a snowbank or an icejam upside down," he wrote. One hard gust "whirled me into a rough patch of ice almost busting my knee, skinning my hands and elbows and broke one of my handlebars." He continued on afoot, pushing the bicycle.

That night, after limping three or four miles, he found company in a party of prospectors holed up in a lean-to. "What have you to eat?" he asked. Not much, it turned out—some tea, beans, hot cakes and mush. Jesson handed over a pound of butter, two cans of milk, a piece of bacon, some crackers and a small frying pan. In anticipation of the feasting to come, he wrote in his diary: "Ah! we will live heigh tonight with butter on the hotcakes and milk on the mush in the morning." All the party now lacked were blankets enough to go around, but that was of little concern, one of the prospectors assured Jesson, "as long as the woodpile holds out." The men cut some spruce boughs for bedding "and everything was fine."

In order to repair his bicycle, Jesson split up "a nice strait grained piece of spruce and with my knife made two nice pieces to tape on each front fork of the wheel letting them extend heigh enough to fasten a cross stick to them to act as a handlebar. I made a real good job of it."

The next day Jesson was wheeling again. At Kaltag, where the looping Yukon makes its closest approach to Nome, he left the river and struck almost due west across the frozen tundra. Nome was still 200 miles away. The tundra made considerably rougher and slower going than the frozen river, and worse, Jesson was now away from the chain of roadhouses. To provide for emergencies he had added 25 pounds of grub to his gear. When it was possible he took shelter at night with Eskimo families along the way. As a precaution against lice, or "seam squirrels" as Jesson called them, he would, before retiring, strip naked outside and leave his clothing in the uninfested arctic night air, then bed down with the family among the sealskins.

A month after he left Dawson, Jesson reached Nome, in good shape except for temporary snow blindness. The newspapers he had brought with him, the *San Francisco Examiner* and the *Seattle Post-Intelligencer*, made him Nome's hero of the winter of 1899-1900, so starved were the icebound prospectors for word of the outside world. Editor John F. A. Strong of the *Nome News* called a public meeting in a dance hall, and several hundred men turned out. The more literate took turns reading the papers aloud, and both Admiral George Dewey—whose victory at Manila Bay dominated the news columns—and Ed Jesson were toasted time and again.

The strike at Nome and the subsequent stampede of prospectors was neither the last big gold rush in the Far North nor the largest. But the bonanza at Nome, for a number of reasons, was the most remarkable. For one thing, it was the richest "poor man's diggings" in history: the dull black sand of Nome's beach was laced with gold that needed no heavy investment or effort to harvest. For another, Nome became the focal point of an epic criminal conspiracy—one that involved powerful lobbyists, a United States district judge and several senators. The conspirators came within an ace of stealing the gold of Nome out from under the shovels of genuine claim holders.

Nome's story begins in the autumn of 1897 when a group of prospectors bound for the Klondike was caught by the freeze-up at St. Michael, the old Russian post on Norton Sound opening on the Bering Sea. Unwilling to stay idle all winter, a few men crossed the sound and prospected the mouth of Fish

Three "lucky Swedes," (from left) John Brynteson, Jafet Lindeberg and Erik Lindblom, triggered a stampede of miners—and claim-jumpers—to Nome when they struck high-grade pay dirt at nearby Anvil Creek on September 22, 1898.

River on Golovnin Bay. They found a little gold, enough to stimulate their interest.

The next summer a small party returned to explore the area more thoroughly. From their base camp on Golovnin Bay, the prospectors ranged across the Seward Peninsula as far as the mouth of the Snake River, 12 miles west of Cape Nome. There too they found a little gold, not enough to excite the whole party but enough to make a Swedish-born prospector named John Brynteson think there might be more. At Golovnin Bay he confided his hunch to two friends, Jafet Lindeberg, a Laplander who originally had been brought to Alaska to herd Sheldon Jackson's reindeer, and Erik Lindblom, a Swedish sailor who had jumped ship to hunt for gold.

Brynteson, Lindeberg and Lindblom made their way to Cape Nome in late September, 1898, and in a gulch on Anvil Creek, three miles from the coast, they panned some $50 worth of gold the first day. After two or three weeks of successful panning, they returned to their base camp to pick up additional supplies and took three more Scandinavian friends and a hired Eskimo into their confidence. Back once more on Anvil Creek, they panned doggedly in the deepening cold and in a few days accumulated $1,800 worth of the precious metal.

That was enough; they had, by performing the legal essentials of work and discovery of a mineral, met the requirements of ownership. The three organized a mining district, elected one of their number recorder, staked out 43 claims for themselves and, under power of attorney, staked 47 other claims in the names of everybody they knew. They returned to camp for the winter, swearing one another to secrecy. But such secrets do not keep.

By the winter of 1898-1899 the rush was on— from the States, from the Klondike, from every corner of Alaska. In midspring the empty beach west of Cape Nome had become a tent town of 250 people; by early summer the population had risen to 1,000. By late summer the 1,000 had doubled. "A city grew between dawns," one new arrival wrote, "a city of gleaming white canvas."

At the end of 1899 Nome had 20 saloons, six bakeries, five laundries, 12 general merchandise stores, three secondhand stores, four wholesale liquor stores, three fruit, cigar and confectionary stores, two meat markets, one boat shop, a bookstore, a bank, two printing shops, four hotels, six restaurants, six lodging houses, four bathhouses, four barbershops, a hospital and a waterworks. In addition to such amenities, it boasted two paper hangers, two photographers, one brewer, two tinsmiths, two sign painters, three watchmakers, three packers, two dentists, 11 doctors, 16 lawyers, a massage artist, and a demimonde that was growing so fast in number that no one bothered

Exodus from the Klondike—a gold rush in reverse

Dawson City, the Canadian boomtown created by the Klondike gold rush, was still prospering in 1899 when word came of the exciting new digs at Nome. Men left Dawson in droves—and they did so without regret. Of all the major gold finds in the Old West, the Klondike was the hardest to reach and the most cruelly disappointing to almost all who made the journey.

Dawson was born at the juncture of the Yukon and Klondike rivers a few weeks after an old sourdough, George Washington Carmack, made his great strike on Bonanza Creek, a tributary of the Klondike. On August 17, 1896, while pausing to drink, Carmack spied a small nugget in the creek and cleared away some of the loose rock. "I could see the raw gold laying thick between flaky slabs like cheese sandwiches," he later reported. "I felt as if I just dealt myself a royal flush in the game of life."

Within weeks of Carmack's find, Bonanza Creek was staked from end to end by sourdoughs who had been working small claims across the border in Alaska. Most of the first-comers scooped up fortunes in gold that winter. At the end of 1896, Dawson had 500 inhabitants; six months later the number had climbed to 5,000. Yet the real stampede was still to come.

The Klondike strike burst upon the outside world in the summer of 1897, when Carmack and several dozen miners showed up in Seattle and San Francisco carrying satchels filled with about three million dollars in gold. Within days the boat fare to

Bound for Nome, stampeders wait to board a steamer at Dawson in 1899.

Skagway and Dyea, the closest access ports to the Klondike, rocketed from $200 to more than $1,000; scalpers bought tickets and sold them for twice that. By the autumn of 1897 at least 100,000 stampeders were on their way to the Klondike.

From the coast the most popular route led over a treacherous 550-mile trail. Hundreds of hikers started out only to turn back after one look at the precipitous White and Chilkoot passes that pointed the way. But others persisted: by the summer of 1898 some 20,000 men and women had struggled into Dawson.

Disillusion awaited most. The Klondike's gold lay within a relatively small 25-by-30-mile area, and the best locations had been staked the

year before. To make matters worse, the Northwest Mounted Police began collecting a Canadian duty on all ore excavated, and soon only rich claims were worth the trouble.

Some of the stampeders made a meager living doing odd jobs or working as laborers on other people's claims. Most did nothing but mill about in Dawson's muddy streets and smoky saloons. By the middle of summer the newcomers were leaving as fast as they had arrived.

The electric news of the gold strikes at Nome galvanized the idlers, providing an alternative to going home. The exodus reached flood stage in July, when fully 8,000 stampeders jammed onto Yukon steamers for the 1,700-mile journey to Nome.

to count. And all this was only the initial wave.

The first of many portents of trouble at Nome arose that summer of 1899. It soon occurred to relative latecomers—stewing angrily in tent saloons along the beach—that, as usual in such circumstances, the best ground had been staked long ago by the early comers. In this case it had been staked by the Scandinavians, who had collectively come to be called the "Lucky Swedes."

In a burst of convenient patriotism, the malcontents concluded that they, true-blue American citizens, had been foully done in by foreigners. Somebody recalled that under United States mining law an alien could legally hold a claim only if he would take an oath, before a qualified United States commissioner, of his intent to become a citizen. Whatever the Scandinavians' intentions might have been about citizenship, Nome had no officer authorized to hear such a deposition. In the heat of inspiration the disgruntled miners decided to take the law into their own hands and evict the Scandinavians.

To achieve this end a miners' meeting was called on July 10, 1899, and a resolution was drawn up that declared all existing claims void and vulnerable to restaking. The plotters sent delegates out to the Scandinavians' diggings on Anvil Creek to await a signal fire in town that would let them know that the resolution had passed and that they were free to jump the claims at will.

The plot did not quite succeed. The only legal authority in Nome resided in the person of a young Army lieutenant, Oliver Spaulding, who had been dispatched from St. Michael with a squad of soldiers and vague instructions to try to maintain order if he could. When Lieutenant Spaulding heard of the presumptive resolution, he concluded that it was a threat to order, and he advanced on the meeting with his soldiers. "Gentlemen," he commanded, "withdraw that resolution."

"What for?" some of the miners shouted. "We make our own laws. What do we care for you and your soldiers?" The belligerent miners began to close around Spaulding. The lieutenant ordered his men to fix bayonets. He turned to the miners and told them they could clear the place in two minutes, voluntarily, or he and his men would clear it for them. Grumbling,

but faced down, the miners shuffled away—and one crisis was past.

Out on Anvil Creek the original claimants went ahead with their work undisturbed, in the shadow of the anvil-shaped rock for which the creek was named. But while they and others labored at their claims, a most unlikely prospector was about to stumble onto the discovery that would obscure the Swedes' finds and render Nome unique.

John Hummell was both old and sick, too feeble to give much thought to going to the creeks and toiling in the permafrost. Still, he was not too far gone to share the common hunger for the yellow metal. One day, a couple of weeks after the miners' meeting, Hummell walked down to the beach and panned a shovelful of black sand in the sea. Gold is where you find it, the old prospectors said, and John Hummell found it at the water's edge.

The gold lay right underfoot, practically in the way. Within hours a throng of men—and a few women—were on the beach, spading up the sands. That first season, the summer of 1899, 2,000 miners along a 42-mile stretch of beach would take out two million dollars, while back on the creeks a few rich claims would yield another million.

On the beach all a miner needed was a shovel and a gold pan or, preferably, a rocker. The latter was a device resembling a baby's cradle, and it functioned on the same principle: pour in a shovelful of sand and a bucket of water; then swing the rocker back and forth. This lullaby motion did for gold what it does for a baby—caused it to settle down.

A miner who had worked on the beach described the rocker process in a letter to home: "At the top is a hopper with holes in the bottom to keep out the coarse stuff. The sand falls through the hopper holes and washes over two 'aprons' slanting back and forth to the bottom where it runs out through a sluice box. . . . The aprons and the whole bottom of the box and riffles are made of blanket so that the finer dust catches in the nap or wool. A man stands dipping water into the hopper with one hand and rocking with the other, while the other man puts in a shovelful of the pay dirt every now and then and keeps the water tub full and the tailings cleared away. To 'clean-up' a

A bargeload of eager gold seekers is greeted by earlier arrivals at Nome in the summer of 1900. At the height of the rush, more than 70 ships anchored in the roadstead, a mile or more off the beach. "Day and night beneath the midnight sun," wrote one newcomer, "they belched forth freight and men of every kind to help in conquering this new realm."

rocker, the aprons and blankets are taken out and washed in a tub and the resulting debris panned out."

On Nome's beach the sands subject to rocker treatment ran from the tundra's edge to the water line at low tide. Sea water stopped the beachcombers there, although many a man, convinced that the sea, too, must be paved with gold, racked his brain trying to think of some feasible way to roll back the tide and harvest the wealth underneath.

Because there was no one in Nome experienced in mining a beach, no one knew quite how to go about allocating claims made on sand. And, because there was practically no law in Nome, the immediate result was close to chaos. With thousands of miners at work on a beach no more than 200 feet wide, the common creekside claim size of 1,320 by 660 feet—or about 20 acres—was obviously impracticable. At one time the miners themselves more or less settled on a space measured on each side by the length of a long-handled miner's shovel—which worked out to about 20 square feet. But all systems of allocation became confusing each day when the tide rushed in, driving the miners back to high ground and smoothing over all traces of their labor before the water receded and let them get back to work.

Then, to nobody's real surprise, organized business reared a hungry head, and for a while everything was more confusing than ever. The Nome-Sinuk Mining Company, one of several corporations hastily formed to exploit the Nome gold fields, asserted that its claims on the tundra behind the beach actually extended all the way across the sand to the water's edge. Miners working the beach were trespassers, the company contended, and to evict them it called upon Lieutenant Wallace M. Cragie, who had succeeded Lieutenant Spaulding as commander of Nome's squad of soldiers. Dutifully, Cragie arrested somewhere between 300 and 400 miners—it was typical of the times in Nome that nobody took an exact head count. Then the question arose of what to do with the prisoners. Nome had no jail or even a building big enough to hold them all for long.

For their part, the arrested men promptly put together a pool of $600 and hired the services of a lawyer. Because most mining camps were highly litigious places, Nome already had lawyers in adequate supply. The prisoners then announced through counsel that they intended to demand individual trials by jury. This brought matters to a pretty pass. Nome had no court, no judge and no authority to impanel a jury. The nearest jurist was United States District Judge Charles S. Johnson in Sitka, about 1,100 miles away, but it was unclear whether even he could try the accused miners, since trespassing seemed something less than a federal offense. The Organic Act of 1884 had placed Alaska under the state laws of Oregon, which meant that if the prisoners persisted in their demands for jury trials, somebody would have to pay to send them to Portland.

Seeing a way out of the dilemma, Lieutenant Cragie called on officials of the Nome-Sinuk Mining Company and advised them that if they wished the miners to be prosecuted, the company would be required to put up a bond to defray the costs of food, lodging, confinement and transportation until the cases were disposed of. The company declined. Lieutenant Cragie thereupon turned the prisoners loose; within an hour they were back on the beach, rocking their cradles, moiling for gold and scurrying like fiddler crabs between high and low tides.

To further complicate legal matters that summer, all up and down the beach men who regarded themselves as legitimate claimants found themselves working side by side with claim-jumpers. The sands of Nome ululated with the sounds of dissent. On August 13, Joseph Grinnell, a claim owner—or so he thought—complained in his diary: "Our claims are now covered with beach jumpers and we cannot get them off. Mob law rules. There are 100 beach combers to one claim owner, and the authorities will not or cannot do anything." The legitimate holders of claims had to take things into their own hands—not that it did much good.

"The lieutenant in charge gave us some notices 'to vacate,'" Grinnell wrote, "but the people pay no attention. It fell to me to go up to one of our claims, and I showed the notice to each of the workers. . . . Some laughed at me. Some sneered. One tough consigned me and the notice to a warmer place than Cape Nome in August. . . . This at my own claim! I never knew I had a temper before, but for a minute then I do not think I would have been responsible. The man

who threatened me was bigger than I, and I went on. And he is still working there, taking out $100 per day, so I am told. He is in a 'pocket.' Our pocket! We have discussed the advisability of using force, but have abandoned it." One of his partners, Grinnell continued, warned that "we 'might get disfigured,' for there are people here just awkward enough to hit a fellow in the face."

Grinnell was one of 20 Californians who, in 1898, had banded together to form the Long Beach and Alaska Mining and Trading Company. They had sailed their own schooner to Kotzebue Sound, chasing a rumor, which proved to be totally unfounded, that gold lay scattered about for the picking on the banks of the Kobuk River. Split into small parties, the men spent the winter of 1898-1899 in camps along the Kobuk. They found no gold, but for 21-year-old Grinnell their expedition was far from being a

total disappointment. He was a bird watcher and amateur ornithologist, and even while the ice on the river was seven feet thick he passed the months happily enough—shooting, skinning and stuffing the birds of the arctic. Still, every now and then he remembered that the stated purpose of his company was to find gold and get rich.

"Ah, I'd like to see a mother lode! She's what we are after," Grinnell wrote wistfully in his diary. "I'd give five dollars for the chance to pan out two dollars' worth of gold dust!" He soon got his chance.

In April 1899 a privately operated mail ship brought news of the Nome strike to Grinnell's group—"Richer than the Klondike. Three men took out $600 in ten hours." Grinnell was pricked by temptation but remained cautious. "I am hard to convert to any gold proposition now," he reported in his diary. "All are excited over this rumor but it is useless to think of travel." April, Grinnell knew, was a bad

month in the open: "Two men came in from Ambler City today with frozen feet. They will be laid up for a month and one may lose his toes. By noon it is thawing. A man's socks and boots become soaked with perspiration and as the afternoon advances, the temperature falls and the wet footgear freezes. Then, too, in many places the river ice cracks and the water flows up through and soaks into the snow so that a traveler steps through into the slush and water deep enough to fill his shoes. Before camp is reached the feet freeze."

For the time being, Grinnell decided to stick to collecting the skins of rock ptarmigans, spruce grouse and three-toed woodpeckers. He did learn that several members of his expedition had set out for Cape Nome and he was content. If they succeeded in getting there, they would stake claims for the entire group. By the end of April only three of the original company still remained on the Kobuk River with the icebound

schooner; the rest were in Nome or on the way there.

Grinnell was not able to reach Nome until July 20, after the ice moved away from the shoreline in Kotzebue Sound and the company schooner could finally get under way. On his arrival in Nome, Grinnell learned that his partners had staked out claims on the beach seven miles west of town. At last, after more than a year, he got his opportunity to pan two dollars worth of gold dust. Probably, if effort could be reckoned in dollars, Grinnell paid more than five dollars for the privilege.

"It is nothing now but 'work' from 7 a.m. to 6 p.m.," Grinnell wrote of his initiation to mining on the beach in Nome. "I do not get a minute to so much as look at a bird except Sunday, which we have voted to observe."

"I am the amalgamator," Grinnell continued, "and have nothing to do with the rockers. I pan out the previous day's clean-up and amalgamate the dust

A prospector wheels a load of Nome sand into a crude, but effective, washing box. Buckets of sea water, poured into the box, carried off sand and clay particles, while heavier gold grains settled to the bottom.

Gentleman miner Joseph Grinnell found Nome living hard. "A man had better stick to $1.50 a day in civilization," he wrote, "than come here and sleep on the damp ground and live on salt-horse and beans."

(combine it with quicksilver), squeeze dry the amalgam and weight it." Grinnell experienced a small disaster when he discovered that gold will stick to almost anything metallic. As he started spooning up some of the liquid amalgam, "the gold melted right into the spoon. I poured the stuff out on to a shovel blade to save what was left. What did it do but melt right into and all over the shovel! The result of this is that the L.B.A.M.&T. Co. has a gold-plated shovel. We are a wealthy company and can afford it."

And perhaps they could. One day in August Grinnell reported that "eight or ten of us are working on the beach claims and are taking out $50 to $60 a day." And again, "The past week we have taken out $250 in dust." A little later: "Sunday I retorted all the amalgam we had on hand and eighty-five ounces of pure gold was the result. Seven pounds of the pretty yellow stuff!" Not enough, by any measure, to make 20 men rich and probably not, for Grinnell at least, as much fun as birds. Still, one could not say the Long Beach and Alaska Company was bankrupt.

But Grinnell could not find much good to say about Nome. "I hate the place," he wrote. "There's the toughest crowd of people, sporting Dawsonites, everyone ready to 'do' everybody else. It is the liveliest, speediest, swiftest mining camp ever seen in Alaska. All sorts of sharks are making fortunes."

Without a true law-enforcement body, almost anything was possible in Nome. The premise that a man owned only what he could hang onto by main force extended to all sorts of property besides mining claims. Town lots were particularly vulnerable. An owner would put up a building on his own property at his peril, knowing that if the lot happened to attract somebody else's covetous eye, his building was likely to be dragged away by a team of horses in the dead of night—often with him still in it.

Not even a man's grave was safe. According to one account, miners tunneled under a new cemetery, digging under the "men buried shallowly in the frozen muck." They even "followed the 'pay' into the city, ripping up streets as they went and tearing down the houses they were still building."

Early on, the more sober-minded citizens organized a chamber of commerce in an attempt to establish

some law and order. Its president, Walter Ferguson, issued a blunt warning: "We will hang the first man who unnecessarily spills human blood, if we have to go to Council City to get the tree to hang him on." (Council City was 55 miles away, and Nome, at the edge of the barren tundra, had no trees of its own.) In spite of Ferguson's threat, there were five murders during the first winter.

In the summer of 1889 the only federal judge in Alaska, Charles S. Johnson, set out to visit as much as he could of his district, holding court in each town along the way. This necessitated a 7,000-mile round trip from Sitka, over the Chilkoot Pass and all the way down the Yukon River to St. Michael, from there across Norton Sound to Nome and home again to Sitka. Recognizing the dimensions of Nome's problem but in a hurry to get away before the freezeup, he recommended that the town organize a government of its own until Congress got around to providing something more permanent.

Two opposing tickets were put up for election, one representing miners, the other businessmen and law-

Tons of freshly off-loaded freight add to the congestion along Nome's beach in 1900. That summer, 20,000 gold rushers swarmed into the town, which two years earlier had not existed. Many of the new arrivals, impatient to strike it rich and clear out, pitched tents right on the sand amid stacks of crated mining equipment and provisions.

yers. The miners won, and Thomas D. Cashel, an outspoken young man who had led the beachcombers in their confrontation with big business, became Nome's first mayor. A municipal court, a police force and a fire department were established; a treasurer and assessor, clerk, surveyor and city council were chosen. The new city attorney was a miner named Key Pittman, later to become a Senator from Nevada.

Nome's next notable civic accomplishment was the invention of a unique garbage disposal system. In the winter of 1899-1900 the town fathers were justifiably apprehensive about the summer to come. Sewers could not easily be built because of the cold, and more people would certainly arrive after the winter ("the scum of the United States will be spewed upon our shores" was the way editor John Strong put it). Garbage, offal and debris of every kind already clogged the streets. The least imaginative citizen could foresee epidemics of disease once the weather turned warm. So the newly organized chamber of commerce raised several thousand dollars to finance the removal of the town's garbage and to have it deposited out on the ice of the Bering Sea. The town officers then sat back and relaxed, comfortable in the certainty that when the ice broke and began to drift south, everything offensive would be carried away.

The town's apprehension of an invasion proved fully justified. Something like 20,000 more gold-hungry pilgrims hit the beach in summer, and if the newcomers did not wholly constitute "the scum of the United States," it had to be admitted that there was among them an overwhelmingly rowdy element.

One woman in the tide of new arrivals to Nome later wrote of her experience with dismay. She reached "that human maelstrom" at night. "We proceeded through the main street, and if ever pandemonium raged it raged there. . . . Drunken gamblers grovelled in the dust; women, shameless scarlet women, clad in garments of velvet, silks, laces, of exceedingly grotesque character but universally decolleté, reveled as recklessly as any of their tipsy companions. From the rough dance halls the scraping of a fiddle rose above the noisy clatter of heavy boots that sounded like a chariot race in an empty attic."

By this time Nome had 100 saloons (though the proprietors of only 22 had troubled themselves to pay their annual town license fees of $1,500), the workload of the municipal court judge had taken on staggering proportions, and the town's three newspapers were bemoaning a crime wave. "While all the officials talk," the *Chronicle* reported, "the burglar and footpad ply their vocations, and honest pedestrians mush home with their hands on large sized guns they carry in outside pockets."

One band of thieves set out to corner the coal market against the coming winter. Driving a team of horses, they hauled away more than half of the 43 sacks of coal owned by a Mrs. Ohahal while she showered them with opprobrium. An hour later, before she could even report the crime, they came back and got the rest.

Sled dogs were choice targets for thieves. The owner of the new Golden Gate Hotel purchased two splendid Malemutes and took them to a dog stable for boarding; there he was informed that the animals had actually been stolen from the same kennel just before he bought them.

"Thieves are so thick that miners have to keep their grub down the shaft," the *News* declared in an anticrime article. Those working the beach, of course, had no shaft to hide their valuables in.

Safe-crackers broke into a store on Front Street; when they could not open the vault, they simply carried the whole thing away. Charles Wooy's most prized possession was a massive four-poster bedstead 10 feet tall. Late one night, weary and more than ready for sweet repose, he reached his tent and discovered that it was empty. Elsewhere a pair of thieves broke into a cabin and stole the stove, with the fire in it still burning.

But the most bizarre crime reported that season took place in a drugstore. Albert Hoepner, the sole owner of the store, found himself groggily signing over 50 per cent of the business to a stranger named Isaac Abramson—and receiving nothing from Abramson in return. Regaining his wits, Hoepner came to the conclusion that Abramson had hypnotized him into giving away half his concern. A timid man to begin with, Hoepner resigned himself to accept his new partner. However, Abramson soon decided that if he could obtain half the store so easily, he could hypnotize Hoepner into turning over the entire enterprise. The

In booming Nome the enterprising J. T. Cosgrove construction crew solicited jobs from a hastily established beach headquarters.

An entrepreneur from Tacoma, Washington, offered basic laundry and bathing facilities to the prospectors of Nome's tent city.

Hardy contenders in a dog-sled marathon

Nome's penchant for rough diversion took organized shape in the spring of 1908 with the first All-Alaska Sweepstakes. This annual 360-mile dog-sled marathon was a test of physical endurance for man and dog and a fine excuse for gambling and skulduggery. Thousands of dollars were wagered, with bettors keeping track of each team's progress via a new telephone line strung along the route.

The racecourse ran through a series of mining camps to the distant settlement of Candle and back, "over frozen tundra, rolling hills and Arctic wastes where," in the words of a young Norwegian miner who was the winner of the 1915 sweepstakes, "calm winds were rare."

Gales, blizzards and temperatures of −20°F. eliminated all but the hardiest drivers and dogs. Even reindeer and moose might become hazards when an unlucky musher's dog team scampered off the trail to chase them.

Drivers were also prey to unscrupulous gamblers. On one occasion they persuaded a driver to stay back in third place by aiming a gun at him. In another race the trail markers were stolen, leaving some teams to wander unguided in the snow.

During the race, the hard-pressed drivers took their first rest period in Timber, about six hours out. Thereafter they snatched brief naps and meals in other camps along the way. At Candle, the turnaround point, judges checked to be sure each team still had its original dogs (it was against the rules to substitute fresh ones). Then the drivers headed back to Nome, taking time out whenever necessary to massage their dogs' stiffening muscles and tend their vulnerable feet.

Waiting at the finish line was a sweepstakes queen. She was elected after a month-long campaign, during which votes were sold for a penny apiece, and voters cast as many ballots as they could afford for the queen of their choice. The money slapped down by Nome's predominantly male population went toward a $5,000 purse that was split among the first three finishers in the race.

When the first driver reached Nome after more than three days on the trail, he was greeted in championship style and paraded through town in a sled that was drawn by small boys before he collected his prize.

A blackboard in the Board of Trade saloon carries detailed bulletins on the 1912 race, won by the team of Allan and Darling.

Gladys Curry was queen of the 1910 sweepstakes; she waved her pennant to signal each team's start. Up to 200,000 votes were cast in the balloting for queen.

Hat-slapping crowds cheer as John Johnson drives a team of Siberians across the finish line in 1910 in record time of 74 hours.

showdown came with Hoepner dodging about the store, trying to avert Abramson's burning gaze. Finally, the mild-mannered druggist grabbed a pistol, turned on Abramson and ordered him off the premises—and out of his sight—forever.

Nome's reputation for crime spread far and wide, but it did not deter people from risking everything to try out their luck on the Beach. Some came with expensive gear, including a few very odd machines. Inventors in the States, fired by the thought of all that wealth under Nome's sands, and intrigued even more by visions of the incalculable hoard that must lie on the ocean floor beyond, had set to work with a will and produced some weird contraptions; editor Strong called it "jackass machinery."

"Pumps of many kinds there are," Strong wrote, "and windmills too in charge of modern Don Quixotes; steam engines of varying horsepower; pipe of diverse colors and assorted sizes; grizzlies, patent sluice boxes—in fact the greatest assortment of mining machinery that has ever been seen in a mining camp. Owners will call sands barren because contraptions won't do the job."

Rex Beach, an enterprising young prospector from Chicago who was later to mine the more lucrative field of literature, was among the owners of such a machine. He had heard of the golden sands while attending law school and, with borrowed money, had commissioned an inventor to devise something that would suck the wealth from the sea.

Man and machine arrived at Nome in June 1900, and Beach engaged a small crew to operate his expensive contrivance. It was difficult going, and the hired hands, who were struggling hip deep in the frigid sea water trying to clear the clogged pipes of Beach's sand sucker, soon grew discouraged. "They shrieked like Vassar girls when that cold surf engulfed them," Beach recalled, "so for weeks I battled with it practically single-handed." His time was spent more underwater than above, and Beach moaned that it gave him the complexion of a tuna—and a similar disposition. In the end, he confessed that "the only suckers that really worked were the owners."

Rex Beach's sanity, if not his solvency, was preserved in September when a three-day gale roared across Nome and demolished all the "jackass machinery," as well as much of the town. Down to Davy Jones's locker, along with Beach's behemoth, went a $74,000 sand sucker belonging to the Mongollon Exploration Company. That machine, at least, had worked—after a fashion. Prior to its demise it had dredged up $350 of gold.

The total harvest of Beach's machine was $25; his other assets after the storm consisted of an oil burner, a useless pump, some hose and a case of canned cherries. No matter. With his own credit and a partner's modest investment, Beach bought another claim. A few weeks later he was offered, and he refused, $30,000 for his share.

For three years Beach lost more money than he made on a number of mining deals. Then he returned to Chicago—materially impoverished. But what he took home in his mind turned out to be far more valuable than what he had failed to bring back in his poke. Throughout his time in Nome, the young prospector had watched while three corrupt politicians repeatedly stole the gold claims of genuine miners. The conspiracy worked so well, Beach observed, that the rightful property owners were left "helpless, dazed and panic stricken. Things had been carried with such a high hand as to institute a reign of terror." Beach fashioned the episode into a novel, *The Spoilers,* and the book made him wealthy and famous.

It was never completely clear who initially thought up the plot to purloin most of Nome's gold; neither was it ever proved just how high the conspiracy penetrated into the upper reaches of the United States government. But there was no doubt about the identity of the archvillain of the scheme: he was Alexander McKenzie of North Dakota.

McKenzie was as imposing a figure as ever was molded by the hardships of America's Old West. He got his start humbly enough, working as a tracklaying subcontractor to the Northern Pacific Railroad in the early 1870s. He entered public service in 1874 as the seventh sheriff of the town of Bismarck in the Dakota Territory. McKenzie held the position for 12 years by sheer force of personality and by such intimidating techniques as making murder suspects lie in a coffin while he interrogated them. By 1883 he had

Friends gather in downtown Nome to bid farewell to a prospecting party, whose provisions are piled high on a lone donkey. Finding the beach played out, the miners headed inland to search for gold in the still largely untapped Seward Peninsula.

become the territory's preeminent political power, and that year his influence helped get Bismarck named the Dakota territorial capital.

By the time of the gold rush at Nome, McKenzie was a familiar figure in Washington and a formidable mover in Republican Party politics. In the nation's capital he was head lobbyist for two great Western railroads, the Northern Pacific and the Great Northern, and he had cronies in high places to serve his purposes. He was a bold man and had the physical presence to back it up: heavy shouldered and portly, taller than six feet in his socks, with hard, shrewd eyes alongside a prow of a nose, and a full moustache above his pugnacious chin.

The plot to appropriate Nome's gold got under way in the autumn of 1899 when a lawyer named

Oliver P. Hubbard, senior member of the Nome firm of Hubbard, Beeman & Hume, embarked for the States early enough to escape being locked in by ice for the winter. The business of Hubbard's firm consisted mainly of conspiring with claim-jumpers to dispossess legitimate miners. One of the firm's clients was Robert Chipps, who had filed suit to take over a lucrative claim, called Discovery, on Anvil Creek that was owned by Jafet Lindeberg, one of the three original "Lucky Swedes."

Hubbard's target was the United States Senate, where a new bill, S.B. 3919, was to be taken up in the spring with a view to enlarging the scope of civil government in Alaska. Contained in the bill was a section proclaiming the right of an alien like Lindeberg to acquire and hold lands for any purpose, and another

Resisting the havoc of fire and storm

Like every jerry-built gold-rush town, Nome was a highly combustible jumble of rickety wooden buildings. Early Nome's worst fire, in 1901 *(right)*, spread from saloon to blacksmith shop to hotel, destroying eight major business buildings and many smaller ones.

But fire was not the town's only peril. Because of its location on the coast, Nome lay exposed to the wrath of the Bering Sea. Each spring and fall, equinoctial storms (sourdoughs insisted the term was derived from *unequaled* and *obnoxious)* shrieked in from the south, driving huge waves onto the shore.

One such gale raged for three days in September 1900, when the beach was covered with the tents of newcomers. The tents blew away, and mining equipment and supplies were swallowed by the waves. Four ships were ripped apart in the surf, and the beach side of Front Street, Nome's main thoroughfare, was completely swept away. The storm took many lives, although the number is not known.

The adventurers who populated Alaska's boomtowns took such catastrophes in their stride; the survivors' first impulse usually was to rebuild immediately. When a fire in 1906 wiped out much of Fairbanks, new construction began by the light of the flames. John Clark, a lawyer whose office had been incinerated, recalled watching a burned-out businessman cart fresh lumber to his lot "while the fire was raging on three sides of him." The man set to work so earnestly that "the floor was laid before the ashes were cold."

A fire that began in a room over a saloon on May 25, 1901, billows through Nome's Stedman Street toward the new Golden Gate Hotel *(left),* which was destroyed—and rebuilt within a month.

A house secured with rope suggests the efforts—usually futile—that were made to keep property from floating away whenever the Bering Sea inundated Nome.

155

The "Nome wonder," a seven-inch chunk of gold, shown here in its actual size, was discovered in 1901 at Anvil Creek, outside Nome, by a man who was digging a posthole. It weighed nine pounds and was worth $1,729—then a very large sum.

guaranteeing an alien's right to sell, mortgage or bequeath those lands to his heirs.

Until somebody—it was never known who—steered Hubbard to Alexander McKenzie, no member of the Senate objected to these provisions or felt strongly about them one way or another. But McKenzie, whose influence was concentrated in the North Central states of Montana, North Dakota and Minnesota, saw the matter in a special light. When the bill came up for consideration, Senator Henry Hansbrough of North Dakota offered an amendment that would not only strike the section on alien land rights but, indeed, would substitute language absolutely prohibiting alien ownership.

Since the amendment obviously was written to implement and legalize a theft, it aroused powerful passions in the Senate. The debate generated such heat that it threatened to sidetrack the entire Alaskan bill. After a month of argument, Senator Hansbrough's amendment was withdrawn as part of a successful compromise that also struck out the earlier version that specifically permitted alien ownership. McKenzie had not achieved precisely what he was

after, but he had rid himself of a serious stumbling block. With no language in the act concerning alien land rights, he now had room to maneuver.

And maneuver he did, with approximately the finesse of the ice breaking up on the Yukon River. The new law—reflecting Congress' growing, though tardy, awareness of Alaska's problems—included provision for two more federal district judges to divide the judicial responsibilities of 586,400 square miles with Judge Johnson of Sitka. Through acquaintances in the incumbent administration of President William McKinley, McKenzie secured the judgeship for the second district, which included Nome, for a lawyer chum from Minneapolis, Arthur H. Noyes. He also got another reliable ally, Joseph K. Wood of Montana, appointed federal district attorney in Nome.

With these key appointments in hand, McKenzie organized a corporation called the Alaska Gold Mining Company with authorized capital stock of $15 million. Then, as president and general manager, he went back to lawyer Hubbard and advised him that the new corporation was taking over the case of Hubbard's claim-jumper client, Chipps, and would compensate Hubbard with stock for the profit he might have earned from the case.

Noyes, Wood, Hubbard and McKenzie arrived by ship in the Nome roadstead on July 19, 1900. Judge Noyes remained secluded in his stateroom, while the others went ashore to prepare for the opening session of the judge's court.

Much later, lawyer William T. Hume of Hubbard's firm, in his testimony before the federal appeals court in San Francisco, related that McKenzie called on him that day and put forward a proposition. First McKenzie informed Hume that he "owned" both the judge and the federal prosecutor, and could therefore prevent Hume's claim-jumper cases from being heard at all if he so desired. Then he said the corporation was taking over the local attorneys' 50 per cent contingent interest in the jumpers' cases and would pay the attorneys with stock in the corporation. He told Hume that his partner Hubbard had agreed to these terms and had assured McKenzie "that the other members of the firm would do likewise." In addition, McKenzie said that he wanted 25 per cent of all the law firm's business for himself and another 25 per cent in silent partnership for District Attorney Wood. McKenzie promised Hume that he would make him deputy district attorney if he complied fully with these demands. Hume agreed to do so.

Thus Hume and Hubbard, who were a couple of swindlers themselves, had been hustled by experts—and had received, in return for their potential profits, stock certificates of dubious worth. And McKenzie added insult to injury. Before he left Hume's office he gathered together the law firm's briefs and pleadings in the claim-jumping cases—which were to be tried that week—and repaired to the ship to consult with the judge. On his return he informed Hume that Judge Noyes wanted to have the papers drawn up in a different form. Hume called in the only public stenographer in Nome and sat down to 36 hours of work without food or sleep, finishing the documents just in enough time for the judge to come ashore and declare his court in session.

Hume, almost too tired to raise his voice, told the court that on behalf of his clients, the claim-jumpers, he pleaded for an injunction and the appointment of a receiver for Jafet Lindeberg's Discovery claim, six other productive claims adjacent to Discovery, plus a claim in nearby Nikkala Gulch. Nearly all of these mines, the cream of the inland claims, were now owned by the Pioneer Mining Company, a California corporation organized by Lindeberg, and by the Wild Goose Mining Company, organized by Charles D. Lane, a California mining engineer. Not a single representative of the defendants was in court, no one having seen fit to notify them.

Even knowing McKenzie's relationship with the court, Hume was astonished at how handily a lawyer could win a case when the circumstances were right. With no hesitation, without even looking at the documents rewritten at his request, Judge Noyes granted the injunctions and put the contested claims in receivership to Alexander McKenzie. He instructed McKenzie to work the mines and to take into custody all personal property he discovered on the premises. To give this transfer the appearance of propriety, the judge directed McKenzie to post a surety bond of $5,000 for each mine—although, as it was later pointed out, Lindeberg's Discovery claim alone was producing three times that much every day. Having delivered, the judge adjourned court.

McKenzie hastened to the street, where he had a gang of men waiting with teams and wagons. The drivers whipped up their horses and McKenzie descended on Anvil Creek. There he took possession and, true to the judge's admonition, seized all personal property, including gold dust and nuggets, and since he was hungry, he even ate the supper awaiting Gabe Price, foreman of the Wild Goose.

The lawyers for Wild Goose and Pioneer, apprised that their clients had lost control of their mines, immediately demanded a day in court. But for them justice proved an elusive commodity. Judge Noyes had sailed away to St. Michael on the other side of Norton Sound to establish his authority in the Yukon Delta. He was gone for two weeks. When he came back he blithely rejected one motion after another by the aggrieved miners to recover control of their property—or at least to get a hearing in federal appeals court in San Francisco.

McKenzie now appeared to be in full command of the richest mines in Nome. "Give me a barnyard of Swedes and I'll drive them like sheep," he remarked

The art-lined, elegantly furnished parlor of Chancy Cowden, a Nome bank cashier, was typical of many homes in town in 1908. It was

lighted by a gas table lamp connected by a tube to the ceiling fixture.

with satisfaction. "I'm too strong at headquarters." Headquarters, of course, was Washington.

The fact was that the fight was just beginning. On August 13, Charles Lane, of Wild Goose, and William Metson, a lawyer for Pioneer, drew up an appeal—in defiance of Judge Noyes—and submitted it to the Circuit Court of Appeals in San Francisco. The arguments in the appeal persuaded Justice William Morrow of the appeals court that something was rotten on the shores of Alaska. Morrow promptly issued a writ removing Judge Noyes from authority over the Nome mines, displacing McKenzie as receiver and commanding him to return to the defendants all the property he had taken.

It was mid-September, close to freeze-up time, when the writ was delivered to Noyes. Characteristically, he made short work of it. The circuit court had no right to allow the appeals and no right to issue the writ, said the judge; both could be ignored. McKenzie, thus encouraged, disregarded that portion of the order directed at him. He kept the mines working, and he continued to fetch the gold each day to the vaults of the Alaska Banking & Safety Deposit Company. By now he had taken $130,000 in gold out of Discovery alone.

Although local law was against them, the Pioneer and Wild Goose people were far from idle. As long as they knew where the gold was they could still hope to recover it, at least in part. What worried them was the possibility that McKenzie would spirit it away before they could regain control. They rented a second-floor room across the street from the bank and installed a 24-hour armed watch. One day when McKenzie was about to leave the bank carrying a moosehide poke filled with gold, he found himself surrounded by determined-looking men with guns in hand. So furious he was speechless, McKenzie was constrained to walk back into the bank and return the gold to the vault.

Meanwhile, except for the confiscated mines, which McKenzie kept producing around the clock, gold mining in Nome ground to a standstill. Any prospector who found a promising lead immediately covered it up and went to town and got drunk. "Miners feared to exploit rich diggings," Rex Beach wrote, "because of the certainty that the court would seize

Alexander McKenzie went to prison for conspiring to take over Nome's richest gold claims in 1900. Soon pardoned, he returned to North Dakota where he became one of the wealthiest men in the state and even had a county named after him.

Arthur Noyes, a pliant drunkard, did McKenzie's bidding during a brief tenure as Nome's only judge. Petitioning for his removal, 54 Nome lawyers described him as "vacillating, dilatory, partial, negligent, careless and absolutely incompetent."

them. There was a common belief that a force of men was employed for the especial purpose of discovering such instances and bringing the titles before the court on some pretext."

At last the officers of the Pioneer company, sure that the law was, in the final analysis, on their side, put together a gang of vigilantes, invaded the disputed claims and drove off McKenzie's men, wounding one of them. For this, Jafet Lindeberg and others eventually were indicted for inciting a riot. Lindeberg, advised of his jeopardy, hired a rowboat in the autumn of 1901 and had himself ferried out to the final ship leaving Nome before the winter freeze set in. The other indictees had their cases dismissed when no jury could agree on a verdict.

Remarkably, considering Nome's shortage of any real law force, the tense situation never broke into open warfare—although it continually teetered on the edge. At one point, during a bellicose conference, McKenzie accused Metson, the Pioneer company's

lawyer, of "stealing" $10,000 in gold when the contested properties were repossessed by force.

"You have kept me stepping," McKenzie told the young opposition lawyer, "and I will fix you for it."

"Turn her loose right now!" Metson answered, on his feet with a gun in his hand. Some cooler participants had to separate the two angry men before anybody's blood was shed.

Supremely confident as he was of his muscle in Washington, McKenzie had not fully taken account of the indignation his actions had aroused in an honest judge 4,500 miles away in San Francisco. Nor had he reckoned accurately the swiftness with which the court could move. Ordinarily, Norton Sound iced up by the beginning of November, and thereafter Nome was frozen solid for eight months. Unfortunately for McKenzie, when the last ship of the season arrived from the south on October 15, aboard were two federal marshals—and a warrant for McKenzie's arrest. They found him having dinner in the Golden

Gate Hotel and took him to the bank where they politely asked him to hand over the key to the vault. McKenzie demurred, saying the key was in the possession of District Attorney Wood. The prosecutor not being readily available, the federal men broke open the vault and turned $600,000 over to the Pioneer and Wild Goose companies.

When the last boat sailed, McKenzie was on it, under arrest for felony. In San Francisco on February 11, 1901, the appeals court found him guilty and sentenced him to a year in prison. But his strength at headquarters did not fail him. Within four months after McKenzie entered the Alameda county jail, President McKinley visited San Francisco and asked one of the judges whether there were any extenuating circumstances in the case.

"Mr. President," the judge is reported to have said, "in going over the evidence, I find 20 reasons why his punishment should have been more severe, but not one why he should be freed."

"But he is a very sick man," one account has the President saying. McKinley then pardoned McKenzie on the grounds that his health was feeble and if he was incarcerated for the full term, he might not survive the ordeal.

"This pardon," Rex Beach noted in a magazine article, "is as remarkable from its unusual pathological effect as from its phenomenal cause, for although released because he lay at death's door, so wonderful was its medicinal stimulus that he was seen sprinting for the first train out of Oakland a few hours later." That train took McKenzie back to North Dakota, where he again became an influential figure in state and national politics—but never again in Alaska.

When navigation to Nome reopened in July 1901, Judge Noyes received peremptory instructions to return to San Francisco and explain his conduct to the court of appeals. At first he refused, protesting his innocence with the galling sentiment that "the golden opinions of my fellow men are treasures far too rich to be swapped for gold dust." But Noyes changed his mind when he was advised that a lynch mob was on its way to his office. Back in California he was found guilty of contempt of his own court but was let off with a fine of $1,000. District Attorney Wood was sentenced to serve a term of four months in jail.

Back in Nome, word of the light sentences brought anger and disappointment but editor Strong was content with the bright prospect of never again having to so much as gaze upon the conspirators. "Their names will be anathematized," he wrote in an editorial, "so long as warm blood runs through the veins of the people of Alaska."

Noyes's temporary replacement was Judge James Wickersham, who had gained a reputation as a stern but fair jurist in the year he had served at Eagle, a gold camp on the Canadian border. When he arrived in Nome in September 1901, Wickersham praised the miners and their lawyers for their success in "fighting the most astounding, vigorous and treacherous attack known to American jurisprudence." Then he set about the monumental task of clearing up the docket, jammed with hundreds of claim disputes that his predecessor never got around to hearing. Wickersham accomplished this in nine months, during which he often held court from 9 a.m. till 10:30 p.m. Having restored Nome's confidence in judicial integrity, the judge went back to his post at Eagle. (He was later elected the new territory's delegate to Congress.)

Gold output from the tundra claims behind Nome continued to provide handsome annual returns until 1906, when production peaked at $6.1 million. Thereafter, as the claims played out, the profits shrank by as much as one million dollars each year—and Nome shrank with them. By 1915 boilers and mining equipment rusted in empty lots. Buildings collapsed from disuse. And the tide swept clean a beach that once, on a single day in 1900, bore the footprints of 8,000 diggers.

The beach had been the drawing card, a geological freak that brought the hordes to Nome and gave up a little more than two million dollars in gold in the two years it took to pick it bare. When the beach gold was gone, fewer than 5,000 souls stayed on to work the tundra, while as many as 20,000 either left for other gold fields or, like the young bird watcher Joseph Grinnell, headed for home. "Yes, home!" Grinnell wrote in his diary. "I am heartily tired of this kind of living. I long to get back to my father's house and up in those cool, high chambers of mine, where I may once more feel like a Christian and a gentleman."

Nome's brief reign of civilized pleasures

By 1906 Nome's most raucous days were over. All the easy gold had been scooped from its beach, the claim-jumpers and tinhorns had moved on, and the rowdy camp had become a respectable mining community. Even this era of stable prosperity would prove fleeting; in barely six more years the underground gold began to give out. But while the money lasted, Nome comported itself in style.

During the eight-month winter, when the freeze-up effectively cut them off from the rest of the world, the prosperous residents of Nome entertained themselves with a continual round of dinner parties, amateur theatricals and dress balls. When the Bering Sea ice finally broke up each June, they went on pleasure outings and imported show troupes from Seattle to perform *East Lynne* and *The Bohemian Girl* at the town's new community center, Eagle Hall.

Evidences of *nouveau riche* gaucherie and display were everywhere: the red woolen underwear showing at the bottom of the ladies' plunging Parisian necklines, the tables heaped with all the courses at once to dazzle guests with a show of plenty, the society columns that listed not only wedding guests but their gifts as well ("Mr. and Mrs. Dave Boyd—bonbon dish").

Every self-respecting household had a cook (preferably Chinese), a parlor piano, cut glass and fine china on the dinner table—every amenity, in fact, except running water and proper plumbing. The citizens had to make do with chemical toilets and a couple of community bathhouses.

But no one really minded such inconvenience. They had come to Nome to build a stake, not a city, and as the gold supply dwindled they left by the shipload. By 1915 the population of Nome had shrunk to 1,000, and its good times were only a memory.

The Nome Brass Band shows its marching stance in a photograph made about 1909,

when the town's tents and shanties had given way to frame houses. The band was a fixture at parades, election rallies and concerts.

The "Merry Masqueraders," as Nome's thriving amateur theatrical company called itself, turns out in a colorful array of costumes

to be photographed on the stage of Eagle Hall in 1907. The placard at rear lists the numbers for a community dance program.

As the ice in Norton Sound begins to break up in late spring, a party of fashionable young Nomeites takes a boat for a picnic on Sledge

Island, just off the coast. Although bleak, the island was at least free of the mosquitoes that began swarming each year with the thaw.

Well-dressed excursionists fill the cars of the Wild Goose Railroad for a Sunday afternoon trip from Nome to the mining community at

Anvil Creek. The rails sagged precariously into the tundra muck, giving riders something of a roller-coaster ride, even at slow speeds.

Unsmiling, yet clearly poking fun at the hardships of their subarctic environment, a well-furred group from Nome presents itself to the

camera complete with American flag, skis and a cozy dog sled. The photographer whimsically called this tableau "Sourdough Picnic."

5 | Last fling for the lawless

Along with thousands of honest adventurers, Alaska's gold rushes attracted a small army of unsavory characters who did their prospecting in the pokes of hard-working stampeders. Thieves, swindlers and floozies crowded the ports and mining camps, ready to make a quick killing—literally, if necessary. Since Alaska had little law enforcement apparatus, they fleeced the newcomers with impunity.

Alaskan lawlessness took many forms. Prospectors were cheated by crooked gamblers and had their pockets picked by dance-hall girls and prostitutes with exotic names—Dirty Gertie, the Chinless Wonder, Nellie the Pig. Innocents were mugged and robbed in town by blackjack-wielding thugs, and were held up on the trail by bandits like the Blue Parka Man.

The most dangerous crooks were ambitious con men who put crime on a business basis. One wild-and-woolly season Skagway—an access port to the Klondike—was ruled by the flamboyant Soapy Smith and his gang of imported roughnecks (right). "Robbery and murder occur daily," wrote a traveler through Skagway in 1898. "Shots are exchanged on the streets in broad daylight. At night the shouts of 'Murder!' mingle with the cracked voices of singers in variety halls."

Such excesses were a product of the gold stampedes, and as the rush subsided, stability replaced disorder in Alaska's towns. The Old West's lawless element had enjoyed its final fling.

Sinister-looking Soapy Smith (center), flanked by four of his henchmen, ran Skagway with guns and cunning in 1898. "People come here with money," wrote a visiting lawman irately, "and next morning haven't the price of a meal."

173

ARRIVAL

TWO MONTHS

FOUR MONTHS

SIX MONTHS

NINE MONTHS

TWELVE MONTHS— SOUR DOUGH.

Progress on the uncertain road to stability

The settlement of Alaska and the emergence of a stable Alaskan society were long in coming about. During its early years of development under the American flag, the territory's few permanent settlers tended to be treasure seekers. Unable to give up their dreams of striking it rich in this big, new land, they had stayed on. But before Alaska could boast a truly stable society, it needed settlers in numbers—enough people with mutual interests to make a commitment to Alaska's future. Gold nearly doubled the territory's population in the 1890s; according to the census of 1900, some 29,500 Eskimos, Aleuts and Indians, and 4,300 white Alaskans had been joined by 26,000 newcomers. Paradoxically, this influx led to widespread lawlessness but hastened the day when law and order would prevail. And soon after the population swelled it began to shrink. Many who came turned around disappointed, leaving behind a hard core of individuals with the stamina and will power to survive the rigors and challenges of Alaska and to build a society they could be proud of.

For a time Alaska's future seemed very much in doubt. A number of thoughtful observers in the United States detected no signs of progress or stability in the lurid reports from Alaska's wild-and-woolly ports and mining towns, which were short on necessities but grossly overstocked with gold-hungry predators—thieves, con men, crooked gamblers, pocket-picking prostitutes and dance-hall girls. The most scandalous town, Skagway, was as chaotic in 1898 as San Francisco had been some 50 years earlier in its hectic gold-rush days. The region's criminals, its unscrupulous trading companies and its many rootless prospectors convinced the noted scholar David Starr Jordan in 1899 that Alaskans cared no more for their "country than a fisherman cares for a discarded oyster shell" and that they were incapable of forming permanent, orderly, law-abiding communities.

Though a few short years of dramatic, tumultuous change proved the skeptics wrong, their concerns were not groundless. Nearly everyone came to Alaska to get rich and get out. Few intended to settle there, build for the future and worry about the establishment of law and order. The newcomers' attitude was typified by some feckless treasure seekers who witnessed a shooting in Skagway in 1898 and cheerfully accepted a townsman's cynical advice against intervening. As one of the young men later put it, "We learned that if you keep your mouth shut and attend to your own business, you are never in danger."

Significantly, however, that newcomer, a Hoosier watchmaker named Lynn Smith, fell under Alaska's spell and stayed the rest of his life. What is more, Smith eventually spent a decade worrying about law and order—as a U.S. marshal. But it took many such committed Alaskans to make a society and many hard lessons to make one committed Alaskan.

By the Alaskans' own definition, any cheechako who was able to survive in the territory for a year automatically was accepted as one of them; he was then a sourdough. However, the achievement of sourdough status by no means meant the individual intended to settle down. More than a few sourdoughs left with the luckless cheechakos when the gold began to dwindle. For most it was easier to leave Alaska than to love its stern climate, its enormous emptiness and its loneliness.

Those who remained and made Alaska their home were, by nature, self-reliant and individualistic almost

A 1907 cartoon traces the evolution of a newcomer, or cheechako, into a sourdough, resembling the frothy pot of starter that gave his bread its leaven and tang.

to a fault. They were fervent chauvinists who revered Alaska's wilderness and took pride in their ability to meet its challenges. Their intensely provincial outlook was epitomized by a special use of the words inside and outside. The Alaskan interior was the "inside," and they believed it had more to offer than the civilized world, where freedom was limited by impersonal institutions and rigid conventions. They called the United States and the rest of the world the "outside."

All the paradoxical traits found in frontiersmen elsewhere were exaggerated in the true Alaskans. They were the toughest of realists and accepted their ordeals as the natural order of things; a traveler who ran out of food thought nothing of eating his faithful dog and remarking later that the animal tasted pretty good. Yet even as young men they were as sentimental as old codgers and glorified their camaraderie and their infrequent celebrations. In fact, Alaskans had a tendency to be loners, and though they joined such social organizations as the Arctic Brotherhood (*page 191*) and the Pioneers of Alaska, many wilderness veterans did not feel comfortable at lodge meetings with so many people around.

The sourdoughs were motivated by a frontier ethic rooted in the Golden Rule. Many would have scoffed at the notion that they were their brothers' keepers, yet they did look after the other fellow if only because their own lives often depended on him. Prospectors shared their meager grub with strangers and lent money to less fortunate acquaintances. Alaskans casually took great personal risks to be helpful. Skagway's dance-hall girls did yeoman duty as nurses during an 1899 epidemic of spinal meningitis. The Right Reverend Peter Trimble Rowe, first Episcopal bishop of Alaska, roamed the snowy gold-rush trails, sharing his food with marooned, half-frozen greenhorns.

In sum, true Alaskans preferred Alaska, hardships and all, to any other place. They found their failures nearly as interesting as their successes and a good deal more informative. They sought gold not just to get rich but also because the searching made them the freest people on earth.

An Alaskan was a man or a woman who could say, as prospector Henry Davis did toward the end of his long life in the wilds, "I have had lots of money but

couldn't keep it, but what is money compared with the life I've had up here?"

The Alaskan spirit and the character of Alaskan life were set by a small group of pregold-rush prospectors—the original sourdoughs. Their numbers grew slowly, from a few score in the early 1870s to perhaps a few thousand two decades later. But their influence increased enormously when the great gold strikes of the 1890s began. As veterans of Alaska's hard times, they were admired and emulated by the hordes who came for the Klondike and Nome strikes. The know-how and traditions they passed on proved indispensable for generations of Alaskans.

The old-timers were predominantly Americans with a sizeable minority of Canadians. Many had

Prospector Robert Snyder (*far right*) put down roots while searching for gold on the bleak northern coast of the Seward Peninsula. He took an Eskimo wife and built a hut of wood and sod to shelter his family.

emigrated from Ireland, Scandinavia, Germany and a scattering of other lands. They usually formed handshake partnerships of two or three men—enough to afford some protection for each other but not too many to share the gold if any was found. Most were experienced outdoorsmen who had no illusions about the perils they faced in the Alaskan unknown. Frank Buteau, a Quebec-born adventurer who arrived in 1886 with 21 friends, told of their trepidations as they chose partners and prepared to go their separate ways in half a dozen groups.

"Before we parted we joined hands and formed a circle. Placing one of our number in the middle of the circle, we said to him, 'Talk.' He spoke the following words: 'Here we are in the land of ice and snow. We know not where we are going. We have seen the tears rolling down from the eyes of our fathers, mothers, brothers, sisters and sweethearts when we bid them goodbye, our hearts full of hope to see them all once again. And now as I see the tears falling here, I feel that it will be the duty of the last one of us who remains alive to tell not only of what we have done but of what we have said.'"

The early prospectors scattered through much of Alaska but tended to concentrate in two regions, where they made modest strikes in the 1880s: in the south around Juneau and in the upper Yukon country where their hunches told them a major gold field lay. Before the onset of their first winter, each group of partners built a cabin. They continued prospecting as weather permitted, but on days when the mercury congealed, at about 40° below zero, they usually stayed indoors, repairing their gear, playing cards and swapping stories.

Come spring, they set out to comb a new area. They found traces of placer gold along many rivers but moved on when it became plain that a claim would not yield important wealth. Partners stuck to rivers whenever possible and thus, in spite of Alaska's enormity, occasionally crossed paths with other groups of prospectors.

These accidental encounters were invariably celebrated with the firing of rifles, followed by some festive hooch drinking and the exchange of news. A rumor begun at such chance meetings or at isolated trading posts would start prospectors converging on a remote place that was said to be promising. Small mining camps would materialize as if by magic, only to disappear in a season.

Before long, cheechakos like Frank Buteau and his partners had confirmed their trepidations about Alaska. They were always conscious of the taxing weather conditions and the testing distances; gold seeking here required more courage, strength and skill than it did anywhere else. The prospectors often had to go hungry; they learned not to be fussy. "If you could see the food we had to eat," Buteau wrote, "you might laugh, but if you found yourself a thousand miles from civilization, without roads, as we were, it might bring tears to your eyes."

Prospecting was hard work. For some it meant standing in an unnamed, icy stream, panning for placer gold in river-bottom gravel and sand. For others who aspired to hit an underground vein of gold, it might involve penetrating Alaska's rock-hard permafrost, which reached to within a few feet of the surface in some places and extended down to bedrock.

The digging of each experimental hole was slow, backbreaking toil. Partners would first build a big fire on a chosen spot and keep it burning all night. Next morning, they would scrape off the embers, shovel away the thawed soil and go to work in the hole with pickaxes. They kept repeating these steps until they reached a depth of 10 feet, when it became necessary to rig up a windlass to haul buckets of water and dirt from the bottom of the pit. Henry Davis, who arrived

from Montana in 1884, said, "If one made 10 inches a day by fires and another six inches by picking he was satisfied." But, of course, many such holes proved utterly worthless. "We finished one hole 28 feet deep but it was not good. We tried 1,500 feet upstream next." And so it went, day after day, month after month. The search for places to dig or pan for gold constituted an education in itself.

By the end of their first year on the inside, prospectors had learned enough from experience and from the Indians to be experts in the arts of survival. They took pains to conserve everything from bits of string to their own strength, which might be needed suddenly to deal with an emergency. To avoid carrying a tiring load, they would divide the season's supplies and store portions in weatherproof, bearproof caches along their route, noting the compass bearings from each cache to prominent landmarks. In winter they pulled on their noses from time to time to prevent that insensitive but vulnerable member from freezing. They used wooden sled runners instead of steel ones, which stuck to the ice in extremely cold weather, and they put water on the wooden blades to form a layer of ice for still easier gliding.

Many sourdoughs were jacks-of-all-trades and became clever improvisors. Frank Buteau, needing a blacksmith forge to repoint his worn pickaxes, made his own charcoal, stitched a moose hide into a bellows to be able to raise the temperature of his fire with oxygen, and then hammered the glowing steel on a rock anvil. When Buteau built a cabin on the Yukon, he installed a window of clear river ice that lasted all winter without melting on the inside or frosting over on the outside. A toothless old prospector named Paddy Meehan fashioned a set of dental plates out of some soft-tin kitchen utensils. He found his new front teeth in the skull of a mountain sheep and took his molars from a bear he killed near his cabin. Alaskans, being connoisseurs of good tales well-told, told this one over and over. They usually finished with the line: then Paddy ate the bear with its own teeth.

Death was always an imminent possibility in the wilderness, and a prospector was steeled to face it — to regret a friend's demise but not too deeply, never knowing whether he himself might be next. In this vein Henry Davis wrote, "Jack Randall and John

Reed came up and told us my old pardner, Neil Lamont, and Indian Tom Jones had upset in the canyon and drowned. My, I am sorry!"

Occasionally an old-timer met his death at the hands of an Indian. The killings usually occurred during the course of a robbery and were followed by swift frontier justice. One victim, a well-liked veteran named John Bremner, was murdered in his camp on the Koyukuk River by a young Indian in 1888. The prospectors in the area were in a vengeful mood when a 22-man posse caught the killer. Jim Bender, who had arrived from parts unknown two years before, reported, "We asked the Indian boy why he killed the old fellow and he said he wanted to go outside and work"—and needed money and grub to do it.

Without formalities, the prospectors took the law into their own hands, as Western pioneers had always done in the absence of any duly constituted authority. "There were two large trees about six feet apart," said Bender. "We tied a pole about 10 feet from the ground and threw a rope over. We hung him and left him hanging as an example to other Indians so they would not ever kill another prospector."

Indian crimes and sourdough punishments sometimes made for strained relations, but not for long. Trading always resumed and so did a practice known as the "squaw dance." Prospectors in a number of mining camps invited unattached Indian women from miles around to attend a shindig in town, and the guests were vigorously entertained and courted. Since there were no white women in the Alaskan interior in the early days, many a sourdough took an Indian mate and raised a family. Prospectors and Indians alike considered the couple husband and wife, and it was the couple's business whether they lived with her people or with his.

Henry Davis, like many other sourdoughs, was woman-shy after years in the wilderness. But he finally succumbed to loneliness and took an Indian spouse whom he called Helen. Davis outlived Helen, married another Indian woman and outlived her, and he felt a strong affection toward both. He wrote late in life, "They were fine pardners, good workers, good fish cutters and I got used to the fish smell and loved them both very much. I busted up when they went to another happy hunting ground."

Necessity forced other sourdoughs to settle down at least for a spell; to earn enough money for another season's supplies, they would do odd jobs at a trading post or work briefly for pay on other men's claims around Eagle and Circle City, where gold production was fairly steady. Throughout the 1880s, very few sourdoughs ended a year's work with more than $1,500 in gold dust and nuggets, and their lives continued to be spartan and chancy.

The great strike that the sourdoughs had been waiting for was finally made in 1896—in the upper Yukon country, as many had prophesied, but across the Canadian border along the Klondike River. Circle City and other mining camps in the Alaskan interior became ghost towns as some 1,500 sourdoughs hurried to the Klondike to stake claims. But, as in almost every gold rush, only the first-comers struck it rich.

In 1898 the last chance to hit Klondike pay dirt was aglimmering as eager cheechakos from the United States arrived in droves, scrambling around the creek beds, staking claims at random, driving local prices sky-high. The sourdoughs relished the companionship, and those who had money caroused in the saloons of Dawson and cavorted with the loose women who came streaming in—dollar-a-dance girls and much more expensive prostitutes. But with all the good claims staked, the Alaskan veterans realized by 1899 that they were wasting their time, and they began drifting back to their old haunts. Almost at once the new strike in Nome started them rushing to the coast, and additional strikes in the Yukon basin kept the territory in a turmoil.

Cheechakos were everywhere. The sourdoughs tried to save them from costly blunders, but it was by no means easy. Lynn Smith, who arrived green as grass in 1898, stubbornly tried to get along without asking for advice. For the most part, the results were merely ridiculous. To cut some firewood, for example, Smith attacked a tree all around the trunk, like a beaver, instead of chopping on one side to make it fall in that direction. Some sourdoughs hooted at his inept performance and thenceforth greeted him with "Hello, beaver." Smith also made the dangerous mistake of not changing a sock after getting one of his feet wet. He reported that after traveling several hours "my heel felt like a thousand needles were sticking me"; he might have lost his foot if some sourdoughs had not thawed it out with an ice-water bath and vigorous rubbing. Finally, Smith and other cheechakos began to solicit the sourdoughs' advice.

Though few of the newcomers arrived with any wilderness experience, many brought skills that Alaska sorely lacked. Bookkeepers, druggists, lawyers and even doctors began to appear, and they could find plenty of gainful employment if they were willing to forego prospecting. Lynn Smith had left Indiana partly to escape a dull life as a watchmaker, and he resolutely resisted offers to work at his old trade. But when poverty weakened his resolve, he fixed some watches and found it so easy to make $10 or $20 a day in his spare time that he never really stopped tinkering.

Nor did Smith stop prospecting. But in 1912, when he set up a jewelry shop at Ruby, Smith ceased to be a prospector who tinkered on the side and became a watchmaker who took a fling at prospecting from time to time. Years later, while serving as a U.S. marshal, Smith paid tribute to the original sourdoughs by collecting and preserving their memoirs.

Slowly, others made the same sort of transition to a settled life. Even Frank Buteau, an inveterate rover, became a townsman when the gold rushes dwindled; friends who heard from him in his later years said he had settled down with a daughter in Fairbanks. But Henry Davis and other intrepid souls clung to the wilderness life to the very end. After he had outlived his two Indian wives and rheumatism had forced him to quit prospecting, Davis selected a wild spot on the Tanana River and, he wrote in his memoirs, "I built a fine cabin and made a fine garden and have been there ever since just getting by. I am 70, and thank God for what I have. I have never been hungry for more than four days at a time."

In many ways Alaska's turn toward respectability was summed up by the early history of two very different towns, Skagway, which was founded in 1897, and Fairbanks, which came into being in 1902. Skagway's first year was a nightmare of lawlessness, and the solid progress the town made thereafter only gradually redeemed its reputation back in the United States. Fairbanks was a law-abiding community from the start, though it had its share of frontier boisterousness.

The first white man to settle on the site of Skagway was William "Captain Billy" Moore, a contentious old riverboat skipper, trader and prospector. In 1887 Captain Billy staked out a squatter's claim to 160 waterfront acres, built a cabin and moved in with

his family. Moore was gambling on a big gold strike on the upper Yukon; he knew that if it came, his claim—the best landing place for overland shortcuts into the interior—was bound to become extremely valuable property. To prepare for that happy event, he went to work building a wharf and blazing trails across White Pass.

But Captain Billy got swamped when news of the Klondike strike reached the outside world. The first boatloads of stampeders arrived in July 1897, and some 100 newcomers decided that running a port right there was a better bet than combing the wilderness for gold. Led by Frank Reid, a rough-and-ready surveyor from Oregon, the opportunists evicted Moore from his land and started laying out the town

of Skagway. Captain Billy had no need for sympathy, however; he grew rich by selling his wharf for $175,000 and later successfully sued the town for reimbursement for his usurped property. Frank Reid did not fare so well. His troubles began just three months after his arrival, when an even less scrupulous man—and one who already was notorious in the Old West—appeared on the scene: Soapy Smith.

Jefferson Randolph Smith debarked at Skagway in late October with five friends, all experienced crooks. Soapy, the suave scion of a prominent Southern family, had earned his nickname by running a street-corner bunco game in which he offered passersby, for the sporting sum of five dollars, their choice of soap bars, some of which had $20 and $50 bills inside the

Skagway was a raw town of mucky streets and plank sidewalks in the summer of 1897. Clancy's Saloon *(below)* for a time became the headquarters from which Soapy Smith and his gang robbed and swindled unwary travelers on their way to and from the Klondike gold fields.

wrappers. Soapy's shills bought the marked bars and flaunted the money, prompting the suckers to spend their cash for nothing but soap. But Soapy was far from satisfied with this small-time swindle; he possessed the education, talent and showmanship for much grander con games. And so, starting in the 1880s, he cut a wide swath through Colorado as ringleader of all sorts of criminal activities in such towns as Leadville, Denver and Creede. But Soapy's fortunes had lately been at a humiliating ebb, and he might not have made it to Skagway had not one of his companions, a thrifty thief named George Wilder, dipped into his savings to finance the trip.

The day after Soapy arrived, he saw a splendid opportunity to establish himself as a steady citizen. A mob was about to lynch a man on muddy Broadway. Soapy, backed by his five armed cronies, broke through the crowd, freed the trembling captive and announced indignantly that lynching would not be tolerated in this fine town.

The rescued man—Soapy quickly smuggled him aboard a boat bound for Sitka—was a bartender named John Fay who had killed two men in a saloon brawl. No matter that Fay was guilty; Soapy had used the incident to create the misimpression that Soapy Smith was a man of high principles. Furthermore, he insinuated that he was a kind man by raising $1,500 to console the widows of the deceased.

The scheme was successful. The hundreds of honest enterprisers who poured into Skagway were so preoccupied with establishing themselves and doing business with the thousands of stampeders that they permitted Smith—that kindhearted, upstanding gentleman—to run their town.

Soapy operated out of Clancy's Saloon and then built one of his own called Jeff's Place. He started crooked gambling games there and sent outside for reinforcements to help him steal everything valuable in sight. Though he cautioned his henchmen against upsetting the townspeople with needless violence, his imported thieves and intimidators were not known for their restraint. In their ranks were gunman Joe Palmer, muscleman Big Ed Burns, opium addict Syd Dixon, bodyguard Yeah Mow Hopkins and a man known as Yank Hank Fewclothes, whose surname was a tribute to the fact that Yank Hank disdained wearing a

coat or vest even in the coldest weather. Soapy's confidence men also included "Reverend" Charles Bowers, a rapacious swindler with a benign smile; Old Man Tripp, a gifted shill who steered moneyed transients to Jeff's Place; and "Judge" Van Horn, a fat, alcoholic lawyer who could subdue a victim's wrath by spouting legal mumbo-jumbo.

Soapy's hoodlums blanketed the area with well-organized criminal operations. His muggers, pickpockets and sneak thieves did their jobs diligently and well, often with tips from bribable prostitutes and favor-currying bartenders. One of Soapy's minions found a new way of getting information on men worth robbing; he opened a travel bureau and sold maps to newcomers for one dollar just to get a peek at their wallets. Soapy's sleight-of-hand artists, disguised as miners with feather-stuffed packs bulging on their backs, prowled the trails outside town, intercepting prospectors and fleecing them at various shell games.

Soapy himself was an inexhaustible font of larcenous schemes. Though Alaska as yet had no telegraph line, Soapy opened a telegraph office and charged cheechakos five dollars for each message home. He even delivered fictitious replies—collect, of course. Under the pretext of raising funds for a newly arrived parson, Soapy and his thugs toured the saloons, gambling halls and bawdyhouses and extorted no less than $35,000 in contributions. Soapy actually handed over this princely sum to the preacher—and that night had the man robbed while he slept.

The townspeople protested these nefarious activities from time to time, especially when someone was accidentally killed in the course of a robbery. But Soapy had no trouble pouring oil on the waters, and early in 1898 he wrote confidently to a friend in Seattle, "We have got them licked, and we mean to rule absolutely."

Soapy scarcely batted an eye when a group of concerned citizens organized what they called The Committee of 101 and published an order to "all confidence sharks, bunco men, sure-thing men and all other objectionable characters" to get out of town while the getting was good. Contemptuously, Soapy replied with a bulletin of his own, announcing on behalf of "the business interests" that "no Blackmailers or Vigilantes will be tolerated." Soapy's procla-

Four days after Soapy Smith rode at the head of Skagway's Fourth of July parade in 1898, he lay dead with a vigilante's bullet through his heart. Below, townsmen watch the coroner begin his autopsy.

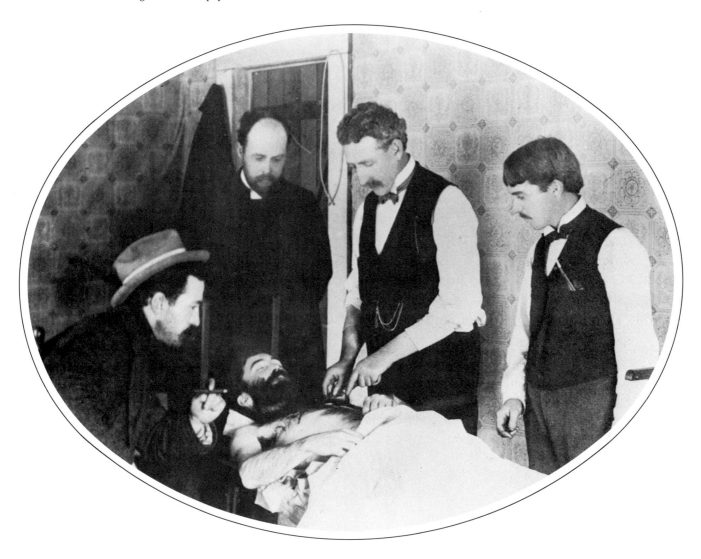

mation was signed by an imaginary "Law and Order Committee of 303."

But Soapy had seriously underestimated the increasing strength of his opposition. By the summer of 1898 Skagway was a prospering—if chaotic—town of 15,000 people. Merchants, craftsmen and restaurateurs had built businesses and homes and brought their families; their spines were stiffened by their wives' passion for decency, order and public education. Perhaps more important, Soapy's depredations were costing the town business, for many stampeders, already warned by stateside newspapers that Skagway was a sinkhole of crime, were landing at Dyea, a rival port located six miles up the coast. Skagway was a tinderbox of pent-up outrage, and it would take only

one spark to instigate a rebellion against Soapy.

The spark was supplied a few days after the Fourth of July, which Soapy celebrated as grand marshal and chief financial backer of a town-wide patriotic celebration. Then prospector John D. Stewart came to town early on the morning of July 8, and by nightfall Soapy's well-built empire of crime lay in ruins.

Except that he arrived at a decisive moment, there was nothing to distinguish Stewart from the hundreds of other miners who came through Skagway with a modest poke. Nor was Stewart's reception unusual; he and his $2,700 of gold were met by "Reverend" Bowers, who advised him that only one man in Skagway would exchange bank notes for gold without taking an exorbitant commission. The bogus clergy-

Wild Westerners who came north for fresh adventure

By the late 1890s the Old West below the 49th parallel had begun to lose its rambunctious spirit. While this change seemed overdue to citizens of a sober turn of mind, it afflicted others with nostalgia for the bad old days. Some of the most restless ones wandered northward to the wide open spaces of Alaska.

No less a figure than Wyatt Earp turned up in Nome in 1899, almost two decades after he had shot it out with the Clantons at the O.K. Corral. For two years Earp promoted prize fights and ran a saloon, until a new gold strike in Nevada lured him southward once again.

John Clum, who as editor of *The Tombstone Epitaph* had chronicled Earp's early deeds, also found his way to Alaska. A man of action in his own right, Clum had forcibly disarmed Geronimo in 1877. His duties in Alaska as a postal inspector seemed prosaic by comparison, but he attacked them with frontier vigor, traveling 8,000 miles in a summer to set up a dozen post offices.

Frank Canton, who had fought rustlers in Wyoming and helped wipe out the fearsome Doolin gang in Oklahoma, traveled up the Yukon as a deputy U.S. marshal in 1897. The next spring he single-handedly rescued the river steamer *Walrus* from a gang of hijackers.

A Westerner of another kind of reputation, Mattie Silks, Denver's Queen of the Tenderloin, scaled White Pass for one profitable season in Dawson in 1898. Her impedimenta included eight soiled doves and a set of gold scales on which she weighed out the exorbitant price of their favors to the Klondike miners.

WYATT EARP

FRANK CANTON

JOHN CLUM

MATTIE SILKS

man led the sourdough to Jeff's Place to meet Soapy Smith.

While waiting for Soapy to show up, Stewart took a couple of drinks on the house and then accepted an invitation from some friendly strangers to step out into the backyard for a look at Soapy's eagle. A stuffed eagle was perched there, all right, but a few moments later—after Stewart's escorts had stumbled into him—the sourdough discovered that he was alone with the bird and his poke had been stolen.

Stewart was not a very well-behaved victim. Angrily, he confronted Soapy's bartender, who explained that it was all a prank and the gold would be returned forthwith. Stewart, unconvinced, went to the recently installed deputy marshal. The marshal said he would investigate but made no move to do so since he was on Soapy's payroll. So Stewart took his indignation into the streets. He stamped around town telling everyone of the wrong done him at Jeff's Place.

With a well-publicized offense to focus on, the town of Skagway began seething with subversive activity. The dormant Committee of 101 woke up and demanded that Smith return Stewart's poke, complete to the last gold flake. Soapy alleged that Stewart had lost his dust fair and square in a game of chance. So the vigilantes sent to Dyea for a judge, George Sehlbrede, who was not on Soapy's payroll. Sehlbrede arrived in a hurry and ordered Smith to surrender the gold by 4 p.m. or he would begin writing warrants. At the appointed hour Soapy, fortified with many shots of redeye, appeared in the streets with a Winchester rifle but no gold. This defiance prompted the vigilantes to call an evening meeting, which started in Sylvester Hall but moved to Captain Billy Moore's wharf, where four guards were posted to prevent Smith's thugs from infiltrating.

At this point the usually cool and resourceful Smith ran out of tricks and lost his head. He stormed onto the wharf shouting imprecations. The guard who

challenged him was surveyor Frank Reid, the man who had seized Captain Moore's real estate a year ago but who had since become one of Skagway's leading citizens. Reid stood with his revolver drawn, and Smith came to a halt in front of him.

Many people saw what happened next, and they regaled listeners for years with their conflicting accounts. The bare facts are these: Soapy Smith and Frank Reid fired their weapons at point-blank range, almost simultaneously. Soapy dropped dead. Reid fell wounded and died 12 days later.

For a few nightmarish days after Soapy's death, Skagway was an even wilder place than it had been during his reign. In the ecstasy of relief and revenge, decent folk swept through town, rounding up gang members and ordering Smith's friends to get out. The enthusiasm for reform was so excessive that a detachment of U.S. Army troops was rushed down from Dyea to prevent lynchings. There were none. The revolution ended, and Skagway settled down to the sobering business of making itself a real town.

Skagway's main problem was no longer law and order; the crime rate plummeted, and the new U.S. deputy marshal, Si Tanner, kept rowdies and drunks in check. The problem was a big backlog of civic needs, especially for public schools and for fire-fighting equipment to protect the highly combustible wooden town. One obvious remedy was taxation, but it remained to be seen whether Skagway's leaders had the authority to prescribe that medicine—and whether the town had the determination to swallow it.

The town council had been elected at a citizens' meeting early in 1898. Although this consent government had done little but accede to Soapy Smith's misrule, it now faced up to its responsibilities and levied taxes on the town's most powerful group—the merchants. The merchants paid. The council went further, soliciting voluntary contributions from

Sled-towing horses trudge through hock-high snow on the Valdez Trail, a 376-mile overland route from Alaska's coast to Fairbanks. Sometimes a driver tied sacks around his horse's hooves and legs to serve as crude snowshoes. In 1906 a stage line was established on the trail, using sleds in winter and coaches when the summer thaw allowed.

individuals and businesses and public support for fund-raising masquerade balls and entertainments. The amateur administrators did so well that the new editor of the *Daily Alaskan* (his predecessor had been deported with Soapy's band) announced in his 1900 New Year's Day edition that the council election scheduled for the spring would not be held "because the people have decided they could not improve on the present membership of the council." That June when Congress finally enacted a civil code permitting Alaskan towns to incorporate, Skagway hurried to file its papers first and proudly announced that it had won the race—a claim hotly disputed by rival Juneau.

The year 1899 had brought a notable increase in civilized activities of every kind. In May alone Skagway hosted more cultural events than many towns see in a year: the YMCA Debating Club and the Skagway Literary Society met in joint session to discuss issues of mutual interest; the Skagway Tennis Club was organized; the Women's Christian Temperance Union held a meeting to deplore the evils of drink; and construction was begun on Alaska's first stone building, to house McCabe College, a private institution financed by the Methodist-Episcopal Church. Though the college failed in 1901, its granite structure later served nicely as a federal courthouse.

Local business got a boost when a company was organized to build the White Pass & Yukon Railroad from Skagway to Whitehorse, 110 miles to the northeast. Shops, hotels and restaurants thrived on the influx of railroad people—office workers and tracklaying crews and their families. Captain Moore's wharf was busy, too, for the railroaders had to rely on supplies and equipment shipped from the States.

The actual building of the road was a king-sized challenge for construction boss Michael Heney; the right of way had to be carved into mountainsides and routed through sinuous gorges. But the crews made rapid headway. In July 1899 the southern part of the route was finished and the first train reached Skagway bearing $500,000 worth of Klondike gold. The whole route was completed a year later.

By 1904 the focus of Alaskan development had shifted again—this time to the Tanana River country in the immense Yukon basin. A new gold field, soon to be recognized as Alaska's richest, had spawned a town called Fairbanks and was drawing capital and manpower from all parts of the territory and the United States as well. The Fairbanks gold rush was slow to gather momentum, but in the end it did more for Alaska than all the other strikes combined.

The Tanana wilderness had been prospected lightly since the late 1880s without encouraging results. Nevertheless, a small group of inveterate sourdoughs elected to give it another try in the aftermath of the Klondike rush. These tough old-timers were the kind of men whom outsiders liked to characterize as eternal optimists. That description certainly fit the man who made the great Fairbanks strike.

He was Felix Pedro, a wiry, mild-mannered veteran who had emigrated from Italy to the United States in 1881 at the age of 23. Drifting westward, Pedro had eked out a living in the coal mines of Illinois, Oklahoma and Washington. In 1893 he tried his luck in a small gold field in British Columbia; he got nothing but experience and a bad case of gold fever. He pressed on to the Klondike, where he earned a reputation as a diligent prospector, albeit a luckless one. Then in 1900 Pedro began combing the hills and riverbanks of the Tanana Valley, finding just enough gold to keep him searching for a big strike.

In 1902 Pedro's stamping grounds were still being prospected by fewer than a dozen men. Most were sourdoughs, and the rest were off-duty workers from a new trading post on a wooded bank of the Chena River several miles above the junction of the Chena and the Tanana.

The trading post belonged to one Elbridge Barnette, a cunning operator with a prison record for larceny back in the United States. The post was known informally as Barnette's Cache, but Judge James Wickersham, whom Barnette had met in St. Michael before he started up the Yukon to the Tanana, had asked him to name the place after Charles W. Fairbanks, a U.S. Senator from Indiana. Barnette had agreed with alacrity; he thought it would be valuable to have a federal judge owe him a favor, and he soon contrived to have the miners approve the name by popular vote.

On July 22, 1902, Felix Pedro finally made a major strike—seven feet of pay dirt at the bottom of a

hole about 16 miles from Barnette's trading post. In the days that followed, Pedro showed a few old sourdough friends where to stake claims that eventually made them fortunes as great as his. The comrades agreed to keep the secret until their claims had been properly recorded. But news got out anyway and traveled like wildfire—thanks to Barnette.

Pedro and his friends revealed no more than that they were going to file some claims in Circle City, 160 miles distant. But Barnette smelled something big. He made an offer, which they accepted, to save them the trip: he would send someone to file their claims for them, confidentially, of course. But Barnette wanted to manufacture a profitable stampede. He dispatched his Japanese cook, Jujuira Wada, to file the claims and instructed him to make sure the word got out. Though the strike was unproven, Wada skillfully let information slip that excited sourdoughs in Circle City and Dawson. Hundreds of

prospectors followed the Japanese pied piper back to Barnette's trading post. Scores of mining camps sprang up in the region. The largest, called Chena, seven miles downstream, soon rivaled Fairbanks as a trading and social center for the miners.

For a while the stampeders found nothing to warrant a gold rush; some talked of lynching Wada, and others departed in disgust. In fact, most of the gold was locked far below the surface, and the strikes of Pedro and his friends were merely superficial clues to the underlying treasure. When deeper digging uncovered the real bonanza, Wada was hailed as a hero. Moreover, the inaccessibility of the gold was a blessing in disguise, for it took heavy machinery and long, hard work to get it out. As a result, Fairbanks' boom lasted a decade and more, bringing huge capital investment and providing steady employment for thousands.

For these very reasons, however, the Tanana gold rush was slow to take hold. Some nine months after

In August 1907, a year after fire devastated Fairbanks, the lights of the reconstructed town glow across the Chena River at midnight. Then the northernmost sizable settlement in North America, Fairbanks enjoyed long hours of summer twilight, and the gloom of its 20-hour winter nights was relieved by electricity from the Northern Commercial Company's power plant (smokestacks at right).

Pedro's initial strike, while Fairbanks was just being built, Judge Wickersham arrived to look for a spot to establish a recorder's office for the midsection of his jurisdiction, which covered well over half of Alaska. The judge wrote: "A rough log structure, with spread-eagle wings, looked like a disreputable pig sty, but was in fact, Barnette's trading post, the only mercantile establishment in the new camp. A hundred yards up the stream, a half-finished two-story building without doors or windows bore the home-made sign on a white cloth—'Fairbanks Hotel.' Two other small log cabins marked 'Pioneer' and 'Northern' made known to miners with wilderness thirst that civilization and its vices were there. A half-dozen new squat log structures, a few tents, and an incoming stream of dog teams and gold seekers, a small clearing in the primeval forest—that was Fairbanks as I first saw it on April 9, 1903."

But the town grew rapidly thereafter, and it was Wickersham more than anyone else who decided that Fairbanks, not Chena, would become the business center of the Alaskan interior. Chena had better port facilities, and the judge might have chosen to build a courthouse there if the merchants had not demanded a stiff price for a town lot. On the other hand, Barnette offered him a free lot in Fairbanks. Wickersham accepted the lot but declined Barnette's offer of an interest in a gold mine in exchange for favorable rulings in certain mining-claims cases. With the courthouse and its region-wide records to attract official business, Fairbanks grew while Chena atrophied.

Three years later Fairbanks was riding the crest of its extended boom. A telegraph line and a road of sorts connected it to the port of Valdez, 376 miles to the southwest. The town, sprawling along a mile of riverfront, boasted 5,000 inhabitants, with another 5,000 distributed among a dozen mining camps in the outlying areas. A narrow-gauge railroad linked Fairbanks to its satellite towns and fed millions in gold onto outbound riverboats.

The Northern Commercial Company, which had bought Barnette's trading interests, built a power plant and supplied Fairbanks with electric lighting, steam heat, water and fire protection. Fairbanks' principal industries were two breweries and three sawmills; it also had three banks, and innumerable wholesale and retail businesses that purveyed a gamut of wares from mining equipment to baby buggies and jewelry made of ancient Mastodon tusks unearthed in the area. The town had three Protestant churches and one Catholic, and their pastors competed for attendance no less aggressively than the hotel men and restaurateurs. John Clark, an observant young lawyer who arrived from California in 1906, remarked with approval, "The law of supply and demand was working under high pressure."

Everywhere Clark looked he saw that Fairbanks was fundamentally different from the lawless gold camps of Alaska's recent past. Not that Fairbanks lacked brothels and gambling houses; it had plenty and they were patronized day and night. But the seamy side of town was not unseemly in its behavior. "There were no gun fights," Clark reported, "as I do not suppose that one man in 500 carried a gun. Fist fights were few, for while men got drunk occasionally, they were not a quarrelsome lot." Best of all, "There were no sneak thieves, no burglars and no criminal element in the common acceptation of the term."

Fairbanks was not orderly and law-abiding by accident. The town was started almost entirely by knowledgeable sourdoughs with too much experience to be fleeced by the usual gold-town predators, and the cheechakos who came later were not greenhorns in search of gold but men like lawyer Clark, shrewd technicians and professional men in pursuit of their chosen careers. Also, the prime motive for chronic crime was missing. As Clark noted, "There was no poverty, for work was plentiful and well paid." Most important, Fairbanks quickly became a family town. The merchants and suppliers, realizing that the deep diggings meant long-term employment, had brought their wives and children and then provided them with the sort of community they deserved. Even the saloonkeepers were responsible citizens. Said Clark, "They gave liberally to every worthy cause; assisted the churches and hospitals. Some were elected members of the City Council and some of them have served on the School Board."

Still, no Alaskan town seemed able to get through its infancy without experiencing at least one devastating fire and a couple of memorable crooks. Fairbanks' great fire started in a dentist's office on May 22,

1906, and quickly burned out most of the business district. The fire-fighting teams were hampered by low water pressure in the town's mains; if the furnaces in the power plant could not soon develop enough water pressure, there was a real chance the whole town would go up in smoke.

Volney Richmond, the local manager for the Northern Commercial Company, responded to the emergency; he saved the town's bacon by literally burning his own. Richmond ordered his men into a company warehouse near the powerhouse, and in a few minutes they were dumping crates of sugar-cured bacon into the boilers. After a ton of bacon had been consumed, the boilers produced sufficient steam to boost the water pressure, and fire fighters soon contained the conflagration. No lives were lost, and Clark reported, "No one was discouraged or downhearted." The work of rebuilding commenced at once and proceeded rapidly. The First National Bank erected a tent over its burned-out site and put miners to work panning the ashes for gold that had been left on the counter in buckskin pokes when the fire started. Several nearby towns offered assistance, but Fairbanks declined with thanks.

Fairbanks' legendary crook was none other than its founding father, Elbridge Barnette, who had become the town's first mayor and its most ubiquitous businessman. After selling his trading post to the Northern Commercial Company, Barnette started a bank and did well enough to speculate in Mexican real estate and to buy a $65,000 horse farm in Kentucky. Though his bank was apparently prospering, it suddenly closed its doors in 1911. About one million dollars in depositors' funds were unaccounted for, and only half that sum was eventually recovered by the sale of the bank's properties.

Not many of the citizens of Fairbanks had doubts that Barnette was guilty of embezzlement. But the evidence against him was sketchy at best. When he was brought to trial, Barnette got off with a $1,000 fine for filing false bank statements. Thereupon he retired and left Alaska.

Compared to Barnette the Blue Parka Man was an almost likeable bandit—a sort of pet crook to the citizens of Fairbanks, who grudgingly admired his daring holdups on the main trail into town. The high-wayman, who concealed his identity with the hooded garment that earned him his name, worked alone with courtesy and flair.

Stories of his robberies tended to improve in the retelling, and the best-known tale was apocryphal, although typical of the bandit. As Judge Wickersham told it, the Right Reverend Peter Trimble Rowe was part of a small group of holdup victims. After he and the others had placed their valuables in a neat pile, Rowe "began with his winning smile and gentle voice to expostulate with the highwayman for robbing a minister of the gospel. The Blue Parka Man asked if he was a minister. 'Yes,' was the reply, 'I am Bishop Rowe, of the Episcopal Church.' 'Oh,' the highwayman said in evident surprise. 'Well, I'm pleased to meet you, Bishop. Of course I won't rob you; take your poke off the heap in the road, Bishop, and take that poke with the shoestring on it, too. Why, damn it all, Bishop, I'm a member of your church.'"

When the Blue Parka Man finally was captured, he turned out to be a bookish fellow who had, when in town, indeed been a frequent patron of the library at Bishop Rowe's church.

Come fire or thievery, Fairbanks hewed to its course and made progress without fuss and feathers. In the first dozen years after Felix Pedro hit pay dirt, the region produced $63 million in gold. That total would more than double before the gold petered out two decades later. Far more important, gold had brought the Alaskan interior what it had sorely lacked: a stable population of deeply committed Alaskans, a permanent commercial and industrial center, and a solid advance base for further development.

The basic settlement of Alaska was now complete. Frontiering would go on for generations, but the territory's pioneering phase had drawn to a close with the rise of Fairbanks. Alaska was already one with the United States in the sense that the age of big business had overtaken it. The dilemma that Alaskans were now faced with was a choice between sound development and ruthless exploitation. Frederick Jackson Turner, the historian famous for his studies of the closing of the American frontier, put the question concisely: "Alaska beckons on the north, and pointing to her wealth of natural resources asks the nation on what new terms the new age will deal with her."

An exuberant outburst of patriotism

The early Alaskans were among the most demonstrably patriotic Americans of their time despite—or perhaps because of—their great distance from home, the rigors of their existence and the federal government's indifference. Independence Day, coming at the peak of Alaska's brief and cherished summer, was a time for exuberant, almost frenetic celebration.

Daylight on July 4 lasted 19 hours or more, and Alaskans, as though unwilling for their favorite holiday to end, kept the festivities going around the clock and sometimes into the following days. The gala's approach awakened civic pride in newly built towns along the edge of the wilderness from Skagway *(right)* to Nome. Merchants festooned their shop fronts with bunting, while workmen built stands along the route of the grand parade. Prospectors and trappers packed into the hotels, and saloons did a roaring trade.

"Every person present seemed proud," wrote a participant in Fairbanks' festivities in 1904. "The new town made a gallant appearance, with clean streets, new buildings, flags flying, the band playing, and fine floats filled with gaily dressed children."

The day's formal ceremonies reflected the traditions Alaskans had brought with them from the States: the Declaration of Independence was read aloud, politicians delivered ringing orations, and everyone joined in singing "The Star Spangled Banner." But the games more often than not emphasized an Alaskan pride in muscular prowess and stamina. There were prize fights, jackhammer contests and a tug-of-war that lasted until one brawny team pulled the other clear off its haunches.

A horse-drawn wagon is transformed into a star-spangled coach to carry Skagway's Goddess of Liberty and her attendants past the bunting-trimmed Elks Club hall in a 1910 Independence Day parade.

197

A schoolgirl (right) sprints down McKinley Street in Valdez to beat her rivals in a Fourth of July game of kick the stone. Valdez' citizens took pride in the fact that their port town owed its very existence to its location at the entrance to the "All-American" trail into the Alaskan interior.

199

All eyes are on a quartet of sack racers as they hop toward the finish line on July 4, 1900, in the mining town of Douglas. Other contestants raced wheelbarrows, climbed greased poles and gorged on pies as preliminaries to Douglas' feature event: jackhammering steel bits into a boulder.

Tug-of-warriors give their all beneath Old Glory on the main street of Fairbanks on Independence Day, 1913. The opposing six-man teams battled on a specially built platform that gave them a chance to dig in their heels.

Trailing smoke, a hot-gas balloon rises above fascinated
onlookers in Juneau on July 4, 1899. High over the
crowd, fireworks tied to the balloon's guy wires exploded
in midair — the climax of Juneau's Independence Day.

6|The perils of exploitation

Blown inshore by an unexpected southwest wind, a massive ice floe tightens its hold on the helpless American whaling fleet, abandoned

Alaska yielded its natural riches grudgingly, and its exploitation usually required organized, large-scale effort. The first Americans to make such an effort—and risk the dangers that went with it—were Yankee whalers.

Each year beginning in 1835 a New England-based fleet sailed into the Bering Sea to hunt the great sperm whales, bowheads and humpbacks. As the whales retreated northward each summer, whaling captains ventured deeper into the ice-pocked Arctic Ocean, remaining perilously close to freeze-up. They always escaped in time—until September 1871 when the ice pack closed in early *(below)* and crushed most of the fleet.

One survivor who may have thought the disaster providential was Captain Frederick Barker, who had been saved from a previous shipwreck by Eskimos and had spent the arctic winter in their care. Barker saw firsthand that the Eskimos were starving because of a lack of walruses, their primary winter sustenance. When whales were scarce, the whalers had turned to slaughtering walruses. Convinced that such butchery meant "the sure death of this inoffensive race," Barker vowed never to kill another walrus and tried to end the practice.

But the slaughter went on while the walrus lasted—a pattern that was repeated a generation later, when entrepreneurs discovered Alaska's bountiful fish and mineral wealth and resisted any attempt to regulate its looting.

at Wainwright Inlet in 1871. When salvagers arrived the following summer, they found that only one of the 32 ships had survived.

The plucking of "a fat goose left unprotected"

Through the 19th Century and well into the 20th, the Americans who gained the most from Alaska's magnificent bounty were men who had the most important requisite for making big money: they had big money to invest. They were businessmen, and most of them had never seen Alaska at firsthand—or ever expected to. As men of means they could afford to send hirelings to harvest the natural plenty and to fetch the profits home.

In the beginning these absentee investors made their fortunes chiefly out of the bodies, bones and hides of Alaska's abundant sea life. The whaleship owners of New Bedford, Massachusetts, and other ports of the American Northeast were among the first to find the Far North profitable. They dispatched their ships on extended journeys into the North Pacific and the Bering Sea, then through the Bering Strait to the edge of the known world in pursuit of the mighty bowhead and other species of whale.

From the 1840s until 1871 (when a mass of ice closed in on the fleet and crushed both the ships and the whaling industry), the Americans took thousands of tons of baleen, the valuable bone in the whale's mouth, and millions of gallons of whale oil. And on the summer days when whales proved too elusive, the whalers trained their gunsights on walruses lazily sunning themselves on the ice floes.

Meanwhile, through Alaska's bays and up its rivers once a year ran incredible numbers of sleek, spawning salmon. In the 1890s West Coast fishing companies built half a hundred canneries along the

Alaskan coastline, and the salmon, like the whale and the walrus, swam into the hands of commerce.

A few years later, when big business penetrated the interior and began to exploit Alaska's great mineral wealth, the largest part of the profits also went to men in the offices and board rooms of distant cities. One of these concerns, the Alaska Syndicate, emerged in the early 1900s as a commercial giant. The Syndicate reached out in any direction, from gold to railroads, that suggested profit—preferably with a monopoly. And, although no stockholder or director took part, the Syndicate was a party to one of the few shooting skirmishes over access to Alaska's riches.

Each of the commercial interests played a vital role in opening up and developing the territory. However, since most of them operated free from taxes or regulation—and, of course, desired to maintain those favorable conditions—they were tremendously influential in depriving Alaska's citizens of the civil government they so eagerly sought. Big business, preferring near anarchy to any form of bureaucratic interference, fought to keep government out. To assure the status quo, the corporations lobbied hard in Washington to prevent Congress from listening to Alaskan cries for self-rule. They argued—effectively and with some truth—that Alaska's white population was too scattered, too poorly educated and leavened with too many unreliable and irresponsible transients to be trusted with its own affairs.

In the face of such arguments, and federal willingness to believe them, Alaska struggled along under its first Organic Act, a modest concession Congress made to the territory in 1884 that had placed Alaska under a jumble of federal laws and special regulations, and the state laws of Oregon. The act provided for a handful of relatively powerless officials, chief among them an appointed governor who had little more to do

Decorative calendars with maps of Alaska on the back and a bit of pulchritude on the front were welcome bonuses for customers of the Northern Commercial Company, which dominated trade in the territory.

209

than issue proclamations and write an annual report.

As early as 1888 the second governor, Alfred P. Swineford, warned Congress that the territory teetered dangerously close to being "nothing more than a national fat goose left unprotected, and to be annually plucked of its valuable plumage by non-resident corporations." That said, the governor made yet another plea for land laws, mail service and other basics of civil government. "It is only necessary that the shackles which fetter the progress of a great empire in embryo be removed—that she be given the same substantial aid and encouragement that has been accorded to every other territory."

But Congress in 1888 proffered neither the aid nor the encouragement the governor asked for. Even the 1900 act that authorized individual towns to incorporate themselves did little for Alaska as a whole. The "shackles" remained until 1912 when Congress at last passed a second Organic Act, which made Alaska a formal territory with an elected legislature. Then Alaskans had at least limited means to control and benefit from the exploitation of natural resources. But until 1912 the guiding ethic of Alaskan business was simply to take the money and run. The first to practice that principle were the whalemen.

The whaleships leaving New Bedford were stoutly built, bluff-bowed square-riggers, running an average 125 feet overall, displacing 300 to 500 tons. For the most part, they were planked with New England yellow pine and to protect them against the ice were sheathed around the water line with Australian greenheart, a particularly tough, crush-resistant wood.

The men on board these ships worked hard and were paid next to nothing. Since the whaleship owners commanded as much as 60 per cent of the net proceeds, and the captains and officers split up to 30 per cent, the crews were left with a miserly residue. Depending on his experience and expertise, a seaman's share varied from 1/150 to 1/250 of the net.

Worse than the appalling pay was the monotony of long months at sea and the separation from loved ones. When a whaleman left the dock he was pretty sure he would be away three to five years.

The whalers customarily reprovisioned in Honolulu and then sailed north along the early-thawing Siberian coast before heading into Alaskan waters. Their quarry, the bowhead, was an awesome beast that could run to better than half the length of a ship and weigh 65 tons or more. The whale's head was a third of its bulk. Its mouth had a 300-barrel capacity, and its tongue alone weighed five tons. A whale strained food from a quarter mile of ocean before swallowing. Such a creature was not to be approached lightly.

When a whale was sighted, crews of six were lowered from the ship in 30-foot boats. As a boat maneuvered alongside the animal's great black back, a harpooner would lean out over the gunwale and drive the iron into the prey as deep as his strength allowed. As spasms of agony shot through the whale's body, it would run and then dive, dragging the iron and line. As the whale sounded the depths, the crew would pay out line. Then, exhausted, the wounded whale would rise, and the force of its final upward lunge would cause turbulence over a quarter acre of sea.

The crewman called the boatheader would set himself for the killing blow. This required precision. The striking point for the lance was just above the shoulder blade. If the lance missed this narrow target and cut into the lungs, there would be a mighty rush of air and the whale, dead or not, would sink for lack of buoyancy. A quick, clean kill was the thing. Otherwise, the whale's flukes—25 feet across—could smash whatever they struck. "A dead whale or a stove boat," the whalers said.

A big dead bowhead was worth having. Its blanket of blubber, up to 18 inches thick to provide insulation in icy northern waters, its tongue and its white, four-foot-thick lips would together yield as much as 325 barrels of oil. In the huge mouth was the baleen—flexible, bristle-covered plumes of whalebone up to 14 feet long that the whale used to strain the plankton it ate. The baleen from an extremely large whale might weigh 3,500 pounds and in a high market could be sold for five dollars a pound. Even the average bowhead, boiled into casked oil and cleaned baleen, seldom failed to bring less than $10,000.

The first whaling ship to thread through the Aleutian chain, cross the Bering Sea and enter the Arctic Ocean was the *Superior* out of Sag Harbor, New York, in 1848. Soon a whole fleet of ships had begun prowling along the arctic ice every summer and early autumn. In 1852, 278 whaleships brought back oil and baleen worth $14,118,900—almost twice what was paid for all Alaska 15 years later.

"By day and night," wrote one whaler in the middle of the 19th Century, "the whale is chased and harassed—the fleet perpetually driving them, until they reach the highest navigable latitudes of the Arctic. The only rest they have is when the fogs are thick and the wind is high."

Each year, as the bowheads retreated farther north and the fleet followed, the whales grew harder to find and still harder to kill. Near the roof of the world, they stuck close to the ice and surfaced to blow only in rifts among the drifting floes where the whaleboats could scarcely get at them. Whaling, never slow or easy in any latitude, became lightning-quick, desperate work when a whale could propel itself under the ice before a man could loose his first harpoon.

In a letter to the *Whaleman's Shipping List and Merchant's Transcript* in 1852, a thoughtful New Bedford shipmaster wondered if there was not something offensive to God about the whole greedy business. "I felt," he wrote, "as I gazed upon the great frozen icefields stretching far down to the horizon that they were barriers placed there by Him to rebuke our anxious and overweening pursuit of wealth."

Few, if any, of the shipmaster's colleagues felt so contrite; in fact, when they were not hunting whales they ventured right onto the ice fields, where the walruses' habit of basking on the ice made them easy to kill. And killed they were, by the tens of thousands, creating great hardship for the Eskimos, who made their living off them as totally as the Plains Indians did off the buffalos.

Compared with a whale, even a full-grown, 2,000-pound walrus bull would appear inconsequential; it took 850 walruses to boil out 500 barrels of oil. But the walrus had something else to offer that made it a valuable prize—ivory. For a time San Francisco received 10,000 tusks a year, shipping most of them to the ivory carvers of China.

Then came the season of 1871 and a climactic disaster that, though it fell short of ending Alaskan whaling—and walrusing—dealt the industry a blow from which it never fully recovered. Every season, as the whales grew warier and fewer, the whalers pushed farther north and stayed longer in their "anxious and overweening pursuit of wealth." In 1871 they pushed too far and stayed too long.

Early in June the fleet was working its way along the coast on the edge of the ice. Already there were portents that might have led a particularly cautious or superstitious man to sense impending danger. Eskimos who came out to the ships spoke darkly of severe and unusual weather ahead. These warnings were ignored; no whaling master could explain to his employer in New Bedford that he had abandoned the season because Toonook, the Eskimo evil spirit, had bade him to do so. Then, in mid-June, the bark *Oriole* got caught in the ice and was so badly stove in that Captain Benjamin Dexter of the *Emily Morgan* bought the wreck for $1,350. It was a profitable deal; he stripped it of everything useful and sold the salvage to other ships for a total of $2,541.17. The other vessels also divided the *Oriole*'s crew.

Whales were few and shy, the skies usually opaque with fog and the ice bothersome. To sail in such circumstances, according to one authority, required consummate skill. "The ship handler had to maintain not only constant vigilance, but a drumfire of steady commands to the man at the wheel for hours on end. It was a matter of perpetual maneuvering when the obstacles themselves were perpetually in motion."

Whalemen recognized the summer ice pack off the Alaskan coast as a phenomenon that was always potentially dangerous. It was old ice, consisting of blocks from six to 16 feet thick. From hour to hour it was opening, closing, piling up in jagged masses as high as a house. An offshore wind moved the ice out to sea and gave the whaleships room. An onshore wind drove it back in on them. But seasons past had convinced the whalers they would never be beached by the action of the ice. Before the wind-blown pack could be driven all the way to shore, it usually grew so dense and deep that it ground to a stop on the sea floor, leaving an avenue of open water between ice and land. This "ground ice" was normally so stable that a ship could actually tie up to it.

By early August, 32 ships of the fleet were off Wainwright Inlet, about 50 miles above the 70th parallel and less than 100 miles from Point Barrow, the northernmost tip of Alaska. Here the ships either anchored or moored to the heavy ground ice, and for five days the whaling was good. But on August 11 the wind-blown ice headed inshore, and the ships moved to shoal water to keep from being stove in. Still the whaleboats went out daily, though whaling under these conditions was more demanding than ever. Miles from their ships, the boat crews slept either on shore or on ice, and if they got a whale, they had to tow it 10 to 15 times the distance they were accustomed to. "Struck a whale five miles from the ship," one mate wrote sourly. "Whale ran under the ice. Lost line. Shut down thick fog. Saw him no more." The mate's mood continued gloomy in a succeeding entry: "Still fast in close-packed ice. Foggy part of the time. Leave one whale floating in the ice."

On August 25 a strong northeast gale set in and drove the ice out eight miles from the coast. The Eskimos once more urged the captains to leave with all possible speed, warning that the sea would not open again. But the warning went unheeded. For four days whaling was excellent and nobody had time even to think of quitting. Then on August 29 the wind shifted, coming now from the southwest. The ice moved back and grounded in shoal water. Between it and the shore lay the ships, strung out along 20 miles of coast with no room to maneuver and no way to leave. The Eskimo prophecy had become reality.

Understandably, nerves were wearing thin. The *Eugenia* took a whale on August 30, and an argument broke out on deck while the crew was boiling blubber. *Eugenia*'s mate wrote in the log: "At 2 finished a-boiling. Ice drifting down past the ship some heavy. At 3 o'clock, two of the men got to fiting. Mr. Coner, the 2d offerser, went forward to stop the row and one of them, George White by name, sayed he wood not for him or eney sun of a bich." The result, when White grew adamant and abusive, was that he and an ally named Dearman were "triced up" to the mizzen rigging. Tricing usually meant that a man was tied by his thumbs to the shrouds just high enough so his toes touched the deck when the ship was still. But when the ship rolled the man being punished would swing by the thumbs and, as one old hand said, "he quick got damn tired of that."

A fresh wind persisted from the southwest, and the open lane between ground ice and the beach narrowed.

Eskimos show off the results of a walrus hunt on the Bering Sea near Nome shortly after the turn of the century. The meat of the walruses was divided among the hunters, but the hides and tusks, once prized by the Eskimos for making clothes, boats and tools, were often sold for cash.

Even there, young ice began to form around the ships' hulls. Then the jaws began to close. At dawn, September 2, the brig *Comet* was caught between two massive floes. The stern was literally crushed out of her. As the *Comet*'s crew took to the ice, her timbers cracked like gunfire. When the ice finally relaxed its grip, the smashed brig sank.

The bark *Roman* was next to go. On September 4, two floes rammed into her. While the crew scrambled for the ice, the gigantic vise lifted the ship out of the water, rolled her until the keel showed, squeezed her three times, then drew apart and dropped her. It was all over in 45 minutes. The disconsolate crew was left on the floes with what few provisions they had been able to save.

The remaining fleet was still whaling in its narrow lane of open water on September 7 (and still expecting a favorable gale to drive away the ice) when two boats from the *Emily Morgan* took a whale. In the process the second mate, preparing to fire at the beast, accidentally shot himself under the jaw with a bomb gun, the missile exiting through the back of his head. While one boat took the body to the ship, the other towed in the bowhead. The mate's death added to the growing sense of uneasiness in the fleet.

Whaling ended that day. Experience had taught the shipmasters to expect the wind to save them, but experience was worth little this year. Three boats were dispatched south along the ground ice to sound the water for a possible escape route. There was none. They found only nine feet of water in many places and over one shoal a mere four feet. The ships drew 15 feet or more.

Whalemen were bred to a school that did not easily abandon hope, much less ships, cargo and responsibility. But, barring a sea-opening northeasterly wind, they were trapped. The crushing of the *Awashonks* on September 8 drove the truth deeper. The wreck was sold to the captain of the *Eugenia* for $16, a pittance that reflected the whaler's deepening pessimism (the bark *Oriole* had brought 85 times that sum earlier in the season).

The shipmasters reviewed their situation. Here were 29 ships still afloat—although some were already damaged—with cargo worth hundreds of thousands of dollars. Here were some 1,200 people who had become prisoners of ice. At hand were provisions for three months. Ahead were nine months of arctic winter. The Eskimos could not help, largely because the whalers themselves had all but wiped out the Eskimos' food supply, the walrus.

"Ice bound on one side and land on the other," noted Captain Lewis of the *Thomas Dickason,* "God have Mercy on this Whaling Fleet."

The captains decided to try lightening the two smallest ships, in the hope of getting them over the shoals. The effort failed; they could not raise the ships high enough in the water to make it through. The only other hope was that there was still open water somewhere to the south where other whaleships might have lingered.

Relays of whaleboats had been sent down the coast, making heavy going through foul weather and the quickly forming new ice. Often the crew had to haul the boats over the ice or along the rocky shore. By September 9 the lead boats reached Icy Cape, a promontory 60 miles to the southwest. Providentially, seven whalers still lay near a field of pack ice south of the cape. They had been having trouble with ice themselves or they would have left days earlier.

On September 11 a boat got back to the marooned fleet and reported that three ships were in open water near the cape and that four more appeared to be fighting clear of the ice there. The masters met again and composed two austere documents. One was meant for their owners at home. "We feel ourselves under the painful necessity," it said, "of abandoning our vessels and trying to work our way south with our boats and if possible get on board of ships that are south of the ice." The second was a plea addressed to the seven captains at Icy Cape: "We now call on you in the voice of humanity, to abandon your whaling, sacrifice your personal interest, as well as that of your owners to receive on board ourselves."

Upon receiving the message, the seven captains made the only humane decision. According to one report, "The masters, with the full consent of all the crews, decided at once to abandon their voyages and to rescue these men, entirely regardless of self and without a murmur. If they had adopted any other course, a cry of indignation would have gone up from the civilized world, which would have justly accused

these claimants of a worse crime than murder, that of abandoning these men to a slow and horrible death."

"Tell them all," said Captain James Dowden of the bark *Progress*, "I will wait for them as long as I have an anchor left or a spar to carry a sail."

The crews of the icebound vessels prepared to run for safety. They, like their rescuers, would also be making a sacrifice: the loss in ships and cargo would be put at $1.5 million. On September 14 first mate Billy Earle wrote in the *Emily Morgan's* log: "If we save our lives we ought to be satisfied and that should satisfy the world. At 12 noon, paid out all of chain on both anchors and at 1:30 p.m., with sad hearts, and with a last look over the decks, abandoned the ship to the mercy of the elements. And so ends this day, the writer having done his duty and believes every man to have done the same."

The problems of the whalers were just beginning. Ahead of them lay a journey of 60 miles through wicked weather and thickening ice. They set out in nearly 200 whaleboats. "As night came on," the *Emily Morgan's* first officer wrote, "the wind in-

creased and as darkness closed around us, heavy black clouds seemed to rest over us and it was not possible to see more than a few feet and we were in constant danger of coming in collision with the many fragments of ice floating in the narrow passage between the land and the main pack. At 10:30 p.m.," he continued, "landed by a fire on the shore, where several boats were hauled up and made some coffee. Shoved off into the darkness at 11:30. The navigation was difficult and dangerous; we kept the land well aboard and sounding continually."

The most dangerous part of the journey still lay ahead, on the raging open sea. "The weather here was very bad," the captain of one of the rescue vessels recorded, "causing a sea that threatened the little craft with annihilation."

"In this fearful sea," the officer wrote, "the whaleboats were tossed about like pieces of cork. They shipped quantities of water from every wave which struck them, requiring the utmost diligence of all hands at bailing to keep them afloat. Everybody's clothing was thoroughly saturated with the freezing

215

Even though the product varied little, each Alaskan salmon cannery promoted its own brand with distinctive labels like the three shown at left. By the early 1900s, Alaska was producing more than half of the world's canned salmon.

brine, while all the bread and flour in the boats was completely spoiled."

The little flotilla finally reached the seven rescue ships on September 16, after a two-day voyage. Then, as scores of abandoned whaleboats bobbed and whirled behind them, the fleet of the whaling ships weighed anchor and sailed south for Honolulu, where the last of them docked safely on November 22.

In 1872, when the whalers returned, they found one ship left of the 32 that had been left in the ice. Miraculously, the bark *Minerva* floated serenely at anchor, unblemished by the winter's ordeal. The returning whalers also found a single seaman who, perhaps hoping to grow rich on salvage, had hidden himself and stayed behind with the icebound fleet. He had been sheltered by Eskimos but had long since come to regret his decision. "A hundred and fifty thousand dollars," he said, "would not tempt me to try another winter in the Arctic."

It was an Eskimo who pronounced the final obsequies over the ill-fated voyage. "Bad. Very bad for you," he told one of the crewmen. "Good. Good for us. More walrus now."

The disaster of 1871 did not stop whalers from returning to the arctic, but the shipowners never again reaped the great profits they had made in the years preceding the destruction of the fleet. Gradually the bowhead was all but hunted out, and long before the turn of the century the revenue from whaling in high latitudes had diminished to an unimpressive $1.4 million or less a year. By then, however, capitalists on the western edge of the United States had discovered, in far less dangerous Alaskan waters, another creature ripe for worldwide commerce. Salmon became the territory's most important resource.

Between the Alexander Archipelago in the far southeast and Bristol Bay just above the tusk of the Aleutian peninsula, Alaska had about 20,000 miles of coastline cut by countless rivers and streams. Some were icy cold and crystal clear; others were greenish-gray because they carried so much sediment from the mountains—glacier milk, it was called. Every year, from late spring until early fall, as certain as fate, five species of salmon came back to these rivers where they had been born. Depending on the species, they

had spent between two and seven years maturing at sea, and now their instincts guided them home.

These fish—called by many Indian names that run pleasantly in the mind: Chinook (king), sockeye (red), coho (silver), humpbacked (pink) and chum (dog)—ran up the streams to spawn and then died.

For centuries the returning salmon had been caught by native fishermen, who had lived on the fish since before time was marked—and often lived very well. It has been calculated that Indian, Aleut and Eskimo consumption of salmon ran to 33.5 million pounds a year before the white man arrived. The Indians fished not only for the day but also put up salmon for the season ahead by drying it in the sun.

The Russians, who called sun-dried salmon *yukola,* had made one effort to exploit the fish commercially, shipping it to California during the gold rush. The venture failed as most of the salmon, unskillfully packed, spoiled on board ship. Thereafter the Russians occasionally salted salmon in limited amounts to send to St. Petersburg as a delicacy for Russian-American Company officials and highly placed friends who might do the company some good at court.

Once again it remained for the Americans to recognize a source of wealth and seize it. In 1868 a saltery was established on Kodiak Island's Karluk River, a magnificent red-salmon stream. Soon more salting stations arose along the coast, tiny isolated settlements reached by boat. At first the fish were brine packed, 800 pounds to the barrel, and shipped mostly to Europe, where salmon was popular as cheap but nutritious fare.

Then, in 1878, putting up salmon in tins—a process already in wide use on the Sacramento River in California—succeeded the not-always-reliable barrel-packing method. That year two canneries were established in Alaska: one at Klawock on Prince of Wales Island, the other at Sitka. The 1878 pack amounted to 8,159 cases of 48 one-pound cans valued at about $50,000. By 1889 Alaska had 37 operating canneries, and their output had risen to 714,196 cases worth about $2.8 million. By 1902 the total Alaska pack was up to 2.5 million cases.

Building a fair-sized cannery to produce 25,000 cases a season was expensive, costing $100,000 to $125,000, because everything from boilers to butch-

Introduced in 1903, the contraption advertised at right butchered and dressed salmon for canning, replacing the Chinese workers for whom it was insensitively named. The machine processed 60 fish a minute, thus doing the work of 15 men.

er knives had to be shipped in from such stateside ports as Seattle, Astoria or Portland. But the construction itself was fairly simple and crude. Mont Hawthorne, a jack-of-all-trades Westerner who, by his own account, "got in on most everything up North except the profits," built four canneries in Alaska at locations from Kasaan Bay, near the southern tip of the Panhandle, to Cook Inlet. In each case he was able to go north in the early spring, pick a site, begin construction and have everything ready when the salmon run began in June or early July. A prime consideration in laying out the plant was to build it on piles over tidewater so the ebb would slough away the "gurry"—the slime, blood and offal that accumulated when the fish were cleaned.

Before the development of automated or semiautomated machinery around the turn of the century, most of the work inside the cannery was done by Chinese—China boys, as the packers called them. The Chinese were hired as a gang from Chinese-owned agencies in California and sent north under their own foreman, called the China boss. They worked long hours, slept in a crowded barnlike structure called the China house and were paid about $165 a season, much of which they sent home to relatives in China.

Hawthorne reported that after working "around Chinaboys for close to 15 years, I got to see their side of things pretty near as good as I could see my own. I used to think it was wrong for them fellows to send their money back to the old country. But the first boy I ever talked to about it said: 'I come here to work so I can send money to my father and my mother. They have a big family in China and only two acres of ground. If I do not work here and send them money, they will starve.' "

The labor assigned to the Chinese was the foulest sort—"the kind of work," Hawthorne confessed, "we didn't want to do ourselves." They asked little in return. "All they expected to get out of life," said Hawthorne, "was hard work and the promise that when they died their bones would be shipped back to the old country to be buried in the graves of their ancestors. And even that wasn't done until they was buried over here long enough for the flesh to waste away. It saved expense and shipping space to dig them up, pack each man's bones in a little metal box, and

send them back home in a sizable consignment."

Each year before the salmon run commenced, the Chinese were given the task of cutting out and soldering cans that were then stored in the cannery attic. A deft hand with a soldering iron could seam 2,000 cans a day. The pace turned feverish with the arrival of the fish. Salmon, weighing more than seven pounds each if they were prime reds, would be dumped on the butchers' table, where it took Chinese workers two seconds per fish to cut off head and tail, flick away the fins and slit the belly.

A team of Indian women, hired locally, would strip out the gurry and let it fall through the fish house floor into the tide. Other Chinese, skilled by long practice, would chop the fish crossways to the exact size to fill a one-pound can. Meanwhile, the cans, each primed with a quarter teaspoon of salt, would be coming down from the attic on a conveyor belt. Once filled, more Chinese would place and crimp the tops before sending them on to a solder bath to be sealed.

The cans were tested for leaks in a vat of boiling water and resoldered if necessary. Next they were cooked twice, the first time at 212° F. for 20 minutes, the second at 240° F. for an hour and a quarter. They were then given a bath of lacquer against rust, and were finally labeled and packed in cases of 48.

Gradually, many of these steps—chopping to length, filling and topping—were turned over to machines, but the manpower used was always Chinese. White men refused the work.

Canners used several methods for catching salmon: purse seines, gill nets and traps. Any of these would take thousands of fish. In 1888 fishermen in Karluk Bay alone caught 2.5 million salmon, enough to fill 200,000 cases. The next year more than three million fish were caught at the same spot.

The assault on marine wealth at Karluk Bay prompted the first government gesture toward regulating Alaskan fisheries. In 1889 Congress passed a limited salmon protection act that outlawed the total barricading of salmon streams. But having made the law, Congress failed to provide any means of enforcement. Not until 1892 did it appropriate funds for one inspector and one assistant, hardly a force large enough to oversee all the canneries along 20,000 miles of coastline. Moreover, the two men had no

The "IRON CHINK"

TWELVE MACHINES NOW PRACTICALLY COMPLETED ARE ORDERED AND WILL BE OPERATED IN VARIOUS CANNERIES AT PUGET SOUND, ALASKA AND BRITISH COLUMBIA.

Any canneryman wishing a machine for this season should place his order at once, so as to enable us to construct it in time for commencement of salmon run.

The illustration above is direct from a photograph of the new model Smith Fish Cleaner. This machine has just been completed, ready for shipment to the Red Salmon Canning Company, Bristol Bay, Alaska. Its capacity is 60 fish per minute. It is operated with two horse-power. As the fish come off the elevator they slide down to operator No. 1, who guides it past a knife which cuts off the head, and thence to operator No. 2, who passes the fish by the knife which cuts off the tail. The fish is then placed in the feeding trough, which is shown on right of wheel. In passing through trough tail first, back down, the back fins come in contact with a self-sharpening knife which trims off both the large and small back fins. In the feed trough is an automatic feed which "times up" with the clamps on the wheel, of which there are six. The fish is caught in the clamp by the tail, carried up through a centering device, when the back clamps close on it, holding it firmly. It travels upward to the self-sharpening, self-adjusting knives which are suspended at top of machine. These knives remove all the remaining fins in a uniform manner. The fish then goes on down to the splitting saw, shown one-fourth of way down from top, splitting very accurately in exact center. The fish then comes in contact with a rotary gutting device, which removes the entrails and stirs up the blood on back bone, leaving it ready to be wiped out with the aid of a stream of water and a rotary hemp brush. The fish then travels on to within three inches of where it entered the wheel, and, released, slides down onto a conveyor which takes it to the gang knives.

Smith Cannery Machines Co.

OWNERS AND MANUFACTURERS

111 Seneca Street   **Seattle, U. S. A.**

boat, so they wound up having to be ferried from cannery to cannery on ships owned by the companies they were there to inspect.

Meanwhile, Alaskans had begun to protest that the spiraling salmon industry was giving the territory absolutely nothing in return—not even jobs. As one writer put it in the 1880s: "The Alaska canners are not held to any restrictions as in British Columbia, not taxed nor hindered in any way. The canneries drain the country of their natural wealth; make no permanent settlements, nor any improvements; spend almost nothing of their profits in the territory."

Governor Swineford reported in 1888 that the canneries "are owned and operated by non-resident corporations, who come to the territory in the spring bringing with them all the cheap Chinese and other labor they require, few if any of their employees becoming actual residents, but nearly, if not quite, all returning whence they came in the fall."

The cannery owners were for the most part based in the States, and some were major corporations. In 1893 a number of them joined forces to form the Alaska Packers Association, with headquarters located in San Francisco. The association hired lobbyists to work in Washington against restrictive legislation and to fend off accusations from critics like Governor Swineford. Another benefit of banding together was the decreased costs in purchasing supplies as well as in marketing the salmon. In 1897 the association's pack came to 669,464 cases—more than 70 per cent of the entire territory's total output. And the profits were tax-free.

Two years later Congress, apparently beginning to listen to critics of the industry, moved to tax the canners, though only lightly—the tax was four cents a case. Under this program, one major cannery paid $5,000 tax on profits of $250,000. The small tax stayed in force, hardly denting profits, until 1912, when the second Organic Act was passed. Then the new Alaska legislature, seeking a handy source of revenue, established a territorial case tax of seven cents on red and king salmon, the most desirable species, and one-half cent per case on the others. The canners resisted at first, and the territory had to haul them into court and win a judgment before it could wring any money out of them. Thereafter, though the

fish industry continued to overlook indigenous labor in favor of cheap, imported work gangs, at least it was forced to help finance Alaska's territorial government.

Though the first Alaska legislature taxed the salmon industry, it chose to tread lightly on corporations engaged in other exploitation, leaving them barely taxed and largely unscrutinized. In the case of mining operations, for instance, the assembly settled on a particularly meager assessment. Miners had to pay the government one half of 1 per cent of their annual net income above $5,000. The legislators defined net income as the cash value of the mining output after deducting leases, royalties, repairs and a loophole-ridden list of other operating expenses. Under this law only the biggest corporations paid taxes, and they paid very little because their accountants could often show that expenses cut the net to below $5,000 a year. One of the largest concerns allowed to operate all but free of taxation was a giant conglomerate called the Alaska Syndicate. The story of its many-tentacled fight to control Alaska's treasures is a story of men not satisfied with anything less than all.

In August 1900 a party of 11 prospectors threaded its way through the Chitina River Valley, a rugged area between the Chugach and Wrangell mountain ranges in south central Alaska that Lieutenant Henry Allen had first explored 15 years earlier. At the 4,000-foot level above Bonanza Creek, a tributary of the Chitina, they came upon a region of stark, green cliffs. When the rock of the strange cliffs was assayed, it turned out to be 70 per cent pure copper. The prospectors staked a mile-long claim.

These men soon chose the path of quickest profit by selling out to a mining engineer named Stephen Birch, who was in the area at the behest of influential backers. Birch bought out the 11 discoverers for $25,000 each and put together a company to explore the area further.

Then in 1905 international banker J. P. Morgan, one of the richest men in the world, joined with the Guggenheim mining family and other lesser interests to create the Alaska Syndicate. It was soon known to resident Alaskans as "the Guggs," or simply "the Syndicate." The Syndicate's first major move was to pay Birch and his backers three million dollars for the mineral rights to the copper cliffs and adjacent properties. Birch's group made a handsome profit on their original investment. For the Guggs it was to be one of the most lucrative mining deals ever negotiated.

Once into Alaska, the Syndicate spread in what appeared to be all directions—copper, gold, canneries, railroads and steamships. Alaskans for the first time were faced with a conglomerate in the modern sense: impersonal, absent, an insatiable combine that seemed bent on swallowing every enterprise in the land.

The Syndicate's first project was to get at the copper it had bought. This was a job of staggering proportions. The green cliffs stood far upriver in a gorge of Bonanza Creek, guarded by the shallow, ice-choked delta of the nearby Copper River and by glaciers on every hand. A railroad was decided on as the only practical way to get the ore out of that defile and down to deep water for shipping.

No railroad ever offered its potential builders more difficulties. The Guggs initially chose the town of Valdez as its seaward terminus because of the town's fine harbor on Prince William Sound. Later, to the bitter disappointment of Valdez, the Syndicate switched its preference to an open roadstead at Katalla, on Controller Bay, and spent about one million dollars constructing a stone breakwater to protect its man-made port from fierce winter gales.

Meanwhile, a promoter named Henry Reynolds sensed a chance for profit in Valdez after the Syndicate pulled out. He won the backing of a former governor, John Brady, and launched an investment venture he called the Alaska Home Railroad in competition with the Syndicate's own line. Banking on the bitterness the Syndicate had engendered in Valdez by teasing the townspeople with the prospect of an economic windfall, Reynolds cried "Alaska for Alaskans" and sold stock in his project by the thousands of shares. His railroad would begin at Valdez and enter the Copper River gorge through a defile called Keystone Canyon.

The Guggs did not abide competition lightly, and before long blood was shed in Keystone Canyon. The Syndicate owned a grade running partway through the canyon, which it had abandoned along with the Valdez route. But it still held the right of way; a cadre of armed guards was posted in the canyon even as Reyn-

olds was announcing that his railroad would pass through. A confrontation was inevitable, and it occurred when 200 of Reynolds' men marched into the canyon and met 40 men employed by the Syndicate. The chief Syndicate guard, Edward Hasey, a deputy U.S. marshal, ordered Reynolds' workers to disperse. When they refused Hasey fired into the crowd, wounding five men, one of whom later died.

To the anti-Syndicate forces the bloody event confirmed the dark suspicion that the Guggs would stop at nothing to gain control of all Alaska. Suspicion grew blacker when Hasey was tried for murder and acquitted. A second trial for assault with a deadly weapon, based on the same evidence and witnesses, ended in a conviction and a short prison sentence for Hasey. Anti-Gugg sentiment deepened when Governor Wilford Hoggatt dismissed from office several government employees who had pushed the Hasey prosecution. After the trial, evidence turned up to indicate that the Syndicate's defense lawyers had entertained both witnesses and jurors. The Syndicate, in Alaska less than three years, had by now become the object of overwhelming hate.

At this point the Guggs were forced to reckon with another rival, a two-fisted engineer named Michael J. Heney, nicknamed the Irish Prince, who had begun building his own railroad with the backing of British investors. Heney was admiringly known to Alaskans as the man who, during the Klondike gold rush, had built the only railroad of any consequence in the area, the 110-mile White Pass & Yukon, between Skagway and Whitehorse. It was Heney's experienced notion that the only workable route to the mouth of the Copper would have to run from Cordova on the Gulf of Alaska. He was convinced, for one thing, that the Syndicate's breakwater at Katalla would not stand up to an Alaskan winter and, for another, that when it came to building railroads in tough country, he could beat Reynolds hands down. Both suppositions turned out to be true.

Reynolds' ill-conceived line failed for lack of funds soon after the shootout at Keystone Canyon. Moreover, when some of the investors' money could not be accounted for, Reynolds was tried, convicted of fraud and sent to prison. As for the Syndicate, its breakwater at Katalla disintegrated under the hammering of

From headquarters in San Francisco, absentee owners Gustave Niebaum, Lewis Gerstle and Louis Sloss directed the far-flung interests of the Alaska Commerical Company. For decades the firm took a million dollars profit a year out of Alaska.

a storm in 1907. With their man-made port destroyed, the Guggs decided to buy out the investment of Heney and his backers in the route from Cordova. They retained Heney to finish the line up the Chitina to the ore-rich cliffs, 200 miles from the sea.

To get through the Copper River Valley, Heney first had to construct a rock-ballast roadbed over terrible topography: mud, quicksand and a multitude of icy streamlets periodically swollen by as much as 200 inches of rainfall a year. Then he had to construct additional miles of roadbed across the top of one glacier—a stretch that would require constant rebuilding because the glacier was always shifting—and between two others that nearly abutted.

If the lay of the land was not problem enough, Heney also had to deal with the chewing and drinking habits of his hard-bitten work crews. Once the railroad gangs walked out on strike because the company store ran out of snuff, an absolute necessity the workmen called snoose. Heney induced his men to return

only after bringing a freight car up the line piled high with snuff. Another time, during slow tunneling in a particularly difficult area, Heney hid a case of whiskey in the bushes near what would be the north end of the tunnel. Then he told the hands they could drink their fill when the bore was finished. By all accounts the tunnel went through in breakneck time.

Building the railroad took five years, from 1906 through 1911, employed 5,000 men and cost $20 million. But when at last it was done, the Guggs took $175 million in copper out of the Chitina cliffs.

Alaskans continued to excoriate the Syndicate, which continued to give them concrete reasons to do so. Spreading its tentacles, the combine acquired a controlling interest in the Northwestern Commercial Company and its sister firm, the Northwestern Steamship Company. It also bought the Alaska Steamship Company, which served the Panhandle. From then on the Syndicate, which now had a fleet of 17 vessels calling at Alaskan ports from Ketchikan to

Nome, gave preferential rates to subsidiaries of the Syndicate. Seeing the Guggs take over a dominant role in shipping, so crucial to Alaska's existence, the *Nome Gold Digger* warned its readers that the "vampire which has already started its blood sucking operation is laying its plans for the complete subjection of the country to its will."

This was a lurid exaggeration, of course, but the Syndicate was indeed on the move. In 1906 it branched into salmon canning and soon owned a dozen canneries along the coast. Turning its attention to gold mining, the Syndicate moved heavy dredges into the Iditarod River area near the lower Yukon, and on a stream called Flat Creek dredged up over a million dollars in gold in one three-month period in 1912.

But when it turned to mining coal, the Syndicate encountered stiffer opposition. In 1906 conservation-minded President Theodore Roosevelt sealed off Alaska's coal fields from private development. The Presidential decree stunned all Alaskans—even those who opposed the Syndicate—for without coal it would be difficult to open up Alaska with new industry and new railroads. The ambiguous wording of the decree, however, left open the possibility that coal claims already staked might still be mined.

The Guggs moved secretly to buy an option on the 27 claims of one Clarence Cunningham and associates. When Cunningham, a prospector and mining engineer, had put together his association it was legal. But Congress had since passed legislation restricting mine ownership, and by the time the Guggs bought in they were flagrantly violating the law. Actual mining of the Cunningham claims, located in the coal-rich Bering River region, was held up first by red tape and then by federal investigations, and eventually the Guggs's illegal involvement was revealed.

This time the issue was not settled by a shootout on the scene but by a power struggle at the highest levels of government in Washington. William Howard Taft had succeeded Roosevelt as President in 1909, and under him served two men who disliked each other: Secretary of the Interior Richard Ballinger and Gifford Pinchot, the chief architect of the conservation program. Ballinger had overseen an impeccably impartial investigation of the Cunningham claims, but Pinchot was able to show that Ballinger once had

In a 1910 cartoon a giant representing the combined Guggenheim-Morgan interests grasps for Alaska's coal as Uncle Sam sits by eating gumdrops. Partly as a result of press opposition, the "Guggenmorgan" syndicate never mined any Alaskan coal.

ANOTHER TRIUMPH IN THE FAR NORTH.
The Great American Trust seems to have discovered Alaska.

performed legal services for Cunningham as a private lawyer. Along with this grain of truth, Pinchot hurled false charges, alleging a connection between Ballinger and the Syndicate that did not exist.

The resulting uproar forced Ballinger to resign. It also added to a widening breach between Taft and Roosevelt that culminated in the formation of a third party in 1912 to run Roosevelt again for President. Roosevelt's challenge split the Republican Party and threw the election to a Democrat, Woodrow Wilson.

The Syndicate never did get to mine Alaskan coal. When the case of the Cunningham claims was brought to trial, the court ruled that they were indeed invalid. The Guggs overcame this inconvenience by importing coal to run their trains. The trains carried the Chitina bluffs copper to Syndicate-owned ships that transported the ore to a smelter in Washington State, which was, of course, owned by the Guggs.

On April 24, 1912, on the floor of the United States House of Representatives, a man who hated the Guggs told his colleagues: "The exploiters of the

223

wealth of Alaska do not live in Alaska at all. They generally live around 45 Broadway, New York."

The speaker was James Wickersham and his credentials as spokesman for the long-abused northern possession were flawless. He had come to Alaska as a federal judge in 1900. After cleaning up the litigious mess left by the spoilers of Nome, he had held court in towns over much of Alaska, dispensing justice with a keen sense of fairness and earning recognition as a man of integrity. In 1908 he sought election as the delegate to Congress, a nonvoting post created two years earlier, and he won largely because in his campaign he swung hard at the Syndicate.

"If ever there was a criminal conspiracy in the United States to get the immense resources which belong to the people," Wickersham said, "it is that of the Alaska Syndicate in Alaska."

When Wickersham got to Washington, he soon came to the realization that Congress and much of the country still held the distorted view that Alaska was a forbidding wilderness, pocked here and there with unruly camptowns that were populated by good-for-nothing drifters. Though he had no vote in the House, Wickersham's statements were given great weight, and he used his office to begin clearing up the territory's bad image. Alaska, said Wickersham, was more than prospectors and trappers, whales and walruses. It had a functioning social order: merchants, editors, lawyers, missionaries, teachers, jurists, independent professionals in a dozen trades.

On April 17, 1912, the House of Representatives opened debate on a bill introduced by Delegate Wickersham—a "bill to create a legislative assembly in the Territory of Alaska, to confer legislative power thereon, and for other purposes." A staunch supporter of the legislation, Representative Harry Flood of Virginia, was first to take the floor on its behalf. Flood cited figures showing that in the 45 years the United States had owned Alaska, the region had yielded $444 million to the United States in products and taxes. By contrast, Flood said, the sum total spent by the federal government on Alaska, including the purchase price, was only $35.7 million.

Flood's presentation ended with a stirring summons: "Fairness and justice and common sense and right demand that we should give to these people what they ask in this respect, and I hope and believe that as soon as this debate is concluded this bill will be passed without opposition." After a spate of oratory that emphasized the beauty and grandeur of Alaska—"wonderland of the world!"—with an ardor that would have shocked the 1867 critics of "Seward's Folly," the House voted unanimously for the bill. Three months later the Senate did too.

In truth, the Organic Act of 1912 was not all that could be hoped for, but it was a sorely needed step forward. Congress retained the power to regulate the salmon fisheries. It kept the right to veto legislation passed by Alaska's new bicameral legislature of eight elected senators and a 16-member house. The territorial governor would continue to be appointed by the President of the United States. The bill did not provide for an Alaskan court system, a system of penal institutions or institutions of higher learning. It prohibited Alaskan towns from issuing bonds to raise capital without Congressional approval and omitted any number of provisions Alaskans would have considered ideal. But, according to Wickersham, a more generous act would not have passed. At one point a senator went so far as to tell him: "I think you have been modest in your requests for self-government. That is, you have not asked for as much as the people in Alaska are entitled to have."

"That we have not," Wickersham replied, "but there are powerful influences that do not want any self-government in Alaska, and when we asked for what other Territories have had they would not give it to us: they would fight us."

Nor did the bill eradicate those powerful influences. The Morgan-Guggenheim Syndicate would continue to multiply its fortune in freewheeling fashion for years to come, as would other exploiters. But slowly, inexorably, Alaskans would come to have a major voice in their own destiny.

On August 24, 1912, President Taft signed Alaska's home-rule bill into law. It was Wickersham's 55th birthday, and the delegate was en route home from the "outside." Arriving in Juneau, he told a packed hall the "birthday present was the biggest and best I have ever received." His audience agreed and celebrated by dancing far into the Alaskan night.

Judge James Wickersham *(below)*, who restored justice to the corrupt court at Nome, left the bench to campaign for election as Alaska's delegate to Congress in 1908. Four years later he introduced the bill that gave Alaska home rule.

FOR
DELEGATE TO CONGRESS
"Alaska for Alaskans"

JAMES WICKERSHAM

Far-flung ports that kept Alaska afloat

With all its remoteness and with 34,000 miles of coastline, Alaska might as well have been an island. Almost anyone who wanted to get there had to go by ship, and virtually everything had to be brought in by sea.

Passenger ships arrived from Seattle and San Francisco packed to the gunwales with gold rushers who paid fares of $100 up to $1,000 and more for a chance to strike it rich.

Even the forbidding interior was penetrated by a doughty fleet of Yukon River steamers before roads or decent trails existed. From the Panhandle to the farthest Aleutian Island and north almost to the arctic, ports became the sourdough's most essential, and often his only, link with the outside world.

Ships discharge their passengers and cargo—including stacks of baled hay for livestock feed—at the wharf in Wrangell in 1898. A former Russian colony located in the lower Panhandle, Wrangell was warmed by the Japan Current and was proud of being a year-round port.

Dock hands and fashionably dressed strollers share busy Moore's Wharf at Skagway in 1904 with two steamers from the States and a recent cargo of sheep. Its rip-roaring days over, Skagway had become a transfer point for goods shipped via rail to Whitehorse and other Yukon towns.

230

The Fairbanks waterfront in 1906 is dominated by riverboats of the Northern Commercial Company, whose initials are boldly displayed on the freight shed at left. The company not only monopolized Fairbanks' shipping, mail delivery and stage lines but also owned its major store and supplied power for its lights, telephones and steam heating.

Almost as lonely and desolate as when the Russians first
sighted it in 1741, Unalaska Island in the Aleutians shel-
ters a few ships at its port, Dutch Harbor, around 1902.
Its fur-sealing days over, Unalaska prospered again briefly
as a refueling stop between Nome and San Francisco.

ACKNOWLEDGMENTS

The index for this book was prepared by Gale Partoyan. The editors give special thanks to Robert De Armond of Juneau who read and commented in detail on the text and to Joanne Dann and Curtis Prendergast who contributed editorial material. The editors also thank Michael Adam, Photographer, Renee Blahuta, Historian, Beverly Davis, Administrative Secretary, University of Alaska Archives, Fairbanks; Ruth Allman, House of Wickersham, Juneau; Georgeen Barrass, Assistant Chief Archivist, Glenbow-Alberta Institute, Calgary, Alberta; F. Frederick Bernaski, Registrar, Kennedy Galleries, New York; Esther Billman, Curator, Sheldon Jackson Museum, Sitka; Jean Bolton, Library, Dr. Frank Roth, Department of History, Sheldon Jackson College, Sitka; Diane Brenner, Archivist, Anchorage Historical and Fine Arts Museum, Anchorage; Isabel Bullen, Photo Archivist, Matilda Dring, Photo Archivist, Kay Saunders, Photo Archivist, San Francisco Maritime Museum, San Francisco; Maud D. Cole, Rare Books, New York Public Library, New York; Dale De Armond, Juneau; Lawrence Dinnean, Curator of Pictorial Collections, Suzanne H. Gallup, Reference Librarian, William Roberts, Assistant Head of Public Services, The Bancroft Library, Berkeley; Zelma Doig, Librarian, Alaska Historical Library, Juneau; Paula Richardson Fleming, National Anthropological Archives, Smithsonian Institution, Washington, D.C.; Laurence Freeburn, Seattle; Lieutenant Colonel W. F. Gabella, Public Affairs Officer, Charles M. Canterbury, Fort Richardson, Anchorage; Betty Gard, Librarian, University of North Dakota, Grand Forks; Herbert S. Green Jr., Los Angeles; Herbert L. Heller, Greencastle, Indiana; Dr. William Jacobs, Department of History, University of Alaska, Anchorage; Marian Johnson, Hazel Jones, Lucy McIver, Eunice Neseth, Baranof Museum, Kodiak; Jerry L. Kearns, Prints and Photographs, Library of Congress, Washington, D.C.; Ron Klein, Juneau; Richard C. Kugler, Director, Philip Harrington, Curator, New Bedford Whaling Museum, New Bedford; Garry Kurutz, Library Director, Terry Mangan, Curator of Photography, California Historical Society, San Francisco; William Leary, Archivist, The National Archives, Washington, D.C.; Margaret Liebowitz, Deputy Director, Alaska State Library, Juneau; Augustino Mastroguiseppe, Picture Librarian, Western History Collection, Denver Public Library, Denver; Virginia McGillvray, Mary Smith, Tongass Historical Society Museum, Ketchikan; Robert Monroe, Head, Dennis Andersen, Assistant, Sandra Kroupa, Assistant, Special Collections, University of Washington Library, Seattle; Alan R. Munro, Chief Curator, Dan Monroe, Deputy Chief Curator, Laura Bracken, Museum Assistant, Alaska State Museum, Juneau; Harold Nesbitt, Manager of Hunting Activities Department, National Rifle Association of America, Washington, D.C.; Edward R. Nolan, Librarian, Museum of History and Industry, Seattle; Dr. Richard Pierce, Department of History, Queens University, Kingston, Ontario; L. J. Rowinski, Director, Dinah Larsen, Curator of Ethnology, University of Alaska Museum, Fairbanks; Martin Schmitt, Carrie Singleton, Special Collections, University of Oregon Library, Eugene; Sister Victoria, Kodiak; Connie Stewart, Administrative Assistant, Governor's Residence, Juneau; Ruth M. Stinemeyer, Assistant Curator, Canon City Municipal Museum, Canon City; Superior Publishing Co., Seattle; David Wellmann, Nome; Janice Worden, Photographs Librarian, Oregon Historical Society, Portland.

PICTURE CREDITS

The sources for the illustrations in this book are shown below. Credits from left to right are separated by semicolons, from top to bottom by dashes.

Cover—From *From Euston to Klondike* by Julius M. Price, published by S. Low Marston & Co., London, 1898, courtesy Library of Congress, copied by Charlie Brown. 2—F. H. Nowell, courtesy the Bancroft Library. 6,7—Courtesy the Dr. Charles Bunnell Collection, University of Alaska Archives, Fairbanks. 8,9—Courtesy Photography Collection, Suzzallo Library, University of Washington. 10,11—Eric A. Hegg, courtesy Photography Collection, Suzzallo Library, University of Washington. 12,13—Courtesy Alaska Historical Library, Juneau. 14,15—Courtesy The C. L. Andrews Collection, University of Oregon Library (AD 825). 16,17—Courtesy the Dr. Charles Bunnell Collection, University of Alaska Archives, Fairbanks. 18—Ron Klein, courtesy Alaska State Museum, Juneau. 20,21—Courtesy Library of Congress. 23—Courtesy Photography Collection, Suzzallo Library, University of Washington, except inset, top, courtesy Oregon Historical Society. 25,26,27—Courtesy Library of Congress. 28—Courtesy Photography Collection, Suzzallo Library, University of Washington. 29—Courtesy California Historical Society, San Francisco/San Marino. 30,31—Ron Klein, courtesy Alaska State Museum, Juneau. 32,33—Robert E. Johnson, courtesy Sheldon Jackson College Museum, Sitka. 36,37—Case & Draper, courtesy Alaska Historical Library, Juneau; courtesy the Bernard Moore Collection, University of Alaska Archives, Fairbanks—courtesy Photography Collection, Suzzallo Library, University of Washington. 38—Courtesy The Barrett Willoughby Collection, University of Alaska Archives, Fairbanks. 40,41—Reuben Albertstone & Co., courtesy Alaska Historical Library, Juneau (2). 42 through 51—Ron Klein, courtesy Alaska State Museum, Juneau. 52,53—Courtesy the U. S. S. Thetis Collection, Alaska Historical Library, Juneau. 54—Courtesy Seattle Historical Society Museum of History and Industry Archives. 57—From *Frank Leslie's Illustrated Newspaper,* April 20, 1867, courtesy Library of Congress. 58,59—Maps by Edward Frank. 60—Courtesy U.S. Signal Corps, National Archives. 61—Courtesy National Archives. 62—Henry Elliott, courtesy University of Alaska Archives, Fairbanks. 63—Barry McWayne, courtesy University of Alaska Museum. 66—Courtesy Photography Collection, Suzzallo Library, University of Washington. 67—Courtesy Library of Congress (2). 68-69—Winter & Pond, courtesy Alaska Historical Library, Juneau. 71—B. B. Dobbs, courtesy Alaska Historical Library, Juneau. 72-73—Courtesy the John L. Powell Collection, University of Alaska Archives, Fairbanks. 74,75—Charles Phillips, courtesy National Anthropological Archives, Smithsonian Institution (2). 76—Courtesy Alaska Historical Library, Juneau; Vaghan & Keith, courtesy Alaska Historical Library, Juneau. 77,78—Courtesy Alaska Historical Library, Juneau. 80,81—Case & Draper, courtesy Alaska Historical Library, Juneau. 82,83—Eric A. Hegg, courtesy Photography Collection, Suzzallo Library, University of Washington, except inset, top left, W. H. Case, courtesy Alaska Historical Library, Juneau. 84 through 89—Case & Draper, courtesy Alaska Historical Library, Juneau. 90,91—W. H. Case, courtesy Alaska Historical Library, Juneau. 92,93—Courtesy Library of Congress. 94—Courtesy the Dr. Charles Bunnell Collection, University of Alaska Archives, Fairbanks. 96,97,99—Courtesy the Bancroft Library. 100—Courtesy the Historical Photograph Collection, University of Alaska Archives, Fairbanks. 101—Robert E. Johnson, courtesy Sheldon Jackson College Museum, Sitka. 102—Map by Edward Frank. 104 through 108—Charles Phillips, courtesy National Anthropological Archives, Smithsonian Institution. 110—Courtesy Library of Congress. 111—Courtesy U.S. Coast Guard. 112—Courtesy the Sierra Club. 113—Courtesy Oregon Historical Society—courtesy the Harriman Expedition Collection, University of Alaska Archives, Fairbanks. 117—Courtesy Library of Congress. 118 through 125—Charles Phillips, courtesy National Anthropological Archives, Smithsonian Institution. 126 through 133—Courtesy the George Y. Wilkinson Collection, University of Alaska Archives, Fairbanks. 134—Courtesy the Bancroft Library. 137—From the *Alaska-Yukon* magazine, courtesy Alaska Historical Library, Juneau (3). 138—Courtesy the Selid-Bassoc Collection, University of Alaska Archives, Fairbanks. 140,141—Eric A. Hegg, courtesy Photography Collection, Suzzallo Library, University of Washington. 143—Courtesy Photography Collection, Suzzallo Library, University of Washington. 144—Lomen Brothers, courtesy Alaska Historical Library, Juneau. 145—Courtesy Library of Congress. 146,147—Courtesy the Edward Mulligan Collection, University of Alaska Archives, Fairbanks. 149—Courtesy Anchorage Historical and Fine Arts Museum Archives—courtesy the Edward Mulligan Collection, University of Alaska Archives, Fairbanks. 150—Lomen Brothers, courtesy Alaska Historical Library, Juneau. 151—Courtesy Anchorage Historical and Fine Arts Museum Archives—courtesy Alaska Historical Library, Juneau. 153—Courtesy the Bancroft Library. 154,155—F. H. Nowell, courtesy the Bancroft Library, except inset, top right, Eric A. Hegg, courtesy Photography Collection, Suzzallo Library, University of Washington. 156—Courtesy the George Y. Wilkinson Collection, University of Alaska Archives, Fairbanks. 158,159—Courtesy Anchorage Historical and Fine Arts Museum Archives. 160—Courtesy Library of Congress (2). 162,163—F. H. Nowell, courtesy Alaska Historical Library, Juneau. 164,165—Courtesy the John L. Powell Collection, University of Alaska Archives, Fairbanks. 166,167—Courtesy Alaska Historical Library, Juneau. 168,169—B. B. Dobbs, courtesy Anchorage Historical and Fine Arts Museum Archives.

170,171—Eric A. Hegg, courtesy Photography Collection, Suzzallo Library, University of Washington. 172,173—Case & Draper, courtesy Alaska Historical Library, Juneau. 174—From the Nome *Nugget,* courtesy Glenbow-Alberta Institute (6). 176, 177—Courtesy Photography Collection, Suzzallo Library, University of Washington. 179—Courtesy The William Hunt Collection, University of Alaska Archives, Fairbanks. 181—Courtesy the Frank Buteau Collection, University of Alaska Archives, Fairbanks. 182,183,185—Courtesy Photography Collection, Suzzallo Library, University of Washington. 186—Courtesy N. H. Rose Collection, Western History Collections, University of Oklahoma Library; courtesy U.S. Signal Corps, Photo No. 111-SC-89517, National Archives; courtesy Denver Public Library, Western History Department—courtesy Arizona Historical Society. 187—Courtesy Dr. Herbert L. Heller Collection. 188,189—Courtesy The C. L. Andrews Collection, University of Oregon Library (AD 1326). 191—Courtesy the Bernard Moore Collection, University of Alaska Archives, Fairbanks. 192,193—Courtesy the Archie Lewis Collection, University of Alaska Archives, Fairbanks. 196,197—Courtesy National Archives Gift Collection (200 [S] MHA [2] 47). 198,199—Courtesy the L. A. Levensaler Collection, University of Alaska Archives, Fairbanks. 200,201—Courtesy Alaska Historical Library, Juneau. 202,203—Courtesy the Lulu Fairbanks Collection, University of Alaska Archives, Fairbanks. 204,205—Courtesy Alaska Historical Library, Juneau. 206,207—Courtesy the Whaling Museum, New Bedford, Massachusetts. 208—From *Flag over the North* by L. D. Kitchener, page 19, published by Superior Publishing Co., Seattle, 1954, copied by Charlie Brown. 212,213—Courtesy the Lynn C. Denny Collection, University of Alaska Archives, Fairbanks. 215—Courtesy San Francisco Maritime Museum, Alaska Packers' Association Collection. 216—Ron Klein, courtesy Alaska State Museum, Juneau (3). 219—John Gilbert. 222—Frank Lerner, courtesy the New York Public Library, Astor, Lenox and Tilden Foundations. 223—Courtesy Library of Congress. 225—Ron Klein, courtesy Mrs. Ruth Allman, The House of Wickersham. 226,227—Courtesy Library of Congress. 228,229—Courtesy the Bernard Moore Collection, University of Alaska Archives, Fairbanks. 230,231—Courtesy the Archie Lewis Collection, University of Alaska Archives, Fairbanks. 232,233—Eric A. Hegg, courtesy Photography Collection, Suzzallo Library, University of Washington.

TEXT CREDITS

For full reference on specific page credits see bibliography

Chapter 1: Particularly useful sources for information and quotes in this chapter: C. L. Andrews, *The Story of Sitka,* Lowman & Hardord Co., 1922; Hubert Howe Bancroft, *History of Alaska: 1730-1885,* Antiquarian Press, Ltd., 1959; Hector Chevigny, *Lord of Alaska: The Story of Baranov and the Russian Adventure,* Binfords & Mort, 1970; Hector Chevigny, *Russian America: The Great Alaskan Venture 1741-1867,* The Viking Press, 1965; Ronald J. Jensen, *The Alaska Purchase and Russian-American Relations,* University of Washington Press, 1975; 19—Sitka's Russian inhabitants, Davis, pp. 1-2; 39—Rezanov describes Baranov, McCracken, p. 252. Chapter 2: Particularly useful sources:

Robert De Armond, "Gold on the Fortymile," *The Alaska Journal,* Vol. 3, No. 2, Spring 1973; Robert De Armond, *The Founding of Juneau,* Gastineau Channel Centennial Association, 1967; Ernest Gruening, *The State of Alaska,* Random House Inc., © 1968; Ted C. Hinckley, *The Americanization of Alaska, 1867-1897,* Pacific Books, © 1972; Jeannette P. Nichols, *Alaska: A History of Its Administration, Exploitation, and Industrial Development During Its First Half Century Under the Rule of the United States,* Arthur H. Clark Co., 1924; 60—military conduct, Bancroft, p. 607; Ushin's report, Hulley, p. 209; 88—Treadwell kitchen, Christoe. Chapter 3: Particularly useful sources: Henry T. Allen, *Report of a*

Military Reconnaissance in Alaska in 1885 by Henry T. Allen, U.S. Army, 1885; Jed Dannenbaum, "John Muir and Alaska," *The Alaska Journal,* Vol. 2, No. 4, Autumn 1972; M. A. Healey, *Report of the Cruise of the Revenue Marine Steamer Corwin in the Arctic Ocean in the Year 1884,* U.S. Government Printing Office, 1889; M. A. Healey, *Report of the Cruise of the Revenue Marine Steamer Corwin in the Arctic Ocean in the Year 1885,* U.S. Government Printing Office, 1887; Isaac Don Levine, *Billy Mitchell: Pioneer of Air Power,* Duell, Sloan and Pearce, 1958; John Muir, "The Discovery of Glacier Bay by Its Discoverer," *The Century Magazine,* Vol. 50, No. 2, June 1895; Frederick Schwatka, *Along Alaska's Great River,* Cassel & Company, Ltd., 1883; Morgan B. Sherwood, *Exploration of Alaska, 1865-1900,* Yale University Press, 1965; 96—exploration, Gruening, p. 27; 98—Whymper's description, Whymper, p. 164. Chapter 4: Particularly useful sources: Rex E. Beach, "The Looting of Alaska," *Appleton's Booklovers Magazine,* Vol. VII, Nos. 1-5, January-May 1906; Joseph Grinnell, *Gold Hunting in Alaska,* David C. Cook Publishing Co., 1901; William R. Hunt, *North of 53 : The Wild Days of the Alaska-Yukon Mining Frontier 1870-1914,* Macmillan Publishing Co., Inc.,©1974; *Nome Chronicle,* August 18, 1900; *Nome News,* November 25, 1900; Ruth Reat, ed., "From Dawson to Nome on a Bicycle," *Pacific Northwest Quarterly,* Vol. 47, No. 3,© July 1956; James Wickersham, *Old Yukon: Tales—Trails—and Trials,* West Publishing Co., 1938; 138—Carmack's discoveries, Mathews, pp. 153, 155; Rex Beach's crew, Beach, *Personal Exposures,* p. 28. Chapter 5: Particularly useful

sources: Howard Clifford. *The Skagway Story: a history of Alaska's most famous gold rush town and of some of the people who made that history.* Alaska Northwest Publishing Co., 1975; William Ross Collier and Edwin Victor Westrate, *The Reign of Soapy Smith, Monarch of Misrule In the Last Days of the Old West and the Klondike Gold Rush,* Doubleday, Doran & Co., Inc., 1935; Herbert L. Heller, ed., *Sourdough Sagas: The Journals, Memoirs, Tales and Recollections of the Earliest Alaskan Gold Miners, 1883-1923,* The World Publishing Co., © 1967; Frank C. Robertson and Beth Kay Harris, *Soapy Smith: King of the Frontier Con Men,* Hastings House, 1961; Wickersham, *Old Yukon;* 172—description of Skagway, Hinton, pp. 14-15; 175—little civic life, Jordan, p. 184; 195—Frederick Jackson Turner, Hinckley, p. 242. Chapter 6: Particularly useful sources: Everett S. Allen, *Children of the Light: The Rise and Fall of New Bedford Whaling and the Death of the Arctic Fleet,* Little, Brown and Company, © 1973; Gruening, *The State of Alaska;* Clarence C. Hulley, *Alaska: Past and Present,* Binfords & Mort, 1970; William R. Hunt, *Arctic Passage: The Turbulent History of the Land and People of the Bering Sea, 1687-1975,* Charles Scribner's Sons, 1975; Hunt, *North of 53°;* Lone E. Janson, *The Copper Spike,* Alaska Northwest Publishing Co., 1975; Martha McKeown, *Alaska Silver: Another Mont Hawthorne Story,* Macmillan, 1951; Alfred P. Swineford, *Report of the Governor of Alaska for the Fiscal Year 1887,* U.S. Government Printing Office, 1887; 220—salmon industry, Hinckley, p. 127.

BIBLIOGRAPHY

Alaskan Boundary Tribunal, British Atlas. U.S. Government Printing Office, 1904.

Allen, Everett S., *Children Of The Light.* Little, Brown and Co., 1973.

Allen, Henry T., *Report of a Military Reconnaissance in Alaska in 1885 by Henry T. Allen.* U.S. Army, 1885.

Andrews, C. L.: "The Real Soapy Smith," *The Alaska Sportsman.* November 1974.
   The Story of Sitka. Lowman & Hardord Co., 1922 (Fascimile Ed. 1973).

Ault, Phillip H., "The (Almost) Russian-American Telegraph," *American Heritage,* Vol. 26, No. 4. June 1975.

Bancroft, Hubert Howe, *History of Alaska: 1730-1885.* Antiquarian Press, Ltd., 1959.

Beach, Rex E.: *Personal Exposures.* Harper, 1944.
   "The Looting of Alaska," *Appleton's Booklovers Magazine,* Vol. VII, Nos. 1-5. January-May 1906.

Bensin, Basil M., *Russian Orthodox Church in Alaska 1794-1967.* Russian Orthodox Greek Catholic Church of North America, Diocese of Alaska, 1967.

Brickey, James and Catherine, "Reindeer, Cattle of the Arctic," *The Alaska Journal,* Vol. 5, No. 1. Winter 1975.

Brooks, Alfred Hulse, *Blazing Alaska's Trails.* University of Alaska Press, 1973.

Cashen, William R., *A Brief History of Fairbanks.* The Lettership, 1971.

Chevigny, Hector: *Lord of Alaska.* Binfords & Mort, 1970.
   Russian America. The Viking Press, 1965.

Choris, Louis, *Voyage Pittoresque Autour du Monde, avec des Portraits de sauvages d'Amerique, d'Asie, d'Afrique, et des Îles du Grand Ocean: des paysages, des vues maritimes et plusieurs objets d'Histoire naturelle.* 1822.

Cobb, John N., *Pacific Salmon Fisheries.* U.S. Government Printing Office, 1930.

Christoe, Alice Henson, *Treadwell, An Alaskan Fulfillment.*

Clifford, Howard, *The Skagway Story.* Alaska Northwest Publishing Co., 1975.

Collier, William Ross, and Edwin Victor Westrate, *The Reign of Soapy Smith.* Doubleday, Doran & Co., Inc., 1935.

Dall, William H., *Alaska and Its Resources.* Lee and Shepard, 1870.

Dannenbaum, Jed, "John Muir and Alaska," *The Alaska Journal,* Vol. 2, No. 4. Autumn 1972.

Davis, William Heath, *Seventy-five Years in California.* John Howell, 1967.

De Armond, Robert: "And a Town Grew," *The Alaska Sportsman.* August 1960.
   "Gold on the Fortymile," *The Alaska Journal,* Vol. 3, No. 2. Spring 1973.
   The Founding of Juneau. Gastineau Channel Centennial Association, 1967.

De Weese, Dall, "A Moose Hunt in Alaska," *Outdoor Life,* Vol. 1, No. 1. January 1898.

Fort Ross, The Russian Settlement in California. Fort Ross Interpretive Association, 1975.

Foster, James C., "The Treadwell Strikes, 1907 and 1908," *The Alaska Journal,* Vol. 6, No. 1. Winter 1976.

Freeburn, Laurence, *The Silver Years.* Alaska Northwest Publishing Co., 1976.

Gay, James T., "Henry W. Elliott: Crusading Conservationist," *The Alaska Journal,* Vol. 3, No. 4. Autumn 1973.

Gibson, James R., *Imperial Russia in Frontier America.* Oxford University Press, 1976.

Grinnell, Joseph, *Gold Hunting in Alaska.* David C. Cook Publishing Co., 1901 (Facsimile Ed. 1964).

Gruening, Ernest, *The State of Alaska.* Random House Inc., 1968.

Healey, M. A.: *Report of the Cruise of the Revenue Marine Steamer Corwin in the Arctic Ocean in the Year 1884.* U.S. Government Printing Office, 1889.
Report of the Cruise of the Revenue Marine Steamer Corwin in the Arctic Ocean in the Year 1885. U.S. Government Printing Office, 1887.

Heller, Herbert L., ed., *Sourdough Sagas.* The World Publishing Co., 1967.

Hinckley, Ted C., *The Americanization of Alaska, 1867-1897.* Pacific Books, 1972.

Hinton, A. Cherry, and Philip H. Godsell, *The Yukon.* Macrae Smith Co., 1955.

Hodge, F. W., ed., *Handbook of American Indians North of Mexico,* Vols. 1 and 2. Rowman and Littlefield, 1971.

Hulley, Clarence C., *Alaska,* Binfords & Mort, 1970.

Hunt, William R.: *Arctic Passage.* Charles Scribner's Sons, 1975.
North of 53°. Macmillan Publishing Co., Inc., 1974.

Janson, Lone E., *The Copper Spike.* Alaska Northwest Publishing Co., 1975.

Jensen, Ronald J., *The Alaska Purchase and Russian-American Relations.* University of Washington Press, 1975.

Johnson, Virginia W., *The Unregimented General.* Houghton Mifflin Co., 1962.

Jordan, David Starr, *Imperial Democracy.* D. Appleton and Co., 1899.

Kitchener, Lois D., *Flag Over The North.* Superior Publishing Co., 1954.

Levine, Isaac Don, *Billy Mitchell.* Duell, Sloan and Pearce, 1958.

Lisiansky, Urey, *A Voyage Round the World.* 1814.

Mathews, Richard, *The Yukon.* Holt, Rinehart and Winston, 1968.

McCracken, Harold, *Hunters of the Stormy Sea.* Doubleday & Company, Inc., 1957.

McKeown, Martha, *Alaska Silver.* Macmillan, 1951.

Muir, John: "The Discovery of Glacier Bay by Its Discoverer," *The Century Magazine,* Vol. 50, No. 2. June 1895.
Travels in Alaska. Houghton Mifflin Co., 1915.

Murtagh, William J., "Some Homes of Nome," *The Alaska Journal,* Vol. 4, No. 1. Winter 1974.

Nelson, Klondy, *Daughter of the Gold Rush.* Random House, 1955.

Nichols, Jeannette P., *Alaska.* Arthur H. Clark Co., 1924.

Nome Chronicle. August 18, 1900.

Nome News. November 25, 1900.

Oberg, Kalervo, *The Social Economy of the Tlingit Indians.* University of Washington Press, 1973.

Osborne, Alice: "Alaska's Early Years," *The Alaska Journal,* Vol. 4, No. 1. Winter 1974.
"Rails Across the Tundra," *The Alaska Journal,* Vol. 2, No. 3. Summer 1972.

Petroff, Ivan, "Alaska: Its Population, Industries and Resources," *Report of the Tenth Census-1880,* Vol. VIII. Bureau of the Census, 1884.

Phebus, George Jr., *Alaskan Eskimo Life in the 1890s as Sketched by Native Artists.* Smithsonian Institution Press, 1972.

Pierce, Richard A., "Alaska's Russian Governors," *The Alaska Journal,* Vol. 1, No. 2-Vol. 3, No. 1. Spring 1971-Winter 1973.

Pierce, Richard A., and Alexander Doll, "Alaskan Treasure: Our Search for the Russian Plates," *The Alaska Journal,* Vol. 1, No. 1. Spring 1971.

Pilgrim, Earl R., "The Treadwell Mines in 1915," *The Alaska Journal,* Vol. 5, No. 4. Autumn, 1975.

Reat, Ruth, ed., "From Dawson to Nome on a Bicycle," *Pacific Northwest Quarterly,* Vol. 47, No. 3. July 1956.

Robertson, Frank C., and Beth Kay Harris, *Soapy Smith.* Hastings House, 1961.

Rochcau, Vsevelod, "The Origins of the Orthodox Church in Alaska," *Orthodox Alaska,* Vol. 3, Nos. 1 and 2. November-February 1971, 1972.

Satterfield, Archie, *Chilkoot Pass.* Alaska Northwest Publishing Co., 1973.

Schwatka, Frederick, *Along Aluska's Great River.* Cassel & Company, Ltd., 1883.

Seppala, Leonhard, "The City of the Storms," *The Alaska Sportsman.* September 1961.

Sherwood, Morgan B., *Exploration of Alaska, 1865-1900.* Yale University Press, 1965.

Sherwood, Morgan B., ed., *Alaska and Its History.* University of Washington Press, 1967.

Spencer, Robert F. et al., *The Native Americans.* Harper & Row, 1965.

Stoney, George, *Explorations in Alaska.* U.S. Naval Institute, 1889.

Swineford, Alfred P., *Report of the Governor of Alaska for the Fiscal Year 1887.* U.S. Government Printing Office, 1887.

Van Nostrand, Jeanne, "The Seals Are About Gone . . ." *American Heritage,* Vol. XIV, No. 4. June 1963.

Van Stone, James W.: "An Early 19th Century Artist in Alaska," *Pacific Northwest Quarterly,* Vol. 51, No. 4. Autumn 1960.
Athapascan Adaptations. Aldine, 1974.

Vaughan, Thomas, *Captain Cook, R.N., The Resolute Mariner.* Oregon Historical Society 1974.

Wallace, Fern A., *The Flame of the Candle.* Sts. Kyril and Methody Society, 1974.

Wharton, David, *The Alaska Gold Rush.* Indiana University Press, 1972.

Whiting, Emma Mayhew and Henry Beetle Hough, *Whaling Wives.* Houghton Mifflin, 1953.

Whymper, Frederick, *Travel and Adventure in the Territory of Alaska.* 1868.

Wickersham, James, *Old Yukon.* West Publishing Co., 1938.

Printed in U.S.A.